Working Through Conflict

A COMMUNICATION PERSPECTIVE

Working Through Conflict

A COMMUNICATION PERSPECTIVE

Joseph P. Folger
University of Michigan

Marshall Scott Poole
University of Illinois

Scott, Foresman and Company
Glenview, Illinois

Dallas, Tex.	Oakland, N.J.	Palo Alto, Cal.
Tucker, Ga.	London, England	

Acknowledgments for all copyrighted material used are given on pages 207–208, which are a legal extension of the copyright page.

An Instructor's Manual is available. It may be obtained through your local Scott, Foresman representative or by writing to the Speech Editor, College Division, Scott, Foresman and Company, 1900 E. Lake Avenue, Glenview, IL 60025.

Library of Congress Cataloging in Publication Data

Folger, Joseph P., 1951–
    Working through conflict

    Bibliography
    Includes index.
    1. Social conflict. 2. Conflict (Psychology)
3. Conflict management. 4. Social interaction.
5. Interpersonal communication. I. Poole, Marshall
Scott, 1951– . II. Title.
HM136.F56   1984   303.6   83–14206
ISBN 0–673–15836–5

2 3 4 5 6—KPF—88 87 86 85

To our parents:
Ed and Virginia, Ed and Helen

Preface

Working Through Conflict: A Communication Perspective examines the forces that generate conflicts and the techniques that can be used to direct these forces toward productive ends. It is written for undergraduate students with little or no background in this area, and it is intended as a core text for courses in conflict and conflict management, or as a supplementary text for applied courses in small group, organizational, and interpersonal communication, and in organizational behavior courses.

Working Through Conflict studies conflict from a communication perspective. It is guided by the premise that people must understand conflicts before they can successfully manage or resolve them. It analyzes conflict as a form of interaction which develops and is managed through communication. The book considers a number of key ideas from traditional conflict research —conflict styles, game theory, and Deutsch's theory of cooperative and competitive climates—in terms of their implications for conflict interaction. Building on these, it advances a model of conflict interaction shaped by four forces —working habits, climate, power, and face-saving.

Working Through Conflict presents a broad theoretical perspective on conflict and a coherent framework that explains the relationship among the various elements. Yet, it is also a highly practical book because it concentrates on face-to-face conflict in groups and organizations. Our examination of the forces that generate conflict cycles suggests numerous strategies and tactics for moving conflicts in productive directions. The final chapter of the book integrates many of these points in a discussion of indirect and direct intervention in conflicts.

Working Through Conflict brings an integrated perspective to the study of conflict. Current work is generally of two types: summaries of studies listed under rubrics like "power," "tactics," and "characteristics," but with little theoretical coherence; and "specialty" books which explain a single method of conflict management, such as problem-solving or negotiation, but give little perspective on conflict in general. In writing this book we sought to address the need for a text with a broad scope, yet a coherent framework that puts the various elements of conflict in clear relation to one another.

Reinforcing the practicality of *Working Through Conflict* are the case examples that appear throughout the book. These cases are intended as material for discussion and debate, and all were drawn from real conflicts, although names and contexts were altered to protect the participants. Our work with ongoing conflicts has given us an appreciation of the complexity of conflict— a complexity that often stymied our best efforts to help people work through difficult problems. We hope the use of real case examples will help ensure that the intricate nature of conflict remains in the forefront of our analyses. If the examples are successful in demonstrating the complexity of conflict, then our analyses of the cases should raise as many questions as they answer. We included the case examples to allay one of our greatest fears in writing the book —a fear that someone might finish reading it and say, "But conflicts are never this easy to analyze or manage."

To further tie the book's concepts to practical considerations, a number of original case studies, role-plays, and exercises are provided in the Instructor's Manual. These applications are linked directly with issues raised in various chapters and should aid in illustrating key concepts and skills. In addition, the Manual contains sample outlines of courses in conflict management and group communication, as well as outlines which show how *Working Through Conflict* can be combined with various texts to design an applied group communication course.

Many individuals have helped immeasurably in the preparation of this book. We owe our greatest debt to our colleagues at the Center for Conflict Resolution in Madison, Wisconsin. The Center gave both of us a start in this area, and many of the ideas and approaches we discuss were developed in long meetings about workshops or mediations. We are very grateful to Lonnie Weiss for her insight and help with our analyses. We also thank Syd Bernard, Jim Carrilon, Jay Herman, Jan Shubert, Rick Sloan, Dennis Smith, and Kathy Zoppi for reading and reacting to parts or all of the manuscript. In addition, we turned to Betsy Densmore, Robert Everett, and Tommy Vines for an evaluation of the manuscript from a managerial perspective. Charles Conrad of the University of North Carolina at Chapel Hill deserves special thanks for his ideas and encouragement. For extremely helpful manuscript reviews, we thank Wayne Beach, University of Nebraska; Robert J. Doolittle, University of Wisconsin—Milwaukee; Dennis Gouran, Indiana University; Thomas J. Harris, University of Evansville; Linda Putnam, Purdue University; Gale Richards, Arizona State University; Michael Sunnafrank, University of California at Davis; and Paul Yelsma, Western Michigan University. We'd also like to thank Linda Klug, Jean Kebis, and Wayne Beach for supplying the transcript of interaction in chapter 5. At Scott, Foresman, Michael Anderson deserves our sincere thanks for astute editing throughout the project, and Lydia Webster, our thanks for seeing the book through production. We are also grateful to our students at the University of Michigan and the University of Illinois who read chapters of the book as we worked on them. Finally, we thank Dianne Haft and Kathy Folger for their help in preparing the manuscript.

The title of the book is an intentional double entendre. Since its major emphasis is on communication patterns people use when attempting to manage conflict, we hope that the book helps people successfully *work through* difficult conflicts. The book is also built on the assumption that people can complete successful work *through the emergence of conflict.* Rather than suppressing or "resolving" conflicts, we hope this book encourages and assists people to confront their conflicts and to creatively work through them.

Joseph P. Folger
Marshall Scott Poole

Contents

Conflict and Interaction

THE POTENTIAL OF CONFLICT INTERACTION

People often claim that conflict can be beneficial. Trainers, counselors, consultants, and authors of conflict textbooks point to the potential positive functions of conflict: conflicts allow important issues to be aired; they produce new and creative ideas; they release built-up tension; they can strengthen relationships; they can cause groups and organizations to reevaluate and clarify their goals and missions; they can also result in social change to eliminate inequities and injustice. These advantages, and others, are raised in order to justify conflict as a normal, "healthy" occurrence and to stress the importance of understanding and handling it properly. But why must such an argument be made? Everyone has been in a conflict at one time or another, and almost everyone would readily acknowledge at least some benefits from conflict. Why, then, do social scientists, popular authors, and consultants persist in attempting to persuade us of something we already know? Perhaps the answer can be found in the following, fairly typical case study of a conflict in a small work group.

_____ CASE (Introduction) _____

Women's Hotline is a rape and domestic crisis center in a medium-sized city; the center employs seven full- and part-time workers. The workers, who were all women, formed a cohesive unit and made all important decisions as a group; there were no formal supervisors. The Hotline had started as a voluntary organization and had grown by successfully soliciting local and federal funds. The group remained proud of its roots in a democratic, feminist tradition.

Generally, the work atmosphere at the Hotline was very informal. The staff saw each other as friends, but there was an implicit understanding that people should not have to take responsibility for each other's cases or the problems related to them. Since each worker's job was extremely draining, having to handle each other's worries could create an unbearable strain. This norm encouraged workers to work on their own and keep problems to themselves.

The conflict arose when Diane, the newest counselor, who had been on the job for only six months, was involved in a very disturbing incident. A client she had been counseling was killed by a man who had previously raped her. Diane had trouble dealing with this incident. She felt guilty about it; she questioned her own ability and asked herself whether she might have been able to prevent this tragic death. In the months following, Diane had increasing difficulty in coping with her feelings and began to feel that her co-workers were not giving her the kind of support or concern she needed. Diane had no supervisor to turn to, and, although her friends outside Hotline were helpful, she did not believe they could understand the pressure as well as her co-workers.

Since the murder, Diane had not been able to work to full capacity, and she began to notice some resentment from the other counselors. She felt the other staff members were more concerned about whether she was adding to their work loads than whether she was recovering from the traumatic incident. Although Diane did not realize it at the time, most of the staff felt she had been slow to take on responsibilities even before her client was killed. They thought Diane had generally asked for more help than other staff members and that these requests were in fact adding to their own responsibilities at the center. No one was willing to tell Diane about these feelings after the incident happened because they realized she was very disturbed by what had happened to her client.

After six months, Diane believed she could no longer continue to work effectively. She felt pressure from the other women at the center, and she was still shaken by the tragedy. She requested two weeks off with pay in order to get away from the work situation for a while, reduce the stress she felt, and come back with greater energy to perform her job. The staff, feeling that Diane was slacking off, denied this request. They responded by outlining, in print, what they saw as the responsibilities of a full-time staff worker. Diane was angry when she realized her request had been denied, and she decided to file a formal work grievance.

Diane and the staff felt bad about needing to address the issue through such a formal, adversarial procedure. No staff member had ever filed a work grievance at the center, and the group was now embarrassed by its inability to deal with the problem on a more informal basis. So, an overall sense of disappointment in their inability to work through the issue themselves now accompanied the feeling of tension between Diane and the staff. The staff committee who received Diane's grievance suggested that they could handle the problem in a less formal way if both Diane and the staff were willing to call in a neutral third party who could help the group discuss the conflict at a staff meeting. Everyone agreed that this suggestion had promise and a third party was asked to help at a meeting where the entire staff would address the issue.

At this meeting, the group faced a difficult task. Each member offered reactions they had been unwilling to express previously. The staff made several pointed criticisms of Diane's overall performance at the center. Diane expressed doubts about the staff's unwillingness to help new workers or to give support when it was requested. Although this discussion was often tense, its purpose was well-directed. At the outset of the meeting, the group changed the definition of the problem from the immediate work grievance (Diane withdrew the formal complaint at the start of the meeting) to the question of what levels of support were needed for various people to work effectively in this difficult and emotionally-draining setting. During the meeting staff members shared doubts and fears about their own inadequacies as counselors and agreed that something less than perfection was acceptable. The group recognized that a collective inertia had grown in the group and that they had consistently avoided giving each other the support they needed to deal with difficult rape cases. They acknowledged, however, the constraints on each woman's time; each worker could handle only a limited amount of stress. The group recognized that some level of mutual support was essential and felt they had fallen below that essential level over the past year and a half. One member suggested that any staff person should be able to ask for a "debriefing contract" whenever they felt they needed help or support from another staff member. These contracts would allow someone to ask for ten minutes of another person's time to hear about an issue or a case that was particularly disturbing. The group members adopted this suggestion because they saw it could allow members to seek help without overburdening each other. The person who was asked to listen could assist and give needed support without feeling that she had to "fix" another worker's problem. Diane continued to work at the center and found that her abilities and confidence increased as the group provided the support she needed to be an effective counselor.

This example is in some ways a "textbook" case in effective conflict management because it resulted in a solution that all members valued and endorsed. It does, however, exhibit several features in common with even the most destructive conflicts and could easily have turned in that direction. First, the situation was *tense* and *threatening*. The weeks during which the incident evolved were an extremely difficult time for the workers. Even for "old hands" at negotiation, conflicts are often unpleasant and frightening. Second, participants experienced a great deal of *uncertainty*. They were unable to understand fully the conflict and how their behavior affected it. Conflicts are confusing; our actions can have consequences quite different from those we intend because the situation is more complicated than we assume. Diane did *not* know her co-workers thought she was slacking. So when she asked for time off, she was surprised at their refusal, and her own angry reaction nearly started a major battle. Third, the situation was extremely *fragile*. If even one worker had acted differently at several crucial points in the conflict, a different result might have occurred. If, for example, the staff had chosen to fire Diane, the conflict might have been squelched, or it might have festered and undermined relationships among the remaining members. If, on the other hand, Diane had won allies, the staff might have split over the issue and ultimately dissolved. The members of this work group were walking a tightrope throughout the conflict; luckily, they managed to avoid a fall.

The tension, unpleasantness, and more importantly, the uncertainty and fragility of conflict situations make them hard to face. Because these problems make it difficult to deal with issues in a constructive way, conflicts are too often terminated by force, by uncomfortable suppression of the issues, or by exhaustion after a prolonged fight—all outcomes that leave at least one party dissatisfied. Entering a conflict is often like making a bet against the odds: you can win big if it turns out well, but so many things can go wrong that few people are willing to chance it. It is no wonder, then, that those who analyze conflict see a need to reassure us. They feel compelled to remind us of the potential outcomes of conflict because all too often the destructive results are all that people experience or remember.

We believe that the key to working through conflict is not to minimize its disadvantages, or even to emphasize its positive functions, but to accept both and try to understand *how* conflicts move in destructive or productive directions. Such an understanding requires a conception of conflict that calls for a careful *analysis of both the specific behaviors and interaction patterns involved in conflict and the forces that influence the direction these patterns take.* Moreover, we can only grasp the fragility of conflicts and the effects tension and misunderstandings have in their development if we work at the level at which conflicts unfold—specific interactions among the members of groups or organizations. Our definition of conflict and our analysis of the major factors that give direction to conflict reflects this emphasis on the need to examine conflict interaction.

Before proceeding, however, it is necessary to clarify the scope of this book. Our analysis is primarily aimed at clarifying how conflicts are handled in *task-oriented* groups, such as organizational work groups, small businesses, classes, clubs, juries, and even therapy or consciousness-raising groups that have clear goals and members who work toward those goals. This focus guides the major issues we examine and the examples we provide. Since group interaction is a primary means for completing tasks in most organizations, institutions, and informal work settings, we believe this book offers a useful framework for understanding a wide and recurring variety of conflict situations. Many of the principles of conflict interaction discussed in this book apply equally well to analyses of conflict in less formal, non-task-oriented settings such as husband-wife relationships, friendship, and families; they could even be extended beyond interpersonal, face-to-face relations and applied to intergroup or interorganizational conflict.

DEFINITION OF CONFLICT

Conflict *is the interaction of interdependent people who perceive incompatible goals and interference from each other in achieving those goals* (Frost & Wilmot, 1978). This definition has the advantage of providing a much clearer focus than definitions that view conflict simply as disagreement, as competition, or as the presence of incompatible interests (Fink, 1968). The most important feature of conflict is that it is based in *interaction.* Conflicts are formed and sustained by the behaviors of the parties involved and their reactions to one another. Conflict interaction takes many forms and each form presents special problems and requires special handling.

The most familiar conflict interaction is marked by shouting matches or open competition where each party tries to defeat the other. But conflicts can also be more subtle. Often people react to conflict by repressing it. They interact in ways which allow them to avoid confrontation, either because they are afraid of possible changes the conflict may bring about or because the issue "isn't worth fighting over." This response is as much a part of the conflict process as the open struggles most of us associate with conflict.

This book deals with the range of responses to conflict and how those responses affect the development of conflicts. We believe conflicts can best be understood and managed by concentrating on specific behavioral patterns and the forces shaping them.

In conflict behavior people perceive that they have incompatible goals or interests and that others are a source of interference in achieving their goals. The key word here is "perceive." Regardless of whether goals are actually incompatible, if the parties believe them to be incompatible, conditions are ripe for conflict. Regardless of whether an employee *really* stands in the way of her co-worker, if the co-worker interprets the employee's behavior as interference, he may move against her or feel compelled to skirt certain issues. Thus, the parties' interpretations and beliefs play a key role in conflicts. Communication, both intended and unintended, looms large because of its importance in shaping and maintaining the perceptions that guide conflict behavior. We do not, however, agree with the old adage "most conflicts are actually communication problems." The vast majority of conflicts would not exist without some real difference of interest. This difference may be hard to uncover, it may be redefined over time, and occasionally it may be trivial, but it is there nonetheless. Although communication processes can worsen or improve conflict interaction, and although they do play a critical role in defining issues, they are rarely the sole source of conflicts.

Conflict interaction is colored by the *interdependence* of the parties. For a conflict to arise, the behavior of one or both parties must have consequences for the other. So, by definition, the parties involved in conflict are interdependent. The conflict at the Hotline would not have occurred if Diane's behavior had not irritated the other workers and if their response had not threatened Diane's position. Further, any action taken in response to the conflict affects both sides. The decision to institute a "debriefing contract" required considerable change by all workers. If Diane had been fired, that, too, would have affected the other workers; they would have had to "cover" Diane's cases and come to terms with themselves as co-workers who could be accused of being unresponsive or insensitive.

But interdependence implies more than this: when parties are interdependent they can potentially aid or interfere with each other. For this reason, conflicts are always characterized by a mixture of incentives to cooperate and to compete. Any comment made during conflict interaction can be seen either as an attempt to advance the speaker's own interest or as an attempt to advance the best decision for the group as a whole. A member can believe that having his or her own point accepted is more important, at least for the moment, than proposing the best idea for the group. When Diane asked for two weeks off, she was probably thinking not of the group's best interest, but of her own needs. In other cases, a participant may advance a proposal designed to benefit the group as a whole, as when one Hotline staff member suggested the "debriefing contract." In still other instances, a participant may offer a comment with a cooperative intent, but others may interpret it as one that places individual interest over the group's objectives. Regardless of whether the competitive motive is intended by the speaker or assigned by other members, the interaction unfolds from that point on under the assumption that the speaker may value only his or her own interests. Subsequent interaction is likely to further undermine the incentives to cooperate and is also likely to weaken members' recognition of their own interdependence. The balance of these incentives to compete or cooperate is important in determining the direction the conflict interaction takes.

PRODUCTIVE AND DESTRUCTIVE CONFLICT INTERACTION

As we have noted, people often associate conflict with negative outcomes. However, there are times when conflicts need to be addressed regardless of the apprehension they create. When differences exist and the issues are important, repression of conflict is often far more dangerous than its emergence. The psychologist Irving Janis points to a number of famous political disasters, such as the Bay of Pigs invasion and the failure to anticipate the Japanese attack on Pearl Harbor, where poor decisions can be traced to the repression of conflict by key decision-making groups (Janis, 1972). The critical question is this: what forms of conflict interaction will yield the obvious benefits without tearing a group or organization apart?

Years ago the sociologist Lewis Coser (1956) distinguished "realistic" from "nonrealistic" conflicts. Realistic conflicts are conflicts based in disagreements over the means to an end or over the ends themselves. In realistic conflicts, the interaction focuses on the substantive issues that the participants must address in order to resolve the underlying incompatibilities. Nonrealistic conflicts are expressions of aggression in which the sole end is to defeat or hurt the other. Participants in nonrealistic conflicts serve their own interests by undercutting those of the other party. Coser argues that because nonrealistic conflicts are oriented toward the expression of aggression, force and coercion are the means for resolving these disputes. Realistic conflicts, on the other hand, foster a wide range of resolution techniques—force, negotiation, persuasion, even voting—because they are oriented towards the resolution of some substantive problem.

Although Coser's analysis oversimplifies the two types of conflict, it is insightful and suggests some important contrasts between productive and destructive conflict interaction (Deutsch, 1973). What criteria could one use to evaluate whether a conflict is productive? In large part, productive conflict interaction depends on flexibility of behavior. In constructive conflicts, members engage in a wide variety of behaviors ranging from coercion and threat to negotiation, joking, and relaxation in order to reach a mutually acceptable solution. In contrast, parties in destructive conflicts are likely to be much less flexible because their goal is more narrowly defined; they are trying to defeat each other. Destructive conflict interaction is likely to have protracted, uncontrolled escalation cycles or prolonged attempts to avoid the issue. In productive conflict, on the other hand, the interaction in the group will change direction often. Short cycles of escalation, de-escalation, avoidance of the issue, and constructive work on the issue are likely to occur as the participants attempt to manage the conflict.

Consider the Hotline case. The group exhibited a wide range of interaction styles, from the threat of a grievance to the cooperative attempt to reach a mutually satisfactory solution. Even though Diane and the members engaged in hostile or threatening interaction, they did not persist in this mode, and when the conflict threatened to escalate, they called in a mediator. The conflict showed all the hallmarks of productive interaction. In a destructive conflict the members might have responded to Diane's grievance by suspending her, and Diane might have retaliated by suing or by attempting to discredit the center in the local newspaper. Her retaliation would have hardened the other workers' position, and they might have fired her, leading to further retaliation. Alternatively, the Hotline conflict might have ended in destructive avoidance. Diane might have hidden her problem and the other members might have consciously or unconsciously aided her in doing so by changing the subject when the murder came up or by avoiding talking to Diane at all. Diane's problem would probably have grown worse, and she might have had to leave the Hotline. The center would then revert back to "normal" until the same problem cropped up again. While the damage done by destructive avoidance is much less serious in this case than that done by destructive escalation, it is still considerable: the Hotline loses a good worker, and the seeds of future losses remain. In both cases, it is not the behaviors themselves which are destructive—neither avoidance nor hostile arguments are harmful in themselves—but rather the *inflexibility* of the parties which locks them into escalation or avoidance cycles.

In productive conflicts, interaction is guided by the belief that all factions can attain important goals (Deutsch, 1973). The interaction reflects a sustained effort to bridge the apparent incompatibility of positions. This is in marked contrast to destructive conflicts where the interaction is premised on the participants' belief that one side must win and the other must lose. Productive conflict interaction results in a solution that is satisfactory to all and produces a general feeling that the group has gained something (for example, a new idea, greater clarity of others' positions, a stronger sense of solidarity among the members) as a result of the conflict emerging. In some cases, conflict interaction with a win-lose purpose stems from clear competitive motives. Members argue vehemently for their stands and attempt to defeat alternative proposals because they believe that if their positions are not accepted they will lose resources, self-esteem, or the respect of other group members. At other times, win-lose interaction is sparked, not by competitive motives, but by the participants' fear of *working through* a difficult conflict. Groups that typically rely upon voting as a way to reach a decision often call for a vote on alternative proposals when the discussion of these proposals becomes heated and the members do not see any other immediate way out of a hostile and threatening situation. Any further attempt to discuss the alternatives or to pursue the reasons behind people's positions seems risky. A vote can put a quick end to the threatening interaction, but it also induces a win-lose orientation that can easily trigger destructive interaction cycles. Members whose proposal is rejected must fight off a natural tendency to be less committed to the chosen solution and may demand the acceptance of their proposals in future discussions to "even the score."

Productive conflict interaction can be competitive at points; both parties must stand up for their own positions if a representative outcome is to be attained. A great deal of tension and even hostility may result as the group struggles with the conflict. The key difference is that although parties in productive conflicts hold to their positions strongly, they are also open to movement if they become convinced that such movement will result in the best decision. The need to preserve power, save face, or make the opponent look bad does not stand in the way of this movement. In destructive conflict interaction parties often become polarized, and the defense of a nonnegotiable position becomes more important than working out a viable solution.

This description of productive and destructive conflict interaction is obviously an idealization. We have rarely observed a conflict that exhibits all the constructive or destructive qualities just mentioned; indeed, many conflicts exhibit both productive and destructive interaction. We maintain, however, that better conflict management will result if group members can sustain productive conflict interaction. Effective conflict management rests primarily on the group or organization's ability to maintain productive interaction patterns.

CONFLICT AS INTERACTIVE BEHAVIOR

Conflict is, by nature, interactive. It is never wholly under one person's control (Kriesberg, 1973). The other party's reactions and the person's anticipation of the other's response are extremely important. Any comment made during a conflict is made with some awareness or prediction about the likely response it will call forth. This predictive basis for any move in interaction creates a strong tendency for conflict interaction to become cyclic or repetitive.

Suppose Robert criticizes Susan, an employee under his supervision, for her decreasing productivity. Susan may accept the criticism and explain why her production is down, thus reducing the conflict and moving toward a solution. Susan may also shout back and sulk, inviting escalation, or she may choose to say nothing and avoid the criticism, resulting in no improvement in the situation. Once Robert has spoken to Susan and she has responded, the situation is no longer totally under Robert's control—his next behavior will be a response to Susan's reaction. Robert's behavior, and its subsequent meaning to Susan, is dependent on the interchange between them.

A behavioral cycle of initiation-response-counterresponse results from the conflict interchange. This cycle cannot be understood by breaking it into its parts, into the individual behaviors of Robert and Susan. It is more complex than the individual behaviors and, in a real sense, has a "life" of its own. The cycle can be self-reinforcing, if, for example, Susan shouts back at Robert, Robert tries to discipline her, Susan becomes more recalcitrant, and so on, in an escalating spiral. The cycle could also limit itself if Robert responds to Susan's shouting with an attempt to calm her and listen to her side of the story. Conflict interaction cycles acquire a momentum of their own. They tend in a definite direction—toward escalation, toward avoidance and suppression, or toward positive work on the conflict.

The situation becomes even more complex when we remember that Robert formulated his criticism on the basis of his previous experience with Susan. That is, Robert's move is based on his perception of Susan's likely response. In the same way, Susan's response is based not only on Robert's criticism, but on her estimate of Robert's likely reaction to her response. Usually such estimations are "intuitive" —that is, they are not conscious—but sometimes parties plot them out ("If I shout at Robert, he'll back down and maybe I won't have to deal with this"). They are always based on the parties' perceptions of each other, on whatever theories or beliefs each holds about the other's reactions. Because these estimates are only intuitive predictions, they may be wrong to some extent. They will be revised as the conflict unfolds, and this revision will determine to a large part what direction the conflict takes.

The most striking thing about this predictive process is the extraordinary difficulties it poses for our attempts to understand the parties' thinking. When Susan responds to Robert on the basis of her prediction of Robert's answer, from the outside we see *Susan* making an estimate of *Robert's* estimate of what she means by her response. If Robert reflects on Susan's intention before answering, we observe *Robert's* estimate of *Susan's* estimate of *his* estimate of what *Susan* meant. This string of estimates can increase without bounds if we try to pin down the originating point, and after a while the prospect is just as dizzying as a hall of mirrors. Several studies of arms races (Richardson, 1960; North, et al., 1963) and of marital relations (Watzlawick, et al., 1967) have shown how this spiral of predictions poses a critical problem in conflicts. If the parties do not take the spiral into account, they run the risk of miscalculation. However, it is beyond the capacities of any human being to calculate all the possibilities. At best, parties have extremely limited knowledge of the implications their actions hold for others, and their ability to manage conflicts is therefore severely curtailed. Not only are parties' behaviors inherently interwoven in conflicts, but their thinking and anticipations are as well.

The key question this book addresses is: *how does conflict interaction develop destructive patterns—radical escalation, prolonged or inappropriate avoidance of conflict issues, inflexibility—rather than constructive patterns leading to productive conflict management?* In a very real sense conflict interaction is always poised on a precipice—one push can send it in a negative direction while another can send it in a positive direction. This book considers several major forces that direct conflicts in groups and examines the problems groups encounter in trying to control these forces in order to regulate their own conflict interaction.

There are a wide array of forces that can influence conflicts. To sort out the forces that are most influential in leading conflicts in destructive or constructive directions, we will turn to the major theoretical perspectives on conflict that have been advanced in a number of different disciplines. In Chapter 1 we will review several theoretical approaches to understanding conflict. We will point to the major contributions of each of these approaches and note where these positions have fallen short of offering a satisfactory explanation of conflict interaction. Based upon this review we will offer four properties of conflict interaction and indicate how each of these properties makes conflict interaction vulnerable to a particular force that can influence the route conflict takes. These four forces (working habits, climate, power, and face-saving) become the focus of Chapters 2–5. In the final chapter, we examine what implications our analysis has for group members or third parties who intervene in group conflicts.

_____ REFERENCES _____

Coser, L. *The functions of social conflict.* New York: Free Press, 1956.

Deutsch, M. *The resolution of conflict.* New Haven: Yale University Press, 1973.

Fink, C. F. Some conceptual difficulties in the theory of social conflict. *Journal of Conflict Resolution,* 1968, *12,* 412–460.

Frost, J., & Wilmot, W. *Interpersonal conflict.* Dubuque, Iowa: Brown, 1978.

Janis, I. *Victims of groupthink.* Boston: Houghton Mifflin, 1972.

Kriesberg, L. *The sociology of social conflict.* Englewood Cliffs, N.J.: Prentice-Hall, 1973.

North, R. C., Brody, R. A., & Holsti, O., Some empirical data on the conflict spiral. *Peace Research Society; Papers I.* Chicago Conference, 1963, pp. 1–14.

Richardson, L. F. *Arms and insecurity.* (N. Rashevsky & E. Trucco Eds.). Pittsburgh: The Boxwood Press, 1960.

Watzlawick, P., Beavin, J., & Jackson, D. *The pragmatics of human communication.* New York: Norton, 1967.

Perspectives on Conflict

Conflict is one of the most dramatic and, at times, traumatic events in life. Because it is often a gripping experience, it has attracted the attention of many researchers. Conflict and related subjects, such as bargaining, negotiation, decision-making, aggression, and social influence, are the focus of literally thousands of studies. Its popularity is an advantage, because we have a firm knowledge base to build on. It is also a disadvantage, however, for two reasons. First, out of the mass of available research only a few theories or explanations emerge, and few of these cover the conflict process as a whole. Research has instead tended to focus on specialized contexts (for example, games) and on only a few variables at a time. As a result, the "big picture" is very hard to grasp. There are dozens of separate theories and findings, yet no way of integrating them into a whole.

A second disadvantage of previous research is that it has surprisingly little to say about interaction *per se.* Most research has focused either on the psychology of people in conflict or on the solutions people arrive at, rather than the *processes* people use to get to solutions. The results of this research are certainly useful: knowing how people think and react tells us a great deal about how they are likely to behave, and knowing what factors (for example, cooperative vs. competitive climate) lead to various solutions is also helpful. But both approaches avoid grappling with the substance of conflict—interaction, the moves and countermoves which constitute it.

As a result, we have several theories and a mass of interesting findings, but no way to link them together. The various theories and lines of research operate on quite different levels and are therefore especially hard to reconcile. This book proposes to integrate them by focusing specifically on conflict interaction. It operates on the assumption that conflict *is* interaction; it assumes that those findings which will ultimately prove to be important and informative are those that carry insights on how people interact in conflicts. Further, as we have noted, we will focus on interpersonal conflict in *groups* and *organizations* and exclude international and interorganizational conflicts, except insofar as they are informative for the study of interpersonal conflict. Although we have narrowed our scope, a huge area is still left to explore. Moreover, it is an area which is "of a piece" and therefore it should be possible to develop a coherent point of view.

In this chapter we will lay the groundwork for the book by considering several key ideas developed in previous conflict research. In the first part of this chapter, we will look at six important research traditions and pull from them insights that are useful in understanding conflict interaction. The six traditions—*psychodynamic theory, field theory, phase analysis, social exchange theory, experimental gaming*, and *research on conflict styles*—advance many propositions relating to conflict interaction; we will evaluate the advantages and disadvantages of each approach for the study of conflict.

In the second part of this chapter we will propose a framework for understanding and working with conflict in groups and organizations. This framework centers on four forces that shape conflict interaction—working habits, group climate, power, and face saving—and attempts to capitalize on the strengths of earlier research without succumbing to their weaknesses or to a fragmented view of conflict.

KEY IDEAS FROM THE STUDY OF CONFLICT

Since the six approaches discussed in this section are extensive, it would be impossible to summarize *all* the important studies in each tradition in a brief review. Instead, we will focus on the basic assumptions of each view as they relate to conflict. We will attempt to evoke the spirit of each position and present its key ideas on conflict. We will return to these basic ideas throughout the book as we examine the major forces that influence interaction in conflicts.

PSYCHODYNAMIC THEORY

Landmark advances in art and science often elicit as much criticism as praise. At the turn of the century, Freud's psychoanalytic theory altered people's vision of themselves as much as French impressionist art had altered people's view of the world. Yet both Freud and the Impressionists became at different times the target of significant criticism, and even ridicule. Freud and his followers (Freud, 1900/1953, 1925, 1923/1947, 1949; Adler, 1927; Sullivan, 1953; Rapaport, 1951; Erikson, 1950) studied the dynamics of the human mind. They try to explain how *intra*personal states and mental activities give rise to behavior in social contexts.

Psychodynamic theories are as controversial as they are ambitious. They have been attacked and ridiculed many times over the years. The crazy psychiatrist in movies and sitcoms is just one example of the harsh reception Freudian ideas have often received. It is certainly true that many psychoanalytic ideas defy common sense and that many writers have used them in unjustifiable ways. However, at its core, psychodynamic theory provides many insights that have become part of our day-to-day thinking, concepts like the unconscious, the ego, and the id, and processes like repression and wish fulfillment. They touch on fundamental aspects of human experience, whether or not we agree with the particulars. Several ideas from psychodynamic theory are absolutely fundamental to an understanding of conflict (Coser, 1956).

To understand the contributions of psychodynamic theory to conflict research, we must first consider some of its basic assumptions. (The account given here is directed to our concerns, but readers may turn to other sources for a fuller description: Hall, 1979; Deutsch & Krauss, 1965; Hall & Lindzey, 1970; Schaffer, 1970). Important for our purposes is a key premise of psychodynamic theory—its "hydraulic" model of human motivation. Freud and his followers portray the human mind as a reservoir of psychic energy that is channeled into various activities. This energy is the impulse behind behavior and can be channeled into any number of different activities, ranging from positive pursuits such as work or raising a family to destructive impulses such as vandalism. But however it is channeled, this energy *must be released*. If it is not released through one channel (for example, vandalism), it builds up pressure to be released through another— hence the analogy to a system of hydraulic pipes, in which turning off one outlet creates pressure on the others. The psychodynamic theorists attempt to describe the mechanisms in the human mind that constrain and channel psychic energy. Their basic model has three components: (1) the id, the source of energy; (2) the superego, the value system designed to constrain this energy; and (3) the ego, the executive function which relates the id and super ego to actual behavior. In order to understand the role of this model in conflict, let us first consider its components and their relationship.

The *id* is "the primary source of psychic energy and the seat of the instincts" (Hall, 1979, p. 26). It is governed by the *pleasure principle,* which aims to reduce the amount of tension in the person by the discharge of psychic energy. Tension is created by two forces, the basic human drives or instincts, and the frustrations the person encounters in attempting to satisfy these instincts. The basic instincts include the drive for self-preservation, needs for love and social support, and the controversial instincts toward aggression and self-destruction. For the id all ways of discharging energy are equivalent, so it is indifferent as to whether energy is used for positive or for destructive tendencies. Energy will tend to flow through which-ever channel offers the least resistance. Because needs and drives must be dealt with in social contexts where others may block their satisfaction, they often go unfulfilled. In such cases the energy originally focused on the drive may refocus on the frustrating person or object, especially if no alternative channels are available. This explanation has been given for vandalism in schools. Frustrated children with no other outlets take out their anger on the institution that constrains them.

People are not just willful, impulsive creatures, however. They often have a great deal of self-control and very high moral standards which route their energy into socially acceptable outlets. Freud called this moral and judicial branch of our personality the *superego.* It consists of two parts, the ego ideal and the conscience. The ego ideal is a person's internalization of who he or she would like to be. It is the person's model for behavior and is usually patterned after his or her parent or some other admired person or leader. The conscience corresponds to what the person believes is morally bad; it is, in essence, a "negative" ego ideal, something the person tries to avoid. The superego is like a parent: it regulates behavior by punishing the person for disapproved activities and rewarding him or her for approved activities. Its punishments and rewards are usually psychological—feelings of guilt and inferiority if a person has done something bad and feelings of pride and accomplishment for good behavior. However, sometimes the superego's control can be physical, as when someone becomes sick from guilt.

Both the id and superego are forceful influences. The id wants to discharge energy, no matter how or what, and the superego wants to constrain behavior to acceptable paths regardless of the consequences. The *ego* mediates between the two and relates them to real-world concerns. According to Freud, the ego is governed by the *reality principle;* its aim is "to postpone the discharge of energy until the actual object that will satisfy the need has been discovered or produced." (Hall, 1979, p. 28). This "actual object" is defined by the limitations of the social situation and by the superego. For example, a member of a decision-making group may be frustrated by the group's slow pace. One avenue for releasing this tension might be to lash out at other members. However, the member's superego might define "ideal" behavior as kind and self-controlled and therefore tend to suppress tension release through attacking others. The member's ego would mediate between the id and superego to find a suitable means of releasing energy, yet maintain a kind, self-controlled demeanor. The member might, for example, throw him or herself into thinking about how to solve the group's problems and therefore speed it up. If this can be done, the member's tension would be successfully diverted. However, the ego can postpone discharge only for so long. If the group's problems are not soluble and no other outlet is found, the energy will eventually either erupt in a tongue-lashing of other members or be turned back on itself and suppressed. Neither result is good for the member. In the former case the member will feel guilty because he or she has violated an ideal, and in the latter the member will feel more tension from suppressing his or her energy. The ego tries to mediate the superego and id, while avoiding these unpleasant alternatives. To do this it must guide the person into successful and effective channels of activity.

However, as we noted in the Introduction, conflict occurs in situations where people perceive incompatible goals and interference from others, that is, *situations in which people fear they will not be able to act successfully.* As a result, the ego is faced with the problem of managing the id and superego when acceptable, effective behavior channels may not be available. The frustrations and uncertainties involved in conflict generate two powerful impulses that the ego must manage, the *aggressive impulse* and *anxiety.* The various ways in which these energies are channeled play a critical role in conflict interaction, because they determine how members react to conflict.

Freud emphasized that the *aggressive impulse* can be directed toward oneself or others. Energy for this tendency may arise from guilt or from frustrations resulting from unfulfilled needs or thwarted desires. Often this aggression is directed at the actual object of guilt or frustration, either back at oneself in the form of self-hate or in attacks on the frustrating other. However, self-hate is very destructive and aggression toward some people is discouraged, either by moral codes or by the negative consequences of attacking them. As a result, individuals develop strategies for redirecting aggression.

One strategy is to attempt to suppress aggressive drives. This is often done simply by not acknowledging them and undertaking a substitute activity. For example, an employee who is angry at his boss for denying him a promotion, may simply suppress his anger and rechannel it into working even harder. Psychodynamic theories stress the benefits of this suppression, because it leads to less anxiety, guilt, or pain than attempting to fulfill a destructive or impossible need. If drives are recognized explicitly, people must make some conscious response to them, and this can increase anxiety or frustration if they go unsatisfied. On the other hand, if a need is never acknowledged, it can be treated as if it were nonexistent, and the energy associated with the need can be diverted into other channels. Despite its benefits, suppression can also be a double-edged sword. Suppressing a need is frustrating and if no acceptable substitute is found, the need can fester and erupt more violently later on. Also, when goals are suppressed, people may still be driven by the need without realizing it. Actions may be guided by unconscious drives or needs, and these may direct behavior in destructive ways. Thus the employee might take out his anger unconsciously by missing the deadline for an important report his boss must give to her superiors. By making his boss look bad, he is getting back at her and assuaging his anger without admitting it; this may have bad consequences for him too, because he might lose his job if his boss believes him to be incompetent or vindictive. Facing up to his anger directly might have been unpleasant for both the employee and his boss, but in this case it would have been less unpleasant than the consequences of suppression.

A second strategy for dealing with aggression is to direct it toward more vulnerable or acceptable targets than the actual source of frustration. This process, which is called *displacement,* is more likely when the true source of frustration is powerful or particularly valuable to the individual. Rather than suffering the consequences of an attack on the true source, people attribute their frustration to other parties so that their impulses can be legitimated. They look for distinctions between themselves and others so that "enemy lines" can be drawn and targets are then available for their aggressive urges. In his insightful book *The Functions of Social Conflict,* Coser (1956) notes that the scapegoating of a few group members may be due to displaced aggression. When members of a group face failure or a crisis, they are often reluctant to blame the whole group, because they fear rejection if they show their anger. In order to avoid losing the benefits of belonging to the group, they attack a weak member or an outsider. This process can be very destructive for the scapegoat, but it serves to keep the group together because it allows members to vent aggressive energy.

In addition to aggressive impulses, *anxiety* is also likely to emerge during conflicts. Anxiety is defined as an internal state of tension that arises when someone perceives impending danger. It arises when people believe their drives or needs will be thwarted. Since people in conflicts anticipate interference from others, anxiety is likely to exist until they have some hope that all parties are trying to reach an agreement that meets each member's needs. If this belief is not present or if members suspect that other parties do not see their needs as legitimate, then anxiety is likely to remain a constant influence throughout the conflict.

Psychodynamic theories also point to two other sources of anxiety in conflict interaction. First, they suggest that anxiety can result from people's fears of their own impulses. As we have noted, many drives are self-destructive or counterproductive. When people suspect they may be acting on one of these deep-rooted impulses, they become anxious. They may be unsure about the limits of their own behavior and try to determine those limits and prove themselves by testing how far they will go with risky or self-endangering behavior. For example, a receptionist in a law office inadvertently overheard an insulting remark one of the lawyers made about her. She was very angry and began to berate the lawyer with insulting jokes in retaliation. Despite the possibility that the lawyer might fire her, she continued to do this for several days. When a friend in the office asked her why she took the chance, she commented that she *was* really afraid the lawyer would fire her.

However, she had to prove to herself that she was not a "mouse," so she continued her counterattack. Persisting in and strengthening counterproductive responses is one way of reassuring oneself that they are permissible.

Finally, anxiety also results from the judgments people make about their own behavior. People have strong behavioral tendencies based on inner needs and impulses, but they also have a clear capacity to make judgments about what they do or do not do to meet these needs. Anxiety results when people disapprove of the very behaviors they are engaging in. In conflict interaction, people can be uncomfortable with their actions and may realize that they would not ordinarily take the stand they are taking or make the moves they are making toward others. They may continue with their actions, however, because at the time there seems to be some legitimate or important reason for doing so. They may, for instance, be trying to save face or may see themselves using a questionable means to achieve a worthwhile end. The anxiety people experience from engaging in disapproved behaviors can decrease the chances that they will stop these behaviors. Anxiety can cloud thinking and prevent people from gaining a clear perspective on their own ambivalence.

Anxiety exerts its major influence on conflict interaction by causing members to be excessively rigid and inflexible. Hilgard and Bower (1966) draw on psychodynamic principles to help explain compulsive or repetitive tendencies that can take hold of people's actions despite the fact that they carry destructive consequences. The mere repetition of unpleasant behaviors is often rewarding because it allows people to achieve a sense of mastery over some activity. Mastery in itself is rewarding and thus behaviors or forms of interaction continue even if they eventually prove to be destructive. Hilgard and Bower note that this sense of mastery, and the compulsive behaviors it promotes, often serve to reduce anxiety. It allows people to cope with a trying situation and it leads to overlearned behaviors that are highly resistant to change. Although the basic notion here is aimed at explaining neurotic forms of individual behavior, it can also explain the nature of interaction cycles. Patterns of interaction which are themselves counterproductive in conflict can persist because they provide a way to deal with the anxiety that conflict produces. As we will see in chapter 2, these cycles, fed by members' rigidity, prove to be threatening.

Psychodynamic theory has generated several important insights into conflict interaction. Most important is its explanation of the role of impulses, particularly aggression and anxiety, in conflicts. The idea that these impulses build up and can be redirected into other activities, including attacks on a third person, is crucial to most conflict theories. Psychodynamic theory recognizes the importance of substitute activities, displacement, scapegoating, and inflexibility in conflicts. It allows us to take many subtle processes into account and therefore greatly enhances our sensitivity to members' behavior. The idea of unconscious or subconscious motivation is also very important. People do not always understand what is driving their conflict behavior. Unconscious motivation underscores the importance of helping members gain insight into their behavior. Once members grasp what is driving conflicts, they can begin to control them.

In addition to these strengths, two caveats must be made concerning the psychodynamic approach. First, although psychodynamic theories do carry important implications for the study of interaction, we should emphasize that the theories themselves are not aimed at the study of interaction per se. They focus primarily on *internal* psychological processes and not on *social* behavior. When the links between mental activity and behaviors are recognized, behaviors are frequently viewed and discussed apart from the interactive context in which they occur. Since psychodynamic theories place heavy emphasis on mental states and the internal motivations that drive behaviors, they often fail to recognize that social behavior is always a response to previous actions of others. In interaction, actions are prompted or shaped as much by previous moves of others as they are by the internal states of the person. In order to get a complete picture we must incorporate others into our explanation and avoid focusing only on internal processes.

The second caveat relates to the first: psychodynamic theories by themselves are insufficient to explain the rechanneling of psychic energy toward different people or activities (Billig, 1976). These theories argue that psychic impulses are often rerouted. There is no question that this is a major insight. However, a problem arises because the psychodynamic approach provides no way to predict or explain in any meaningful way *what substitute person or activity will be chosen.* Psychodynamic theories merely show that rechanneling does occur and give vague explanations of how substitutes are chosen. For example, psychodynamic explanations have been advanced for the transfer of frustrations into aggression against the Jewish community in prewar Germany. However, they do not account for why the Jews, *in particular,* were chosen rather than other minorities or non-Germanic nations. In order to predict which substitutes are chosen—and why—we must consider social factors outside psychodynamic theory. In the case of scapegoating, for example, factors such as the person's power relative to others, the person's habitual style of conflict behavior, the degree to which the expression of anger is socially acceptable, and the characteristics of available weaker parties must be taken into account. As powerful and interesting as they are, psychodynamic theories by themselves offer only a partial picture of conflict interaction. We must move to the social arena to grasp fully the nature of conflict.

Many of the social scientific theories discussed later in this book have rejected psychodynamic approaches. However, despite their explicit rejection of psychodynamics, they are often based on many of its insights. Few theories of conflict could function without ideas derived from psychodynamic concepts such as *rechanneling* or the *subconscious.* Psychodynamic theories are a little like an offensive but rich uncle—family members benefit from the relationship, but no one wants to admit it.

FIELD THEORY AND THE CONCEPT OF CLIMATE

Ever since Kurt Lewin's work on Field Theory surfaced in the 1950s, the concept of climate has held an important, although somewhat elusive place in the study of conflict (Lewin, 1951; Deutsch & Krauss, 1965, Chap. 3; Neel, 1977). Lewin represented human behavior as movement through a "life-space" under the influence of various fields of force. The life-space consists of the person's conception of important goals and the barriers and requirements necessary to attain them. For example, Figure 1 shows a space for a worker who wants to become chair of a union committee. To reach this goal she must pass through or around four regions of the space, each of which corresponds to a requirement or barrier: Region (a) representing the actions necessary to be elected to the committee; region (b) representing serving on the committee and becoming prominent; region (c) corre-

————— **Figure 1** —————————————————————————————
A Sample Life-Space

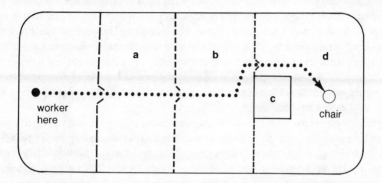

sponding to opposition expected from Hank, a power-hungry member of the committee; and (d) representing the "politicking" needed to be elected to the committee. The dotted line represents one path the worker could take in order to achieve the chairmanship. It includes cutting around Hank's opposition and therefore avoiding his field of force. This might be done by studiously avoiding Hank's challenges and instead concentrating on other members or issues.

A critical feature of the life-space is that it is determined by how the individual sees the world at a given time; the life-space is not determined objectively, but rather, *psychologically*. Lewin and his co-workers identified a number of properties of life-spaces and of the forces which shape them. For the study of conflict, one of the most important properties is the overall character of the social field. As Lewin puts it:

> To characterize properly the psychological field, one has to take into account such specific items as particular goals, stimuli, needs, social relations, as well as . . . more general characteristics of the field as the *atmosphere* (for instance, the friendly, tense, or hostile atmosphere) or the amount of freedom. These characteristics of the field as a whole are as important in psychology as, for instance, the field of gravity for the explanation of events in classical physics. Psychological atmospheres are empirical realities and are scientifically describable facts (1951, p. 241).

Climate is a quality of the field "as a whole." As such it pervades all thought and action in the situation; it gives a "flavor"—for example, of warmth, safety, fear, or distrust—to everything that happens.

Perhaps the best analysis of the role of climate in conflict was provided by Morton Deutsch (1973), one of Lewin's students. In the opening pages of his discussion, Deutsch notes that "the processes of conflict resolution that are likely to be displayed will be strongly influenced by the context within which the conflict occurs" (p. 10). Deutsch argues that the critical contextual feature of conflict situations—the one that makes the difference between cooperative resolution and potentially destructive competition—is the *type* of interdependence established between the persons involved. For Deutsch, climates are defined by interdependence.

Deutsch defined two basic types of interdependence: a) *promotive* where the persons involved in the conflict perceive that gains by either one will promote gains by the other, while losses will promote losses, and (b) *contrient,* where everyone perceives that one's gain will be the other's loss. It is important to emphasize again that interdependence is not defined objectively, but by the perceptions and beliefs of the conflicting persons. If they perceive the situation as promotive, they will act as if it is promotive; if they perceive the situation as contrient, they will act as if it is contrient. Perceptions of promotive interdependence, Deutsch argues, tend to promote *cooperative* interaction, whereas perceptions of contrient interdependence tend to produce *competition.*

Deutsch identifies several further consequences of interaction occurring under promotive and contrient interdependence. Under promotive interdependence (cooperative climates), people will stress mutual interests and coordinated division of labor, exhibit trusting and friendly attitudes, perceive similarity in their beliefs and goals, and communicate more openly and honestly. Under contrient interdependence (competitive climate) people will focus on antagonistic interests and on constraining each other, exhibit suspicious and hostile attitudes, overemphasize differences, and communicate in a misleading and restrained manner. Studies by Deutsch and later researchers largely confirm these hypotheses and show that eventually these consequences "feed back" to influence interaction, thereby strengthening the dominant tendency in the conflict: "cooperation breeds cooperation, while competition breeds competition" (Deutsch, 1973, p. 367).

Other research enlarges upon Deutsch's analysis by suggesting additional climates that arise from and ultimately guide interaction in conflict. White and Lippitt (1968), for example, describe an *individualistic* orientation where members do not believe they are dependent on each other at all; it is characterized by a lack of common motives, autonomous behavior, rather indifferent attitudes towards others, and selfish preoccupation with one's own affairs. As a second alternative, Janis and Mann (1977) warn that overly cooperative orientations can lead to unthinking agreement among members, resulting in poor, unreflective group decisions. They propose instead a *vigilant* attitude, in which members are aware of common interests and trust and respect one another but are wary of each other's ideas (see also Gouran, 1982). Rather than easy cooperation, there may be sharp conflicts in vigilant groups, as members push each other toward the best decision through criticism and debate.

Deutsch's analysis is built on two assumptions particularly useful in understanding the general direction and underlying coherence of conflict interaction. First, as described above, Deutsch stresses that the pervasive climate of a situation influences parties' conflict behavior. According to Deutsch, this generalized quality or force emerges as shared perceptions of interdependence develop. Perceptions of interdependence are generalized through parties' assumptions about their common interests, their level of trust, their friendly or hostile attitudes toward each other, their perceptions of similarity or difference in positions, and their communication. These perceptions constitute an overarching climate, a sense of the situation that shapes how parties calculate their moves and perceive each other.

Second, Deutsch points to the cyclical relationship between perceptions of interdependence and interaction. Deutsch suggests that generalized perceptions of interdependence arise from interaction, and once established, they in turn guide interaction. In other words, he assumes that interaction, cooperative or competitive, creates the climates just mentioned and, in turn, that parties' trust, attitudes, beliefs, and so on, rebound to influence interaction and reinforce themselves. This cycle is common in groups and organizations. For example, a manager and an employee with a bad work record are likely to come into a performance appraisal interview with the expectation that it will be an unpleasant competitive situation, where the boss rebukes the employee and the employee tries to evade responsibility. It is this *contrient,* suspicious climate that causes both to interact mistrustfully and competitively in order to "protect themselves"; this reinforces the climate, which reinforces the interaction, and so on in a deadly spiral. Similar spirals also work for cooperative, trusting climates, as we will see in Chapter 3. This is an important insight for an interaction-centered approach to conflicts, and we will expand on it considerably in Chapter 3.

Deutsch's two basic assumptions provide a strong footing for understanding the general direction conflict interaction takes. However, we must also consider certain limitations of his analysis. Deutsch isolates one feature of conflict situations, interdependence, and derives his entire analysis of cooperative and competitive processes from this feature. Although this has the advantage of permitting a simple, orderly description of cooperation and competition, it carries the disadvantage of an overly narrow focus. Other features of group situations, such as dominance or emotional relationships, are underemphasized in Deutsch's discussion. These omissions can lead to serious misdiagnoses of conflicts. Several features of climates discussed in Chapter 3, including dominance relations, supportiveness, group identity, and goal interdependence, are crucial aspects of group experience that are not directly accounted for in Deutsch's analysis. Each of these aspects of climate has its own particular flavor, and each can affect conflict in its own right. Interdependence alone is not always the key to understanding climates.

A second limitation of Deutsch's analysis stems from his overemphasis on perceptions. Deutsch views participants' perceptions as the immediate cause of cooperative or competitive behavior. Although he recognizes that interdependence is exhibited in the interaction between people, he chooses to emphasize participants' *perceptions* of interdependence as the primary "cause" of conflict behavior. This leads to two problems. By focusing on perceptions of individuals, the analysis shifts away from a focus on a *quality* of the situation. This makes it very difficult to explain behavior in cases where individuals' perceptions disagree. Deutsch explicitly states that his analysis holds only for cases where both persons' perceptions are the same; where individuals differ it is not possible to predict their behavior. This assumption may rule out a considerable number of important cases, because individuals often have very different perceptions of what drives the group's interaction. Deutsch's focus also has the disadvantage of diverting attention away from behavior and towards individual psychology, thereby making it less likely that we will recognize forces that shape conflict as they are produced in interaction.

Bearing these limitations in mind, we can take away several critical insights from Deutsch's work. The importance of *interdependence,* the role of *climates* in conflict, and the *cyclical flow between climate and interaction* are certainly important pieces of this puzzle called conflict.

PHASE THEORIES

A number of theorists emphasize that conflicts are not so much events as processes. They stress that conflicts occur over time as people act and react to each other. To capture the development of conflicts, these researchers have tried to describe series of phases or stages that conflicts tend to pass through. Some phase analyses (Kriesberg, 1973; Rummel, 1976) are based on studies of societal or international conflicts, while others are drawn from studies of organizations (Walton, 1969), bargaining and negotiation (Morley and Stephenson, 1977) and small group processes (Ellis & Fisher, 1975). Although there are some differences in the phases described in each analysis, all suggest that conflicts can be broken down into recognizable, sequential periods marked by different behaviors and sequences of behaviors.

Rummel, for example, takes a very broad view of conflict when he suggests that conflicts pass through five sequential phases. In the earliest stage, Rummel says, conflict is *latent*. In other words, individuals hold different dispositions or attitudes which carry the potential for conflict. Differences in values, objectives, outlooks are present and lay the groundwork for future behavior. During the *initiation* phase, some "triggering event" causes the individuals to act. At this point, the potential differences become the basis for interaction. After the conflict has been initiated, the interaction turns towards an attempt at *balancing power*. In this third phase, individuals assess each other's capabilities and willingness to use force, threats, rewards, and so on, and they actually confront the issue as they try to reach some accommodation or settlement. The accommodation leads to a *balance of power* phase, in which the participants come to understand the consequences of the resolution and learn to live with the outcomes. This phase is characterized by the "set expectations" of individuals and may last for some time until significant changes in circumstances, attitudes, or goals arise. Such evolving changes lead to a *disruption* stage where parties realize that circumstances are ripe once again for the emergence of potential conflict and eventual confrontation. This model implies a continual cycle from latency to initiation to balancing power to a balance of power to a disruption back to a new latency, and so on, until the issue is ultimately resolved.

Based on a much narrower study of how small, decision-making groups settle conflicts, Ellis and Fisher identified three recognizable conflict phases, each "distinguished by characteristic patterns of interaction" (1975, p. 206). As groups attempt to reach agreement over possible decision-making proposals, they tend to move through an initial *interpersonal conflict* phase. During this stage, members attempt to orient themselves to the issue. There are relatively low levels of disagreement, a considerable number of comments that reveal members' ambiguity about the issue and many attempts to seek information about the various proposals that the group is considering. Since any conflict during this phase is based on the original, individual differences between the members rather than issues generated by the group as a whole, Ellis and Fisher called this stage the interpersonal conflict phase. The second conflict phase begins when there is direct *confrontation* on the issue. During this period, there is a marked increase in the number of comments favoring or disfavoring alternative proposals. There is also a high incidence of favoring comments following favoring comments and disfavoring comments following disfavoring comments. The interaction, in other words, is characterized by members' attempts to make a direct assault on the issue and to determine how much support there is for the various proposals that have been suggested by group members. Finally, groups tend to move through what Ellis and Fisher call a *substantive conflict* phase where there is a noticeable increase in the number of agreement statements as members try to reach a final decision. As in the first phase, there are numerous comments revealing members' ambiguity about the issue. In this last stage, however, the ambiguity usually signals that members are changing their minds as the group moves closer to a final choice on the issue at hand. The conflict de-escalates as they make this choice.

The Rummel and Ellis and Fisher studies are just two examples of phasic analyses of conflict, but their general similarity should be evident. Both characterize conflicts in terms of two broad phases, a *differentiation* phase followed by an *integration* phase (Walton, 1969). In the differentiation phase latent conflicts emerge and the differences between the group members come into sharp relief. Usually members struggle to the point that further escalation seems fruitless. At this point a process of integration begins. Members move toward some solution, hopefully one that meets everyone's needs, but sometimes simply one that they can live with. If integration is not completely successful the conflict may later cycle back to a new differentiation phase. This *differentiation-integration* pattern is important because it indicates what individuals must cope with to move successfully through a conflict. Phase analyses have also led to several other important insights:

_____ **Figure 2** _____
Three phase analyses of conflict

Walton	Rummel	Ellis & Fisher
	latent conflict	
differentiation	initiation	interpersonal conflict
	balancing of power	confrontation
integration	balance of power	substantive conflict
	disruption	

(1) Phase research suggest that conflicts have a definite pattern or rhythm. The pattern often seems to depend on participants' expectations about likely directions conflicts will take. These expectations seem to be governed by an underlying logic of progressions that conflicts go through and serve to make even apparently confusing interaction understandable over the long run. Looking back and forward simultaneously, members can see an ambiguous situation of latent conflict growing into a test of power and can anticipate the need to de-escalate the conflict by compromise or at least by "backing off." Phase analyses imply that an understanding of the direction and pattern of conflict behaviors can only be gained if conflicts are looked at broadly with an eye towards the sequence of behaviors that occur over time. Phase analyses lead to a conception of conflict that includes not only

confrontation and discussion of differences between parties, but also intermittent periods of equilibrium and calm when the parties "settle into" new arrangements resulting from the conflict.

(2) The same patterns or forms of interaction can serve different functions in different conflict phases. Each phase provides the broader, meaningful context that makes behavior understandable in light of what is going on at any particular stage of the conflict. Ellis and Fisher note, for example, that ambiguous comments occur in both the first and third phase of decision-making conflict in small groups. In phase one, these comments reflect the ambiguity of indecision; people are unsure about their attitudes and are trying to orient themselves to the issue before the group. In the final phase, however, the ambiguous comments reflect members' moves from one position to another. Members are changing their minds so that agreement can be reached in the group and a decision can be made. So, an understanding of the general phase guides interpretation of the more specific comments or sequences of acts occurring at any moment in the conflict.

(3) Phase research also suggests that certain events can ignite confrontation, not because they carry any particular importance in themselves, but because they occur at a critical point in the conflict interaction. As a conflict ripens and people feel pressure to face up to the issues, seemingly common and inconsequential events can trigger rapid escalation. A misplaced criticism, teasing, or even a casual reference to a touchy subject can be the "straw that breaks the camel's back," that forces members to address an issue or act on previously unacknowledged differences. While latent differences may influence interaction in subtle and destructive ways, the issues themselves remain veiled until the triggering event brings them out in the open.

(4) Conflict often includes a "testing" period before any direct confrontation occurs. This testing period allows parties to reduce their uncertainty about what others will do if they make certain moves. For example, in the face of an impending conflict one person may want to cooperate, but fears being taken advantage of. By making certain subtle cooperative overtures the individual can assess likely responses without opening him or herself up too much. By "testing the waters" parties gain knowledge of the likely consequences of moves they might make. This knowledge allows people to develop broad strategies and to choose specific tactics as the conflict unfolds. Phase analyses suggest that these testing periods can play a critical role in determining the direction conflicts take; they offer a chance for people to flirt with various approaches without overly exposing themselves.

The preceding points indicate that phase models are built on close analyses of interaction. Phase analyses are, by definition, concerned with the *sequence* of moves as conflicts unfold. They attempt to outline meaningful segments of interaction based on analyses of series of actions and reactions.

The main problem with phasic theories of conflict is that they may be too simplistic. Recent research suggests that phasic analyses may sometimes overemphasize the role of a "logical" step-by-step sequence in the development of conflicts. Poole (1981), for example, found that the assumption of a set sequence of phases was often not correct for decision-making groups. Instead of a single set of phases applicable to all decisions, he found numerous different sequences, depending on how the group chose to attack its problem. This finding is also likely to apply to conflicts. Instead of finding that all conflicts go through, say, three phases—interpersonal conflict, then confrontation, then substantive conflict—we are likely to observe more complex sequences as well—for example, interpersonal conflict, then confrontation, then interpersonal conflict, then another confrontation phase, then substantive conflict. We will still observe the cycles and several other characteristics found by phase analyses researchers, but there may be more complexity than current theories suggest. Factors such as the particular strategies adopted by group members or attempts to jockey for power may make conflicts considerably more complicated than phase theories assume. These additional factors must be taken into account in forming expectations about how conflicts will go.

Nonetheless, phase theories point to the ways in which members' behaviors tend to perpetuate conflict cycles and illustrate how conflicts develop a thrust that leads interaction in constructive or destructive directions. The concepts of *latent conflict, triggering incidents, differentiation and integration,* and *interaction cycles* will play an important role in our analyses of conflict interaction.

EXCHANGE THEORY AND EXPERIMENTAL GAMING

Social exchange theory and experimental gaming are two separate, but closely-related approaches to the study of conflict. Each has spawned a huge body of research in its own right, with over a thousand experimental game studies alone (Pruitt and Kimmel, 1977) and literally dozens of books summarizing social exchange research (for example, Homans, 1961; Blau, 1964; Thibaut and Kelley, 1959; Roloff, 1981). Despite the fact that researchers in either approach often seem unaware of studies conducted in the other, the two approaches are based on similar assumptions and lead to complementary conclusions. In this section we will discuss the two approaches together. Because of the size and importance of these research traditions this section will be longer and more complex than the others.

Both approaches are based on a recognition of two important facts about conflict: (1) conflicts involve people who are *interdependent,* and (2) conflict behavior involves *rewards and costs* for participants. They attempt to explain conflict behavior (and, indeed, all behavior) in terms of the individual's calculations of the potential rewards and costs associated with different actions. Both theories assume that people prefer those behaviors which promise rewards and avoid those for which costs are greater than benefits. Interdependence is critical because (as we noted in the Introduction) how others act and respond determines, in large part, the individual's rewards and costs. Both approaches define interdependence as the degree to which two people can influence each others' rewards or costs. In order to show the relationship of the two approaches, we will first discuss the assumptions of Exchange Theory and then show how they translate into those of Game Research.

Social exchange theory is built on two basic assumptions. First, it assumes that the guiding force behind behavior is *self-interest.* It presumes people monitor their rewards and costs during interaction and strive to achieve a relationship which meets their needs in terms of outcomes. Outcomes are defined as rewards minus costs. There are various ways to define what "meets people's needs." The most obvious way is to assume that people attempt to maximize their profits regardless of the other's loss (cf. Lewin's individualistic climate). However, social exchange occurs in the context of a relationship between people, and few relationships could survive for long in this dog-eat-dog situation. Instead, individuals often seem to seek outcomes that are fair in relation to the other's outcomes. This rule of fairness, which has also been called distributive justice (Homans, 1961) and equity (Walster, Walster, & Berscheid, 1978), states that rewards should be proportionate to costs or contributions made to the relationship. Whether people seek to maximize their outcomes or to achieve fair distributions of outcomes, they are assumed to alter their own behavior and to attempt to alter others' behavior so as to achieve their desired outcomes. Social exchange theory does not imply that rewards or costs can always be absolutely or objectively defined. People are often unaware of or mistaken about the consequences of their behavior. Rather, it is the parties' *perceptions* of benefits and costs that guides their behavior.

Second, social exchange theory assumes that rewards and costs stem from *exchanges of resources* among participants during interaction. Roloff (1981, p. 21) defines social exchange as "the voluntary transference of some object or activity from one person to another in return for other objects or activities." A wide range of social resources may be exchanged in interaction, including liking, love, status, information, help, approval, respect, and authority. Exchange theory assumes that people exchange or deny resources every time they interact. When Sherry compliments Herb on his new tie, she gives him approval; when Herb smiles back at Sherry, he gives her liking. In the same vein, when Sherry yells at Herb to pick up his socks she gives him disapproval; when Herb refuses, he denies Sherry his cooperation.

A corollary to the two assumptions is that parties exchange resources in order to influence others to behave in ways that yield acceptable outcomes. Thus Sherry might compliment Herb so that he will wear his tie again; this will make him look attractive and be more pleasant for Sherry to be with. In the same way, Herb might refuse to pick up his socks in order to frustrate Sherry and show her that shouting will not work; if she stops yelling and asks him politely, Herb's outcomes will be better. From a social exchange perspective interaction is a complex transaction in which individuals calculate present and desired outcomes and act in a manner that will maintain or improve these outcomes. It applies an economic metaphor to interaction.

This analysis suggests that conflict will emerge when one person (1) feels his or her outcomes are too low and (2) perceives or anticipates resistance from another when attempts are made to raise those outcomes (Roloff, 1981, Ch. 4). Outcomes may be too low because the person did not receive an expected reward, or received an unexpected cost, or because the person perceives inequity between his or her rewards and those of others. Conflict is triggered when the individual comes to believe that the other is responsible for low outcomes or that the other stands in the way of future improvements. As we will see below, both individuals can take several alternative paths in dealing with this conflict.

Because social exchange theory is based on an economic metaphor, it dovetails nicely with *experimental game research* which is based on theories originally developed in economics (Von Neumann & Morgenstern, 1947). Thibaut and Kelley's version of exchange theory (1959, Kelley & Thibaut, 1978) is strongly influenced by the economic theory of games and is often utilized in game experiments. Basically the experimental gaming approach likens interaction, particularly conflicts, to games of strategy (for example, chess), in which the results of each player's moves depend on the other player's moves. In its most basic form the experimental gaming approach makes the following assumptions:

1. The structure of a game is composed of choices (options) available to players and the rewards or costs (payoffs) they receive from selecting a given choice.
2. The choices available to players are limited in number, and players know what these choices are.
3. The payoffs associated with a given move depend not only on the player's choice, but also on the choice made by the other.
4. Players know the payoffs associated with each combination of choices and these payoffs are interesting and meaningful to them.
5. A player's choice is determined by calculation of payoffs (rewards and costs). Rational game behavior consists of the selection of choices that yield favorable outcomes, either the maximization of gain or the attainment of a beneficial norm, such as distributive justice.

Based on these assumptions the motivational structure of any conflict can be represented as a payoff matrix like that in figure 3. The particular game portrayed in figure 3 is called *prisoner's dilemma,* after a well-known situation. Consider two criminals who have been apprehended by the police. They are put in separate rooms and kept incommunicado. The police instruct each that they have two choices: confess or keep silent. If only one confesses, he or she can turn state's evidence and go free, with a reward for nailing the culprit; the other prisoner will "take the rap" and receive a heavy sentence. If both confess they both go to prison with lighter sentences. If both remain silent, they go free because the police cannot make a case without a witness. In figure 3 (a) represents a payoff matrix for this game, and figure 3(b) expresses the payoffs in verbal terms. Notice that within this structure there are incentives for each to betray the other and a lesser reward for remaining faithful.

The numbers in matrix (a) represent the values of outcomes for the prisoners for each pair of choices. In each cell of the matrix, the number in the upper corner is prisoner B's outcome and that in the lower corner is prisoner A's. To determine the outcomes associated with each combination of A's and B's choices, locate A's choice on the left side of the matrix and B's choice on the top of the matrix and then find the cell corresponding to the two choices. For example, if A confesses and B remains silent, the cell for this choice is the one in the lower left-hand corner of (a). (The entries in this cell are A's and B's outcomes.) So, the possible outcomes are shown as follows.

1. If A remains silent *and* B remains silent, then A's outcome is $+1$ and B's outcome is $+1$.
2. If A remains silent *and* B confesses, then A's outcome is -2 and B's outcome is $+2$.
3. If A confesses *and* B remains silent, then A's outcome is $+2$ and B's outcome is -2.
4. If A confesses *and* B confesses, then both have outcomes of -1.

All payoff matrices for experimental games can be understood in this fashion.

As this discussion shows, because the two prisoners are interdependent they also face a dilemma. If one confesses and the other does not, the first goes free. If both confess they both go to prison. Can each trust the other to stand fast and not be

Figure 3

Outcome Matrices for *Prisoner's Dilemma*

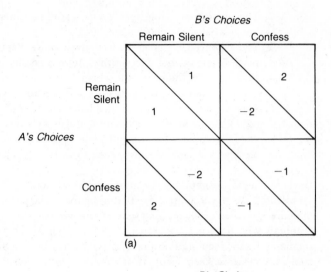

(a)

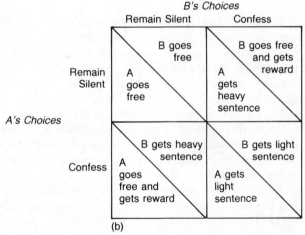

(b)

a traitor? Misplaced trust may result in a severe penalty. The prisoners are thus in a situation where there are incentives both to cooperate and to compete—a *mixed-motive* situation in the terminology of Game Research. Because, as we have noted, almost all conflicts have incentives for both cooperation and competition, mixed-motive games provide a good experimental model for conflict situations.

There are several ways in which the prisoners can attempt to resolve their dilemma, and the particular strategies they choose for doing so are the real interest of experimental game research. If each is only allowed one move, they could attempt to predict or infer what the other would most likely do and base their strategy on that prediction. However, in most experimental games, as in most conflicts, the parties are permitted to make more than one move. Hence, they can use the other's previous moves as information for predicting his or her next move. They can also use their own response to the other (competitive or cooperative) to tell the other what his or her choice should be: if, for example, A always confesses and B wants A to change, B can also consistently confess, which gives A -2 outcomes and an incentive to move toward cooperation. If they are allowed to communicate with each other, as they are in many experimental games, they also have other strategies available for maximizing their outcomes. For example, one might persuade the other to remain silent and then betray him or her. The numerous resolution strategies available to parties make it evident that a great many of the processes involved in conflicts—*prediction, persuasion, interchanges of moves, bargaining*—can be simulated with experimental games.

The versatility of games becomes even more apparent when we consider other variations. For one thing, many incentive structures other than the Prisoner's Dilemma can be built into the matrix. Figure 4 shows two other structures. Matrix (a) shows a situation where cooperative *matching* is encouraged. Individuals both receive rewards when they select the same choice and penalties when they make different choices. An example of this situation would be a couple very much in love who are considering whether to move to a different city or stay where they are. If one moves without the other, they both suffer, the mover somewhat more than the stayer. Matrix (b) shows a game called *chicken,* in which one party can win big if he or she can bluff the other, but loses big if the other calls the bluff. This matrix is illustrated by the game of "chicken," in which players drive their cars toward each other at high speeds. If one swerves and the other does not, the first is "chicken" and the other wins admiration for being brave. If both swerve, they lose face, but at least escape unharmed. If both do not swerve they collide. This game also has parallels to the thinking behind nuclear deterrence. Each nation must put itself in danger of annihilation in order to threaten the other. If the threat convinces the opponent to back down the nation scores a great gain. If, however, the opponent responds in kind, the consequences for both are unthinkable. Many other matrices expressing almost any kind of incentive structure are possible (Kelley & Thibaut, 1978). Game research assumes that all types of interdependence can be translated into these terms.

It is also possible to relax the assumption that members know all options or outcomes equally well. As Kelley and Thibaut (1978) point out, many behaviors can be interpreted as attempts to "explore" the outcome matrices. People ask others what they think of alternatives, observe them interacting with other people, and tentatively test out certain alternatives in order to find out more about the outcomes they are likely to receive from interacting with the other. It is also possible to expand the available alternatives to include mutually rewarding options. Just as people sometimes narrow the options available to others with "either-or" type statements ("Either we go to that movie or I'm staying home!"), so too they can widen the range of alternatives ("Why don't we try _____?"). As long as we can get a reasonably small set of options, the game approach is workable.

Finally, games do not have to be confined to the matrix format outlined above. As Pruitt and Kimmel (1977) note, there are three main types of experimental games: (1) *matrix games,* (2) *negotiation games,* which simulate formal negotiations over some issue like an award in a legal case or the price of a used car (points are awarded on the basis of the final agreement), and (3) *coalition games,* in which more than two subjects play a game or bargain and subjects can form coalitions to defeat others (the coalition is awarded points and members then bargain to split

---

Figure 4

Outcome Matrices for Two Conflict Situations

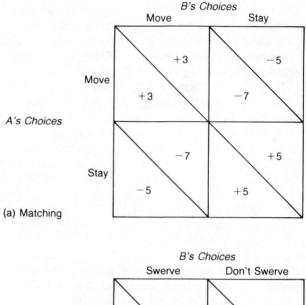

(a) Matching

(b) Chicken

their rewards). Although these games have different formats, for all practical purposes they are equivalent: their outcomes are determined by numerical assignments, the choices available to players are limited, and multiple trials are run.

The similarities of the experimental game approach and exchange theory are evident in the preceding discussion. As Thibaut & Kelley (1959) observe, game matrices can be regarded as explicit, numerical formulations of exchange principles. The advantage of games lies in the fact that the numerically-specified outcomes allow easy control over experimental situations. This advantage has generated an immense amount of research on conflict interaction using experimental games. As this section and the remainder of this book shows, a great deal of our knowledge about conflict is based on bargaining and negotiation research.

The large body of research in the experimental gaming and social exchange traditions has produced numerous interesting and useful findings. Unfortunately, these are far too extensive to summarize completely. Instead we will focus on the three lines of research in these traditions that are the most useful for the study of conflict interaction: (1) research on the *tactics* parties use during conflicts; (2) research on general *strategies* in conflicts; and (3) studies of *coalition formation*.

Tactics. One line of research has been concerned with explaining people's choices among various strategies in cases of conflict or potential conflict. Marwell and Schmitt (1967) studied the sixteen "compliance-gaining" techniques listed in Table 1. They gave subjects four situations with potential conflicts and asked them to rate how likely they would be to use the techniques in the situations. From these ratings they were able to group the techniques into sets which represented how subjects viewed them. The sets they obtained were the following:

1. Rewarding Activity: promises, liking, and pre-giving
2. Punishing Activity: threat and aversive stimulation
3. Expertise: expertise (positive) and expertise (negative)
4. Activation of Impersonal Commitments: moral appeal, self-feeling (positive), self-feeling (negative), altercasting (positive), and esteem (positive)
5. Activation of Personal Commitments: debt, altercasting (negative), altruism, and esteem (negative)

After further analysis, Marwell and Schmitt grouped the sets of techniques into two general types, one representing socially-acceptable techniques (sets 1, 3, and 4) and socially-unacceptable techniques (sets 2 and 5). Miller, Boster, Roloff, and Seibold (1977) did a study replicating the Marwell and Schmitt study, but using situations that were clearly distinguishable in terms of how well the subject knew the other and whether the exchange had long-term or short-term consequences. Miller et al. found considerable differences in use of tactics across different situations. Among other things their analysis suggested that Rewarding tactics and those Impersonal and Personal Commitment tactics with positive connotations are more likely to be used in situations where the party knows the other well, while Punishing tactics, Expertise, and Impersonal Commitments with negative connotations are more likely to be used in situations where the other is not well-known. Once again, a positive (rewarding)—negative (punishing) distinction emerges among the tactics.

Roloff (1976) reports a study of conflict resolution methods which also isolated sets of conflict responses. He gave forty-four possible responses to a sample of high school students and asked them which ones they would use if "something important were taken from them." He also asked them how likely their favorite television character would be to use each of the forty-four responses in a similar situation. Roloff clustered their responses to obtain general types of tactics and obtained the five clusters displayed in Table 2, which he labeled revenge, regression (behavior "similar to that of children"), verbal aggression, physical aggression, and prosocial behavior. In looking for basic dimensions or themes running through these clusters, Roloff, too, categorized them into prosocial responses (which promote the growth and development of relationships) and antisocial responses (which undermine and impede relationships).

These studies suggest that people distinguish conflict response modes on the basis of how rewarding and punishing they are for others. The Miller et al. analysis

TABLE 1. Sixteen Compliance-Gaining Techniques with Examples from Family Situations

1. Promise	(If you comply, I will reward you.) "You offer to increase Dick's allowance if he increases his studying."
2. Threat	(If you do not comply, I will punish you.) "You threaten to forbid Dick the use of the car if he does not increase his studying."
3. Expertise (Positive)	(If you comply, you will be rewarded because of "the nature of things.") "You point out to Dick that if he gets good grades he will be able to get into a good college and get a good job."
4. Expertise (Negative)	(If you do not comply, you will be punished because of "the nature of things.") "You point out to Dick that if he does not get good grades he will not be able to get into a good college or get a good job."
5. Liking	(Actor is friendly and helpful to get target in "good frame of mind" so that he will comply with request.) "You try to be as friendly and pleasant as possible to get Dick in the 'right frame of mind' before asking him to study."
6. Pre-Giving	(Actor rewards target before requesting compliance.) "You raise Dick's allowance and tell him you now expect him to study."
7. Aversive Stimulation	(Actor continuously punishes target making cessation contingent on compliance.) "You forbid Dick the use of the car and tell him he will not be allowed to drive until he studies more."
8. Debt	(You owe me compliance because of past favors.) "You point out that you have sacrificed and saved to pay for Dick's education and that he owes it to you to get good enough grades to get into a good college."

also suggests that people select different tactics in different situations in an attempt to maximize the effectiveness of their attempts to influence outcomes. Roloff (1976, p. 181) puts it as follows:

> Prosocial communication strategies reflect people's attempts to obtain relational rewards by techniques that facilitate understanding of their attitudes and needs. . . . Antisocial communication strategies represent people's attempts to obtain relational rewards by imposing their position on another through force or deception.

Sillars (1980) conducted a study which tested these suggestions. He tested a Subjective Expected Utility (SEU) Model of tactical choice. In common with the game research and social exchange assumptions, SEU models assume people choose behavioral options on the basis of their *expected utility* (the usefulness of the outcome). The more positive the outcome a person expects from a course of action, the more likely he or she is to undertake it. Sillars found that SEU was a

9. Moral Appeal	(You are immoral if you do not comply.) "You tell Dick that it is morally wrong for anyone not to get as good grades as he can and that he should study more."
10. Self-Feeling (Positive)	(You will feel better about yourself if you comply.) "You tell Dick he will feel proud if he gets himself to study more."
11. Self-Feeling (Negative)	(You will feel worse about yourself if you do not comply.) "You tell Dick he will feel ashamed of himself if he gets bad grades."
12. Altercasting (Positive)	(A person with "good" qualities would comply.) "You tell Dick that since he is a mature and intelligent boy he naturally will want to study more and get good grades."
13. Altercasting (Negative)	(Only a person with "bad" qualities would not comply.) "You tell Dick that only someone very childish does not study as he should."
14. Altruism	(I need your compliance very badly, so do it for me.) "You tell Dick that you really want very badly for him to get into a good college and that you wish he should study more as a personal favor to you."
15. Esteem (Positive)	(People you value will think better of you if you comply.) "You tell Dick that the whole family will be very proud of him if he gets good grades."
16. Esteem (Negative)	(People you value will think worse of you if you do not comply.) "You tell Dick that the whole family will be very disappointed in him if he gets poor grades."

*From Marwell & Schmitt (1967), pp. 357–58.

good predictor of which response a subject will choose in a conflict. Subjects evaluated outcomes by considering how likely it was that the tactic would gain compliance and what impact it would have on their relationship. Thus there is evidence that which conflict response mode an individual chooses is based on people's calculations of rewards and costs, both for themselves and for others.

Strategies. Conflict interaction cannot be reduced to parties' choices of single moves. The give and take of move, countermove, and response is integral to conflict, and experimental games are well-suited for studying these interchanges. Consistent with the basic design discussed above, most studies on conflict interaction have focused on *sequences* of moves, that is, sequences of choices from an outcome matrix, or series of moves in bargaining games. A great number of variables which influence these sequences and the strategies used to play them out have been studied, including the incentive structure of the game, the presence of outside audiences, the sex of the parties, the availability of third parties, the type

TABLE 2. Roloff's Modes of Conflict Resolution

Revenge

Hate the person
Destroy something that the person has
Cheat the person
Get drunk
Take a pill
Take something from the person
Turn others against the person
Chase the person away
Lie to the person
Give the person something for returning
    the object
Ignore the missing object
Joke about it

Regression

Ask someone what to do
Cry
Plead with the person
Pray for return of the object
Worry
Pout
Feel guilty that someone took something
    from you
Not know what to do
Run away

Verbal Aggression

Argue with the person
Trick the person
Shout at the person
Insult the person
Take the object back
Threaten the person
Tell someone about it
Make the person feel guilty
Ask others' help

Physical Aggression

Shoot the person
Hit the person
Stab the person
Kick the person
Punish the person
Shove the person

Prosocial

Help the person reform
Feel sorry for the person
Forgive the person
Talk to the person
Be honest with the person
Think about what to do
Try to persuade the person
Let the person alone

"Roloff's Modes of Conflict Resolution and Their Items" from "Communication Strategies, Relationships, and Relational Changes" by Michael Roloff in *Explorations in Interpersonal Communication*, edited by Gerald R. Miller. Copyright © 1976 by Sage Publications, Inc. Reprinted by permission of Sage Publications and Michael Roloff.

of communication allowed, the importance of the issues, and the personality attributes of the bargainers (see Rubin & Brown, 1975, for an extensive summary of many of these studies). We will refer to these studies throughout the remainder of this book. At this point we want to concentrate on one important area that offers a clear illustration of game findings and their value—the study of *strategies* employed by members with approximately equal power. The literature on strategies in experimental games is voluminous, and somewhat confusing, but three particularly effective strategic options emerge.

The first strategy is *toughness*. A tough bargainer makes extreme opening demands, relatively few concessions, and small concessions when he or she does move (Bartos, 1970). Generally, the negotiator attempts to convey strength and determination and to discourage others sufficiently so that they will yield first. The strategy is designed to maximize the person's gains, if need be at the expense of the other. It is consistent with the competitive, compromising, and collaborative styles discussed above: all three orientations imply that the party is assertive of his or her own needs, a necessary prerequisite of toughness.

The research on tough strategies indicates that a party can obtain a more favorable final agreement by being tough (Chertkoff and Esser, 1976, 480–481). Indeed, Bartos (1970) has shown that if both bargainers are tough, other things being equal, they will achieve the optimal solution. However, there are limitations on this result. Tough bargainers must not be too uncompromising, or their partners may respond with counterattacks or equal intransigence. When there is little pressure on the bargainers to come to an agreement or when time is short, excessive toughness can lead to impasses. In general, it seems best to convey an impression of "tough, but fair" and give on less important points. Toughness encourages the other to take one seriously, but excessive toughness may seem foolish and bull-headed.

A second strategy is the *reformed sinner*. Unlike toughness, which simply aims to maximize the individual's outcomes, the reformed sinner attempts to induce an uncooperative partner to cooperate and thereby enhance outcomes (Pruitt & Kimmel, 1977, pp. 377–78). In this strategy the person initially competes for a period of time, and then shifts over to cooperation. The method demonstrates that the individual could compete if he or she wanted to, but that they chose instead to cooperate and reward the other. In most studies this strategy, or a similar one in which the individual is initially tough and then relaxes his or her demands, is unusually effective in inducing the other's cooperation. Of course, for the strategy to work, there must be an incentive for the person responding to the reformed sinner to cooperate rather than exploit the weakness. Thus the reformed sinner must maintain a "stick" and be prepared to resort to it again if the "carrot" does not work.

Why does the reformed sinner strategy work? One explanation points to the respect that such a strategy creates for the person using it. By initially competing, the person demonstrates an ability to punish the other. Voluntarily giving up this punishment and exposing oneself to the other generates respect and also a sense that the person must be sincere in his or her offers of cooperation. This explanation is illustrated in the strategy used by many elementary school teachers who want to have an "open classroom" atmosphere, yet do not want students to abuse this openness. The teachers often try to be somewhat stern at the beginning of the year and make an effort to show the students that they can punish them if need be. Only after respect for the teacher's authority is established does the teacher gradually relax and attempt to promote a more open atmosphere. The second explanation is simpler than the first and goes hand-in-hand with it: it posits that once the other has experienced the negative consequences of competition, sudden cooperation will be attractive and motivate the other to cooperate. If this explanation is valid, it implies that the person employing the strategy should take care to make the other recognize the disadvantages of competition and the advantages of cooperation.

The third and final strategy is *tit for tat,* or matching. In this strategy one person matches the moves made by the other. If the other makes a competitive or hostile move, so does this person; if the other makes a cooperative or conciliatory move, so does this person. This strategy is also effective in persuading the other to cooperate, but it can also backfire and trap both parties in an escalating spiral. Two explanations of this result can be offered. The first is based on Leary's (1957) conception of matching, which will be discussed in the next chapter. Briefly, Leary argues that partners in a relationship tend to reciprocate similar levels of hostility or friendliness almost unconsciously. This *interpersonal reflex* leads to perpetuation of the hostile or friendly tendencies in relationships. Hence, by matching cooperativeness one partner may induce the other to unconsciously continue cooperative moves. The second explanation assumes a more conscious process of inference. By matching, the partner is demonstrating to the other that he or she is responsive and therefore could be persuaded to cooperate. This encourages the other to exercise any impulses he or she may have to cooperate, to see if the partner can be induced to respond (Apfelbaum, 1964). This interpretation is strengthened by the finding that if the first person is slow to reciprocate matching behavior (giving the impression that he or she is deliberating whether to reciprocate or not), the other is more likely to remain cooperative. Apparently, reluctant cooperation suggests conscious or deliberate intention and thereby implies a stronger commitment to cooperation.

There are infinite variations on the strategies members can use in conflict games, but the three reported here show the most reliable and consistent results. We will expand on them in chapter 4 when we discuss power, moves, and countermoves in conflicts.

Coalition Formation.   Consider the following example: Ed and Janet are members of the Affirmative Action Committee of a large corporation. In the two years they have served on the comittee both have grown to dislike Thelma, the committee's chairperson. Thelma is an assistant administrator from the President's office and tends to be very careful in her recommendations on grievance cases, because she is afraid to offend her superiors. Janet and Ed have seen Thelma's caution result in the dismissal of several good cases and they are determined to try to counteract Thelma's slowdown of the committee. What should they do?

Although either Ed and Janet could try to control the group by themselves, it is more likely that they will form an alliance or coalition. Since both have less power than Thelma, they have a greater probability of success if they team up. There are also costs involved, because both Ed and Janet give up a certain amount of freedom when they form a coalition. Since their effectiveness depends on joint action, each must trust the other and each is vulnerable if the other decides to betray them. However, in this case the benefits are likely to outweigh the costs, because a coalition greatly enhances Ed and Janet's chances of influencing their group. Half a loaf is better than none at all.

These considerations suggest that the principles of game and social exchange theories would be very useful to explain coalition behavior. Game and exchange researchers have conducted numerous studies of coalition choices, and this research gives us some clues to how coalitions form.

The earliest theory of coalition formation was advanced by Caplow (1956), who argued that coalitions formed on the basis of *minimum power* necessary to defeat the opponent. Caplow assumed that parties are guided by a motivation to maximize the number of others they control (and therefore their ability to control the rewards they obtain). If this motivation holds, then relatively strong members will seek to form a coalition with the weakest member (or members) who still has enough power to defeat their opponent. For example, for three members A, B, and C whose ratio of power is 4(A) to 3(B) to 2(C), the principle of minimum power would predict that coalitions between A and C, or B and C, would be more likely to form than between A and B. Caplow's theory suggests that, "weakness is strength"; the weakest member of the triad is the only one who will always be included in a coalition. Evidence from several studies supported this prediction and the minimum power theory.

Gamson (1961) advanced a theory that is different from Caplow's but still grounded in exchange theory. Gamson chose to refer directly to the rewards received from coalitions. He theorized that rewards depended on the resources a person could contribute to the coalition—the greater a person's contribution the greater the share of rewards the person would be entitled to. On the assumption that each person in the coalition desired to maximize his or her rewards, Gamson predicted that coalitions would form on the basis of *minimum resources*. This principle predicts that the most likely coalition would be the one capable of controlling the group which involves minimum resources contributed by the two members. In this case members would attempt to maximize their own rewards by preferring those coalitions where their own contribution is as great as possible relative to other members. In the case of A, B, and C the most likely coalition would be the B-C alliance. Both A and B will seek to ally with C, but C will prefer B, because this alliance will maximize C's contributions relative to the other and therefore entitle C to a greater share of rewards.

The minimum power and minimum resources theories make somewhat different predictions about coalition formation. Minimum power theory argues that coalitions A-C and B-C are equally likely, while minimum resources theory predicts that B-C is much more probable than A-C. This difference permitted comparison of the two principles. Generally, the evidence has favored Gamson's minimum resource theory. For example, one way of studying coalition formation is to create a political game simulating a political convention. Subjects are assigned different amounts of power by varying the number of votes they control, for example, A might control 40 votes, B 30 votes, and C 20 votes. In these studies all three possible coalitions form, but A-C and B-C form much more often than A-B, and B-C is much more likely than A-C (Gamson, 1964; Komorita & Chertkoff, 1973; Murnighan, 1978; Baker, 1981). Hence, *minimum resource* theory seems a more plausible explanation than minimum power theory.

Minimum resource theory assumes members of coalitions divide rewards in proportion to their contributions. If B contributes 30 votes and C only 15, then B is entitled to twice as much benefit as C. However, Komorita and Chertkoff (1973) studied the division of rewards in coalitions. They found that members bargain over the division of rewards prior to joining coalitions. This bargaining is not always open—it may be done "under the surface" without people's admission that it is occurring. The bargaining process determines what coalitions form, and it may result in distributions of rewards that differ considerably from the proportion of resources contributed. Minimum resources still seem to determine what coalitions form, but it does not necessarily *determine* the division of rewards.

Going back to Ed, Janet, and Thelma, these findings would suggest that the Ed-Janet coalition was more likely to form than the Ed-Thelma or Janet-Thelma alliances. As Ed and Janet talk about working against Thelma we would also expect them to refer to their contributions as a way of setting the division of rewards. For example, Ed might refer to his own verbal skill by saying "I'll try to point out the flaws in her case, and you back me up." In saying this, Ed implicitly assigns to Janet the supporting role and, hence, a weaker contribution. If Janet accepts this, she may be granting Ed a greater claim to any benefits that result, such as the gratitude of other members for stopping Thelma. Of course, Ed and Janet may address the issue of division of rewards directly. Many coalitions depend on members' openly agreeing to do X in exchange for Y. However, there does not have to be an explicit agreement for minimum resource theory to apply. Unspoken agreements may hold just as strongly as spoken ones.

However, as much support as it has received, the minimum resources theory is not sufficient to explain all coalition behavior. There are cases where Janet or Ed would join forces with Thelma rather than with each other. In every coalition experiment, there are at least some A-B coalitions, a fact which runs counter to both Caplow's and Gamson's predictions. What accounts for this? Research by political scientists (Gamson, 1961; Axelrod, 1970) has disclosed that *similarities of attitudes and beliefs can also motivate coalition formation*. These political theories assume that parties join coalitions not only for rewards, but also because they are interested in getting certain policies or measures enacted. For example, it assumes Ed and Janet form a coalition not only to obtain rewards, but also because they desire to change the committee, independent of rewards. From this assumption it follows that parties will prefer coalitions with others with similar preferences: if both favor similar goals from the beginning they have a common ground for cooperation, and they are less likely to be sidetracked from their original ends.

The similarity principle implies a considerably different explanation for coalition formation than the minimum resource principle, an explanation not directly tied to rewards. Lawler and Youngs (1975) compared the two explanations with an experimental game simulating a political convention. They found that both rewards and attitude-similarity determined coalition choice, but attitude-similarity was "by far, the most important determinant." This finding may not hold for other situations where specific platforms are not so important, but it does show that similarity must be taken into account as well as reward.

The study of coalition formation is important, because coalitions are the primary path to power for weaker members (Janeway, 1980). Because of this fact stronger members often move to head off coalitions among weaker parties, either by forming coalitions themselves or by confusing issues and sewing seeds of discontent among their weaker counterparts. The findings discussed here underscore the importance of communicative processes in coalition formation. Members must convince others of rewards to be won and of their similarities in order to promote coalitions. In addition, they must downplay or make plans against any costs or problems they might face. However, these strategies cut both ways. Just as weaker members can use them to band together, so can the stronger members use them to win over weaker ones or prevent their alliances. Conflict interaction is an arena for the struggle over allies between strong and weak. In chapter 4 we will explore the evolution of power through coalitions in more detail.

Experimental game research and social exchange theory give us several critical insights into conflict interaction. (1) Both approaches focus on the role of *strategic calculation* in conflicts. They recognize that people usually play an active, controlling part in conflict interaction, rather than the passive, reactive role assigned to them by psychodynamic theories. Moreover, the two approaches attempt to specify the principles governing people's choices, in this case the attainment of positive outcomes. These theories make it possible to identify factors which may predict others' behavior in conflict situations.

(2) The two approaches also emphasize the importance of *interdependence* in conflicts. They underscore the fact that conflicts almost never occur in wholly competitive or wholly cooperative situations. There is almost always a mixture of incentives to compete and incentives to cooperate. If parties focus on the former, they may be drawn into an ever-escalating spiral; if they recognize the latter, they have grounds for a productive resolution.

(3) The two approaches also give a good picture of conflict as an *exchange of moves and countermoves*. They show how later moves are shaped and constrained by earlier ones and how each party's *power*—in the form of control over the other's rewards and costs—determines the moves they can make.

(4) Finally, the game and exchange approaches recognize that the rewards and costs associated with moves depend not only on the direct, instrumental gains they yield (for example, a raise in salary), but also on the effects the moves have on the relationship between the two parties. The exchange theorists recognize that resources obtained from relationships—such as love, liking, and self-esteem—are critically important sources of rewards and costs. People's calculations are based not just on gain, but on *consequences for their relationships* as well.

Clearly, game research and social exchange theory offer a powerful and useful analysis of conflict. Like all scientific theories, however, they have limitations as well. In effect, both approaches argue that conflict interaction can be reduced to a series of exchanges governed by participants' calculations of potential outcomes. This implies that other aspects of interaction may be interesting, but they are important only insofar as they influence the outcome structure or participants' practical reasoning. This is quite a claim. Can it be sustained?

At least three problems revolve around the issue of human rationality. Both game and exchange perspectives assume people (a) know their options, (b) know the outcomes associated with them, and (c) perform calculations of gains and losses. Let's consider these three assumptions in turn. As Wilmot and Wilmot (1978) observe, one shortfall of game theory is that it does not take into account the extremely wide variety of choices people face in real life. Games usually assume there is a relatively small set of options that remain stable over time. Consider the case of John and Steve who own a business together. Steve, who keeps the books, has let another check bounce because he doesn't keep up with deposits and balancing the account. The bank has just called John, and he is very angry about it. Here are just a few of his choices:

1. Ignore the problem
2. Leave in disgust and go get a drink
3. Shout at Steve
4. Leave Steve a note so Steve won't see how angry he is
5. Tell a mutual friend so he can let Steve know how angry John is
6. Call a financial consultant to help straighten out the books
7. Dissolve the partnership
   etc.

These are just some of John's choices. Depending on how Steve reacts to his move, John may face a totally different set of options later. John may, for example, choose response number 4 in the hope that things will cool off. But Steve may feel a note is impersonal and get angry. In the face of Steve's counter-accusation of his coldness, John faces a whole new array of problems. Real-world conflicts are often not fought out of small, well-defined game matrices that remain stable over time. The "option" problem becomes even thornier when we consider that parties often create entirely new options as they interact. The structure of options changes constantly as the conflict interaction unfolds.

Second, these theories assume that parties know the consequences and outcomes associated with each option and make choices on the basis of expected outcomes. However, this is a much more complex process than it seems at first. Most resources or behaviors are neither totally rewarding nor totally noxious; instead they have complex sets of properties, some of which are rewarding and some of which entail costs. For example, threatening to break up their partnership may be rewarding to John because he would be free of Steve's sloppiness, he could get out of a business that has become boring, he has the satisfaction of having shown Steve how he feels, and he would have more time to spend with his kids. At the same time this threat may be costly, because John would miss Steve if Steve agreed to the breakup and because bad feelings might arise even if they didn't break up the partnership. If John could consider all these possible consequences prior to acting, he would probably have trouble assigning positive or negative values to them. Is the reward of freedom from Steve's sloppiness greater than the cost of missing his friendship? How much greater? It is one thing to numerically rate rewards on a questionnaire concerning a hypothetical conflict; it is quite another to place values on possible consequences in the flux of an ongoing, highly-emotional conflict. People simply do not know what they want sometimes.

Third, these perspectives assume that behavioral choice is based on calculations of gains and losses. However, consider John's situation. If he considers three or four positive and negative consequences for each option, as well as the probability that the option will yield each consequence, he faces a formidable calculating task. This task, as Simon (1955) notes, is far beyond the available capacities of the human brain. It is simply impossible to weigh thirty to forty items of information for every act we undertake.

There is an easy answer to the first three objections. It can be argued that people do not consider a wide range of confusingly similar options, consequences, and outcomes. Instead they focus on just those few elements that they find salient in the given situation; they simplify issues to fit what they are capable of doing, and if they select a given outcome it is because it is rewarding given their limited perceptions of the situation. This explanation, however, opens the door to the problem of circularity (Skidmore, 1979).

When we see someone doing something, we can conclude that it must be because they expect rewards from doing it. We can then identify the rewards or functions of this behavior for them. However, this is circular. Why is Bob doing X?—because it's rewarding to him. Then how do we know it really is rewarding to him?—because he's doing it. According to this logic *any* behavior is rewarding by definition. Skidmore (1979, pp. 105–06) summarizes the implications of this:

"Reward" and "value" are indeed used as explanatory terms [in Exchange theories]; but in every case they are used to explain something that has already happened, and they are used *ad hoc.* That is, we might observe a man doing something and, to explain his doing it, suggest that it might have been rewarding to him or else he would not have done it. Knowing nothing about the man's values or his previous state of reward or punishment, adding the concept of reward is really to add nothing. We could say, "He did it; I saw him." What more do we know, or what more can we predict, when we add, "It must have been rewarding to him"? Whatever he might do, the explanation remains the same. There is no way to prove the theory wrong, if it is.

Thus we can either try to define options and consequences in the full sense, which entails an impossible calculative task or we can assume people "narrow their fields," which opens us to the charge of circular reasoning when we try to determine how rewards motivate them. If the theory is accepted and we assume that people act because they feel rewarded by something, rewards can always be identified. Either way, however, we are faced with a thorny dilemma if we operate solely from this point of view.

A final problem with the experimental game and social exchange perspectives is their oversimplification of complex issues. According to these theories, options and outcomes are the critical explanatory factors in conflicts. Other variables like power, climate, and the previous history of the conflict are assumed to influence conflict interaction through their effects on rewards and costs associated with options, that is, through their effects on the outcome matrix for the conflict. But this seems to be an oversimplification. As we will see below, climate does influence the rewards and costs associated with various moves: for example, in an open trusting climate, being honest about one's feelings is not as likely to evoke ridicule as it would in an "ordinary business climate." But climate also has other effects on interaction. It influences group members' perceptions of one another and their predictions of what others will do, as well as their attitude toward the group. To focus exclusively on members' choices and not on other aspects of the situation seems too narrow and simplistic. This narrow focus filters our perceptions too much and causes us to ignore or trivialize a number of important aspects of conflict interaction.

We have discussed the limitations of social exchange theory and game research in great length. We have not done this to refute these approaches. On the contrary, the two approaches provide what are probably the most important set of findings we have regarding conflict. We believe it is important to consider the limitations of these approaches because they are so often accepted "whole cloth" as the correct way to look at conflict. Like the other perspectives considered in this chapter, exchange theory and game research provide a suggestive but incomplete view of conflict. It is important to see their limitations and attempt to build on their strengths.

Given their limitations, what is the ultimate value of game research and social exchange theory? First, they provide a *metaphorical* analysis of conflict. Even if they are not accurate in their particulars, the game and exchange metaphors bring out the important characteristics of conflict listed above—conflict as a *sequence of moves and countermoves, the active role of parties* in the development of conflicts, *interdependence,* and the *relational consequences* of conflicts. We will return to these points throughout this book.

In addition, there are cases where these theories are directly applicable, that is, cases where options are well-defined, outcomes fairly clear, and parties are capable of calculating gains and losses. Conflicts in fairly advanced stages, after the parties have clarified their positions and have developed a "working relationship," are probably the most important case for which these theories apply. For example, late stages of labor-management negotiations, where only a few options or proposals remain, can be modeled as games. So can conflicts in personal relationships once issues are heading toward a "moment of truth"—for example, to split up or stay together. A second case is when one party narrows the other's options with a statement such as "either you move to California with me or I'm leaving you!" This can happen very early in an interchange, but it has the function of projecting alternatives into a few choices and pressuring parties to focus on them exclusively. Whenever choices are simplified or narrowed game and social exchange approaches are applicable.

STYLES OF CONFLICT INTERACTION

One labor mediator recently observed that during negotiations he is most confident that the parties will find a settlement when they have lost any basis for predicting each other's behavior. Although the implications of this statement are intriguing in many ways, one point in particular has long captured the attention of conflict researchers. The mediator's observation implies that people enter disputes or negotiation sessions with set expectations about how others will react. Based on their past experiences, they assume that others will adopt predictable styles to deal with conflict. One line of research has tried to identify recognizable styles or strategies people use in conflict and to determine how effective these styles are in different situations. The concept of style originated with Blake and Mouton (1964), Hall (1969), and Kilmann and Thomas (1977). These researchers identified five distinct types of conflict behavior. Their classification is based on two independent components of conflict behavior (Ruble & Thomas, 1976): (a) *assertiveness,* defined as behaviors intended to satisfy one's own concerns, and (b) *cooperativeness,* defined as behaviors intended to satisfy the other individual's concerns. These components combine to specify five styles, shown in Figure 5:

(1) A *competitive* style is high in assertiveness and low in cooperativeness—the party places great emphasis on his or her own concerns and ignores those of others. This orientation represents a desire to defeat the other, and has also been called the *forcing* or *dominant* style. Filley (1975) has referred to those who regularly use this style as "tough battlers."

(2) An *accommodative* style is unassertive and cooperative—the person gives in to the other at the cost of his or her own concerns. This orientation has also been called *appeasement* or *smoothing* and those who follow it attempt to avoid conflict for the sake of maintaining the relationship. It is a self-sacrificing approach, but may also be viewed as weak and retracting. Filley (1975) has called those who usually accommodate "friendly helpers."

(3) An *avoiding* style is unassertive and uncooperative—the person simply withdraws and refuses to deal with the conflict. In this orientation the person is

_____ **Figure 5** _____

Five Conflict-Management Styles and Their Relationships

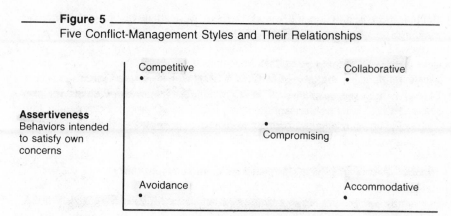

indifferent to the outcome of the conflict and can be described as apathetic, isolated, or evasive. This style has also been called *flight*.

(4) A *collaborative* style is high in both assertiveness and cooperation—the person works to attain a solution that will meet the needs of both people. This orientation seeks full satisfaction for all and has also been called *problem-solving* and the *integrative* style.

(5) A *compromising* style is intermediate in both assertiveness and cooperativeness—both people give up some and "split the difference" in order to reach an agreement. In this orientation both are expected to give up something and keep something. It has also been called *sharing* or *horse trading*.

The five styles have been an enormously useful tool for understanding conflict. They provide a common vocabulary and almost every major writer on interpersonal or organizational conflict has used the styles extensively (for example, Blake & Mouton, 1964; Filley, 1975; Thomas, 1975; Wilmot & Wilmot, 1978). In addition, this classification is grounded in experience: Blake and Mouton developed it from their own experience with organizational conflicts, and later research has supported the existence of the two dimensions and five styles (Filley, 1975; Cosier & Ruble, 1981). Several tests have been developed to enable people to identify their predominant style (Kilmann & Thomas, 1977; Lawrence & Lorsch, 1967; Putnam & Wilson, 1982).

Several studies have also evaluated the *effectiveness* of the styles in various situations. Cummings (reported in Filley, 1975) studied the consequences when pairs of different styles interact with each other. Among other things, he found that competitive versus competitive styles generally resulted in stalemates in bargaining and that competitive versus collaborative styles led to mutual agreement in many cases, though the competitive person still won in over 50 percent of the cases. Phillips and Cheston (1979) compared the effectiveness of forcing (competitiveness) and problem-solving (collaboration) strategies in fifty-two conflict cases reported by middle-managers. Their managers used forcing twice as often as they used problem-solving, but also reported more "bad" solutions with forcing than with problem-solving (about half the incidents in which forcing was used had "bad" results, whereas all instances of problem-solving yielded "good" results).

Phillips and Cheston concluded both methods were effective, but under different circumstances. Forcing was more successful under the following conditions:

- there was one best solution to the problem
- there was a value conflict between the manager and a subordinate
- the manager was fair and could give an objective explanation of his or her reasons for forcing a solution
- the ultimate outcome benefitted the organization rather than one person or a small group

Problem-solving was more successful under these conditions:

- the parties were highly interdependent and had to work together in the future
- there was mutual awareness of the potential for conflict
- those involved were open-minded
- there was a willingness to ignore power issues
- formal procedures for problem-solving were available
- one or both people detected the conflict early and initiated problem-solving before things got bad
- attention was focused on solving a common problem rather than defeating or adopting one person's preferred solution

These studies yield important clues about how we should react to conflicts. However, they are only useful if people *can* adopt the recommended styles in the appropriate situation. Since researchers disagree about what the styles really are, trying to use them may present a problem.

Some writers, like Filley (1975), define style as *the way a person usually responds to conflict.* In this view the styles identify types of people—the "tough battler," the "friendly helper," "the problem-solver"—who are predisposed to handle all conflicts in the same way. This tradition has strongly influenced how the tests that measure a person's predominant style of conflict-handling behavior have been interpreted. Although the way the tests are scored allows people to fall under more than one style (for example, people are often classified as compromisers *and* problem-solvers), styles are interpreted as a relatively *stable* aspect of the individual's personality. We believe this view is misleading: while people certainly develop habitual ways of responding to conflict, they also have a capacity to change or adapt their behavior from situation to situation. Studies of leadership (Hill, 1973; Stogdill, 1974) and conflict behavior (Phillips & Cheston, 1979) have shown that people *change* in response to their situation, and that more effective people are more flexible. In the larger view, an extensive body of research on personality traits has shown that they do not lead to consistent behavior in all situations (Mischel, 1968; Endler & Magnusson, 1976). Two recent studies showed very low correlations between conflict styles and personality traits such as dogmatism, deference, and Machiavellianism (manipulativeness) (Jones & Melcher, 1982). People can and do adapt and change, and denying this capacity through the assumption of fixed styles denies an important human potential.

Taught to large numbers of people this view could be harmful. If people assume their styles are stable traits, they may not be motivated to change in order to break out of destructive patterns. If a supervisor assumes an employee is a "tough battler" and will always be one, he or she is likely to go into any disagreement with the employee with a belligerent, "they're-not-going-to-run-over-me" attitude that greatly increases the possibility of destructive escalation. Alternatively, the supervisor may just give in to avoid the employee's wrath but later resent this act of submission. Neither response is a good one; not only do they increase the probability of destructive conflict and bad decision-making, but they also deny the worker's ability to change. Assuming that the other person is inflexible discourages parties in conflict from trying different approaches that may cause him or her to act differently. The boss's anticipatory attack may make the employee respond as a "tough battler" just to defend him or herself, even though the worker would actually have preferred to discuss the issue quietly. Expectations about "how people are" too easily turn into self-fulfilling prophecies: they lead individuals to act toward others in ways that cause others to respond with the undesirable but expected behaviors. They freeze others into a mold that prevents the flexible and responsive behavior needed for effective conflict management. This problem is compounded when people believe they themselves have a characteristic personal style. "I'm a battler," they say and assume they cannot or do not have to be flexible, because "that's just the way I am." Thus, conflict training programs and tests which purport to identify "characteristic styles" may worsen the very conflicts they are intended to help. People do fall into habits, but they can also change.

A second view of style turns away from personal characteristics and defines styles as *specific types of conflict behavior* (Cosier & Ruble, 1981). In this view, any behavior intended to defeat the other—for example, making a threat—is competitive, while a behavior designed to achieve a mutually acceptable solution—for example, restating the conflict in problem-oriented terms—is collaboration. The styles refer to *categories of behavior*, not types of people. This definition is an improvement over the previous one, because it neither assumes nor encourages inflexibility. However, it too has a problem: the same behavior can fall under different styles. A threat, for example, can be classed under forcing, but it could also be classed under avoidance if it was intended to keep an opponent from raising a conflict ("I'll leave if you bring that up any more"). Postponing a conflict is often advocated as a problem-solving tactic because it gives both sides a "cooling off" period, but it can also be an avoidance tactic if used persistently. An offer to "split the difference" is certainly a compromise, but it can also be accommodation if what the offerer gets is of little value and he or she did it simply to avoid losing. There is a good deal of truth in the definition of styles as behaviors, but there is a broader conception of styles that has also been discussed.

The third, and most useful, position defines styles as *orientations people can take toward conflict* (Thomas, 1975; Phillips & Cheston, 1979). In this view a style is a general expectation about how the conflict should be approached, an attitude about how best to deal with the other party. *A competitive style is oriented toward defeating the other, toward achieving one's own goals without regard for the others,* and it dictates certain behavioral choices to achieve these ends. *A collaborative style reflects an orientation toward mutual benefit.* It favors moves that enhance cooperation and creative thinking toward this end. The definition of styles as orientations solves the problem of classifying specific behaviors under one or the other style: the same tactics can serve different intentions and attitudes. Moreover, this definition is true to the observations showing that people exhibit definite, consistent strategies or thrusts during conflicts without denying their capacity to change. Choosing an orientation is making a decision about the principles that will guide one through the conflict; it is choosing the degree to which parties will be cooperative and/or assertive.

The ultimate problem with this definition—or with any definition of style, for that matter—is its focus on the individual. Style refers to the orientation of the individual in conflict; it reflects one person's approach independent of the other person. However, in the long run, it is self-defeating to talk of orientations or behavior without taking both people into account. Styles represent the "mind sets" parties have in the conflict, but what another person does often changes one's attitudes and intentions, almost without the individual realizing it. Someone may go into a disagreement with a firm intention to collaborate, but if the other person betrays, or viciously attacks, or refuses to talk about the conflict at all, it is hard to keep collaborating. The other's reactions make one want to defend oneself, or strike back, or scream in exasperation, or withdraw completely. Whatever the response and reaction to that response, it makes no sense to talk of behavior as if it were independent of the other's actions. *Moves are a response to another's actions.*

Styles by themselves are not sufficient to describe conflict behavior. We must focus on interaction, and recognize that even descriptions of styles are not sufficient to fully capture what happens when two people act together in conflict. The five styles can be used as reference points; they allow for a classification of moves that can be made. But they are in some ways a static framework: they are certainly not sufficient to explain all the directions conflict takes. To explain conflict behavior in full, we must grapple with the *forces* that shape conflict interaction, and this will require a more comprehensive approach than any we have discussed thus far. The next section lays out the basic framework for this approach.

GUIDING PRINCIPLES IN CONFLICT INTERACTION: AN OVERVIEW

The theories and key concepts we have overviewed in the preceding section start from diverse sets of assumptions and seek to explain different aspects of conflict. Some of these approaches are concerned more directly with explaining conflict interaction than others. As we stated in the Introduction of this book, our major objective is to examine the factors that influence the direction conflict interaction takes. Based on our review of the major theoretical approaches that have been taken to explain conflict, we will summarize four key properties of conflict interaction that help to explain the thrust and direction of conflict:

1. Patterns of behavior in conflicts tend to perpetuate themselves.
2. As senseless and chaotic as conflict interaction may appear, it has a general direction that can be understood.
3. Conflict interaction is sustained by the moves and countermoves of participants; moves and countermoves are based on the power participants exert.
4. Conflict interaction affects the relationships between participants.

There are two main reasons why these properties in particular emerge as central principles. First, these four properties map a fairly comprehensive and unified approach to understanding how conflicts are pushed in constructive or destructive directions. The first property deals with the *momentum of conflict behavior;* it recognizes the tendency for conflicts to build their own thrust as they progress. The second property points to the *underlying coherence of conflict interaction* and thus helps to explain direction. The third concerns the *mechanics of interaction* itself; it demonstrates how behaviors in sequence, moves and countermoves, are the means through which conflicts unfold. The fourth property focuses on the *interplay between conflict interaction and the relationships between participants;* it emphasizes the consequences that result when conflicts head in either constructive or destructive directions.

There is a second reason why these four properties, in particular, emerge as keys for understanding conflict. Each property suggests a place where conflict interaction is vulnerable to *constructive or destructive influences;* each points to a *force* that influences the route conflict interaction takes. We describe these forces in the discussions of the conflict properties below. These forces then become the major topics of the following four chapters in the book.

1. Patterns of behavior in conflicts tend to perpetuate themselves. Almost inevitably, conflict interaction gains a momentum or life of its own. It tends towards repetitive cycles. In part, this tendency is present in any type of human interaction —conflict or otherwise. Any message is based on some, perhaps only barely conscious, assumption about how it will be received. Each assumption or prediction about the reaction is based upon an estimate, a best guess, about the other person, or group as a whole. The choice of message anticipates and reflects the response it seeks and thus promotes the reaction included in its construction. A predictable sequence of act-response-counterresponse gets established quickly in conflict interaction because each message in the sequence helps to elicit the response it receives.

This tendency towards self-perpetuation is encouraged and reinforced by its own usefulness. People in conflict find it useful to "know what to expect." *Any* basis of predictability is more assuring than not knowing what the group will do next. One can prepare counterresponses and strategies during a conflict if one can predict reactions to one's own statements. For this reason, people are often willing to make assumptions about the way others will act before any move is made (Kriesberg, 1973; Sillars, 1980). They therefore run the risk of eliciting the response they assume will occur. As we discussed earlier, anticipating that someone will react with a certain style, like tough battler, can encourage a battling response. It becomes the *appropriate* response, given the previous comment. Since *all* members of the group can find this predictability useful in preparing their own responses, the cycle feeds on itself across members. In some cases a cycle may be helpful to the group: cycles can be productive if they include a periodic check for possible inflexibility or if they lead to success on "easy" issues which then carries over in more difficult disputes (Karrass, 1970). In many other cases, however, the cycles become the basis for inflexibility and lead to uncontrolled destructive interaction.

The self-perpetuating nature of conflict interaction makes conflict highly sensitive to any force that prevents the group from stopping or reversing a conflict cycle.

For this reason, the *working habits* of groups can be influential in moving conflict interaction in either destructive or constructive directions.

Working habits are the habitual interaction strategies a group uses to accomplish its tasks or solve problems, for example, decision procedures such as voting, leadership styles normally employed in the group, or the practice of frequently joking during meetings in order to vent the frustrations of work. Sometimes these are formally and consciously adopted by the group, but more often the group is not conscious of its habits or their effects. Members employ them without thinking. These habits are a critical force in conflicts because they establish a framework for group interaction. As habits, they encourage interaction cycles to continue once they start despite changing events or circumstances that may call for new approaches. They establish expectations about how the group will obtain ideas for consideration and how alternative proposals will be evaluated as the conflict is addressed. Working habits may be beneficial or harmful depending on the situation. The most troublesome habits are those that normally yield benefits but backfire when the conflict situation changes and members fail to take these changes into account.

When confronted with conflict, parties often fall back on behaviors that have proven effective in other contexts. However, behaviors effective in some circumstances may actually worsen conflicts. For example, the common practice of openly evaluating ideas or proposals in an attempt to reach a decision can deepen parties' feeling of anger or competition in conflicts, resulting in escalating hostilities. These behaviors hold a "catch"—because they seem ordinary and have proven useful so often that the group may be blinded to problems they create. The social critic Kenneth Burke (1954) has termed this "catch" a trained incapacity. He argues that we become so well trained in our strategies that they begin to serve as blinders. We think we know what to expect, so we ignore signs that something is wrong. These incapacities are particularly pernicious because group members assume they are doing the right thing when actually they are worsening the situation.

In the Hotline case we described in the Introduction the workers had a "standard operating procedure" which discouraged workers from taking problems with their cases to each other. When Diane asked for time off, the other workers disregarded her problem as irrelevant and evaluated her request only on the basis of its implications for work loads at the center. As a result, the staff concluded that she was slacking off and responded by defining "worker responsibilities," hoping they could get her back in line with "normal" procedures. It was only when Diane escalated the conflict further that the workers were jolted out of their "task-centered" frame of mind and forced to address the issue at hand. In another group where work habits were more firmly entrenched, Diane's grievance may not have broken the habitual interpretation of her behavior, and she might have been fired.

Understanding the role of *habits* in group behavior helps to explain why conflicts get out of hand, why in many cases people cannot see that their behavior is becoming destructive and change it. It is definitely true that people sometimes choose to use force to defeat their opponent, and in these cases a destructive conflict can be stemmed only by altering the motives or power of the participants. However, in many cases, conflicts move in negative directions because people are *incapable* of diagnosing the conflict and altering their behavior. Once people are in a conflict cycle, they may be trapped by their own interaction patterns. Several observers of the arms race between the U.S. and the U.S.S.R. have argued that even though both sides see its pernicious consequences, neither is able to stop escalation, because they are caught in an increasing spiral of matching weapons systems. In the same vein, group members sometimes find themselves in an ever-worsening cycle of arguments, building arsenals of evidence to support a point they may no longer be able to articulate. There is convincing evidence that people develop their perceptions and beliefs from observing their own behaviors, so even destructive patterns tend to begin seeming "normal" or justifiable after a while. The useful appeal of working habits sometimes undermines parties' ability to recognize they are trapped. Since conflict leans heavily towards self-perpetuating cycles in the first place, a group's working habits can hold a strong influence over the route interaction takes.

  2. *As senseless and chaotic as conflict interaction may appear, it has a general direction that can be understood.* Although certain types of interaction (like shouting matches or heated discussions) are often the first images that come to mind when we think of conflict, our conception argues for a more broadly based understanding of conflict interaction. Active suppression of issues, an exchange over who is an authority on some issue, a round of comments explaining positions to a third party, a discussion of the decision-making procedures the group should adopt, or a series of comments which back the group away from a stand so that one member is allowed to "win" a point are forms of conflict interaction as well. *Any exchange of messages that represents an attempt by participants to address some incompatibility of positions is conflict interaction.*

  Although conflicts can emerge and be played out in many forms, they are not chaotic or anarchic. As confused and irrational as the conflict situation may seem to participants and observers, nearly every conflict exhibits definite *themes* that lend coherence to the exchanges and make certain forms of interaction more likely to emerge than others. Even in a brutal, cutting free-for-all, a competitive coherence can be discerned. We have noted earlier in this chapter that these themes, the generalized character of the situation, have traditionally been termed its *climate* (Lewin, 1951; Taguiri, 1968).

  Climate emerges from the enduring and momentary pursuits of the group; it is a *generalized composite of properties that arise from and guide the group's interaction.* The climate in the group provides important information to the members about how conflict is likely to be handled; more specifically, it sets expectations about what participants can safely say, it establishes the emotional tenor of the interaction, influences how much tolerance for disagreement seems possible and determines whether the emergence of any conflict will be an immediate threat to the interpersonal relationships in the group. A change in climate in the group most often means a noticeable difference in the way the group interacts. Consider the following illustration of a shift in group climate and its influence on interaction.

CASE 1.1

  An editorial columnist from the *New York Times* was asked to participate in one of a series of brown-bag discussions that a university's department of journalism hosted over the course of a semester. Faculty, students, and journalists from the community attended these noon-hour seminars. While some speakers in this series of talks gave formal presentations and then left a few minutes for questions afterwards, this columnist said, at the outset of his talk, that although he had prepared comments on a number of different topics he would rather spend the entire hour responding to questions.

Within a few minutes after the session began, a climate of open interaction was established in this group of twelve people. The speaker responded to a wide range of questions. People asked about national economic policy, press coverage of news events, politically-based indictments of the press and the use and misuse of the term "the media." Despite the potentially controversial nature of many of these issues, there was an expectation set in the group that the questions would seek information or opinions from the columnist, who had over thirty years of experience on the prestigious newspaper. In his first answers, the speaker told amusing anecdotes, gave background information about recent news events, and offered unmuted commentary on key issues. The atmosphere was relaxed, almost reverent, and the speaker himself continued to eat his brown-bag lunch as he spoke.

In the last ten minutes of the question-and-answer discussion, there was a sudden shift in climate that brought about a remarkable change in interaction in the group. A student sitting in the back of the room sat up and leaned forward in his chair. Speaking more loudly than anyone else had during the previous forty-five minutes, he said he had a question about editorial responsibility. He said that the *Times* ran a story about atrocities in an African tribe but the paper made no editorial comment on the killings until three years after they occurred. He wanted to know if the paper had the editorial responsibility to comment on this event at the time it happened. It soon became clear that both the student asking the question and the columnist knew, as the question was asked, that American arms had been used in the killings. The student did not, however, explicitly mention this as he asked the question.

With the student's question and the first response it received, the previously established climate in the group changed. The expectation that questions would seek information or a desired opinion from the speaker was overturned by the student's entry into the exchange. The question sought a defense of the paper's policy and assumed that the speaker would take a stand supporting the paper.

The group resented the attempt to change the tone of the interaction. Almost immediately, a journalism professor who had introduced the speaker and was instrumental in getting him to visit the campus, defended the paper's policy before the guest speaker had a chance to respond. Neither this professor nor anyone else in the group had previously interrupted the "question-answer-question" format that the group came to adopt; no one had made a comment in response to any other person's question. The professor was visibly upset by the student's question, said he had worked on the paper himself at the time the story broke, and contended that the editorial decision was justified because insufficient information was available about the incident for quite some time. The student came back with a pointed declaration of mistrust in the paper. The columnist then took the floor and commented that, although the paper had made several editorial blunders in the years he worked at the paper, he could not accept the accusation that editorial comments were withheld because U.S. arms were involved. There were, he said, too many editorials to the contrary in the paper.

The whole climate for the presentation clearly shifted as this exchange occurred. People sitting in the room turned to look back at the person who was asking the questions, some side comments were made, and a few people smiled uncomfortably at each other. A second professor interrupted the columnist and said, in a somewhat self-conscious tone of voice, that "we had better leave the seminar room because another class had to meet in it soon."

The climate of this discussion shifted in midstream, with profound effects on group interaction. In order to understand how conflict interaction unfolds, it is necessary to explore how climates are created and changed in groups and the effects this has on the direction of conflicts.

3. *Conflict interaction is sustained by the moves and countermoves of participants; moves and countermoves are based on the power participants exert.* Conflicts emerge as a series of actions and reactions. All of us have heard someone using the "He did X—and then she said Y—and then he said Z—and then . . ." formula to explain a quarrel. When an incompatibility of positions arises members try to cope with it and the way in which their actions mesh plays an important role in the direction the conflict takes. Moves and countermoves in conflict are often based on the participants' ability and willingness to exert *power.* Power can be defined as the *capacity to act effectively.* Power sometimes takes the form of outward strength, status, money, or allies, but these are only the most obvious sources of power; there are many others that operate in a much more subtle fashion. In the Hotline case, for example, Diane might have used the other workers' guilt to try to get her way and the workers did use their seniority and familiarity with their jobs to pass judgment on her by drafting a list of worker responsibilities. In both cases, power is used much more subtly than is commonly assumed. More generally, a person is powerful when he or she has the *resources* to act and to influence others and the *skills* to do this effectively (Deutsch, 1973). The third party in the Hotline case provides a good example of the effective use of power: she had certain resources to influence the group—experience with other conflicts and knowledge about how to work with groups—and made skillful use of them to move both sides toward a solution.

Power exerts an important influence over conflict interaction; people's attempts to mobilize and apply power can drastically shift the direction conflict takes. As possible solutions to the conflict are considered, members learn how much power members are willing to employ to encourage or prevent the adoption of various alternatives. This is critical in the definition of conflict issues and solutions, because it signals how important the issue is to the member involved. When Diane filed a grievance in response to the Hotline staff's definition of worker responsibilities, the other workers realized she was committed to having her problem aired. This act certainly contributed to the group's realization that a third party was needed.

The balance of power in the group often tips the scale in a productive or destructive direction. If a member perceives that he or she can dominate the other members, there is little incentive to compromise; a dominant member can get whatever he or she wants (at least in the short run), and negotiation only invites others to cut into the member's solution. In the same vein, feeling powerless can sap members' resolve and cause them to appease more powerful members. Of course, this method often encourages the powerful members to be more demanding; only when *all participants have at least some power* is the conflict likely to take a productive direction. At the Hotline agency the third party was only called in after both sides, Diane and the workers, had played their first "trumps"—the workers by informing Diane of her responsibilities, and Diane by filing a grievance. The use of power could have prompted further moves and countermoves: rather than calling in a third party, both sides could have continued to try to force each other to yield, and the conflict could have continued escalating. However, in this case the two sides perceived each other's power and, because they wanted the Hotline to survive, backed off. As risky as this process of balancing power is, many social scientists have come to the conclusion that it is a necessary condition for constructive conflict resolution (Deutsch, 1973).

Power feeds on itself. Those who have resources and the skills to use them wisely can employ them so their power increases and reinforces itself. Those with little power find it hard to assert themselves and build a stronger base for the future. Yet, as we have noted, for conflicts to maintain a constructive direction there should be a *balance of power*. This requires members to *reverse the usual flow:* the weaker members must build their power; the stronger ones must share theirs or at least not use it to force or dominate the weaker ones. As we will see in chapter 4, managing this reversal is both tricky and risky. It is tricky because power is hard to identify and sharing power may run against members' natural inclinations. It is risky because the process of increasing some members' power and decreasing or suspending others' is a sensitive operation and can precipitate even sharper conflicts.

Regardless of how unpleasant or risky it may be to deal with power, power is a fact of life in conflicts. Ignoring it or pretending power differences do not exist is a sure formula for failure, because power *is* operating and will direct the moves and countermoves in the conflict.

4. *Conflict interaction affects the relationships between participants.* It is very easy to focus only on the substantive issues in a conflict, on the problem and its proposed solutions. In fact, centering only on issues and ignoring the other, "emotional" aspects of a conflict has sometimes been recommended as the best way to deal with conflicts. However, focusing on the "bare facts" of the case can cause one to overlook the important effects conflict has. Conflicts are often emotionally-laden and tense. This is in part because participants are concerned about getting (or not getting) what they want, but it also stems from the implications the conflict has for their present and future relationship to the other party. The conflict in the Hotline case had the potential to drastically alter the relationships in the group. Until the staff openly challenged Diane for not living up to her responsibilities, she felt she was doing adequate work and was regarded as an equal by the other workers. The reprimand called her competence and responsibility into question and told her that others felt she was not on an equal footing. It challenged her attitudes and assumptions about her relationship with the other workers and caused her a great deal of self-doubt and soul-searching, as well as stimulating her angry retaliation against the center. The workers' judgment of Diane also affected their attitudes and assumptions about her. Coming to the conclusion that Diane was slacking off generated distrust for her in the minds of the other staff members; it also made her an object of anger, and some members admitted a tendency to want to "gunnysack," that is, pile up a long list of problems with Diane and then attack her with it. Luckily this never happened and the third party was able to restore some of the trust and encourage a more open and understanding approach among the parties.

This case illustrates two levels operating in all communication: every message conveys not only substantive content, but also *information about the relationship of the speaker to the hearer* (Bateson, 1951; Watzlawick, Beavin and Jackson, 1967). If Diane angrily says, "I don't deserve this reprimand, I'm filing a grievance!" to her co-workers, her statements convey two levels of meaning. First, and most obvious, is the information that she is angry and is filing a grievance to challenge the reprimand, a countermove in the conflict. But second, Diane's message also carries the information that she believes her relationship with the workers has deteriorated to the point that she must file a formal grievance—it redefines the relationship between Diane and her co-workers.

This relational aspect of communication is critical because it affects both present and future interaction. It affects present interaction because members often respond to relational messages immediately and emotionally. If someone insults us, we may become angry and want to retaliate. If someone implies that our friendship is in jeopardy because of an argument, we may back down and become conciliatory. However, relational communication has its most profound effects through influencing future interaction. How people interact in conflicts is colored by their assessments of others, judgments about such things as others' trustworthiness, intentions (good or bad), and determination to win. These assessments bear directly on the relational aspects of communication and, because of this, people often try to project a certain image in order to shape others' assumptions about their relationship. For example, one person may act very defiant and angry to project an image of cold determination that tells the other, "Our relationship is not that important to me, as long as I get what I want." If this projection is successful, the second person may back down because he or she believes the first has no regard for them and will go to any lengths to win. Of course, this tactic could also backfire and make the second person resentful and defiant, because the first seems cold and ruthless. Attempts at *managing image and relationships* prompt many moves and countermoves in conflict.

As important as relational management is in conflicts, it is not surprising that it plays a critical role in generating the direction conflicts take. *Face-saving*, people's attempts to protect or repair their images to others, has great potential to send conflicts into destructive spirals. One particularly dangerous form of face-saving stems from people's *fear of losing ground in an exchange* (Brown, 1977). Parties in conflict can perceive that if they move from a stated position or back away from a set of demands, they will appear weak or vulnerable in the eyes of the group. This concern for face—a concern for how one appears to others during the conflict interaction and the effects this will have on future relationships—can encourage members to keep arguing for a position even though they no longer believe in it or they recognize it is not contributing to a workable resolution to the conflict.

A second form of face-saving can prompt groups *to continually ignore or avoid an important conflict issue.* In groups that have had a history of resolving conflicts in a friendly and cooperative manner, a concern for face may prevent members from raising an issue that is far more threatening than any conflict the group has previously addressed. People may believe that if they raise the issue the group will see them as a person who is trying to destroy the friendly relationships that have been cautiously protected and valued. This concern for face may prevent groups from calling in a third party when intervention is needed because the group is reluctant to admit that it cannot resolve an issue on its own.

People's ability to define and maintain positive working relationships during conflict interaction depends heavily on how much concern they have for saving face as they approach the issue, take stands, and try to construct a resolution. For this reason, it is important to understand how groups create pressures or incentives that heighten or lessen members' concern for saving face during conflict interaction.

_____ **SUMMARY** _____

From our review of the major theoretical approaches to conflict and the four principles we have distilled from this review, we have drawn the beginning of a complex net of ideas which we will explore in the remainder of this book. Throughout, we will constantly return to the point that conflict interaction, deceptively simple and clear on the surface, is incredibly complex and can only be understood by analyzing its flows and the forces which shape them. Conflict, like any other form of behavior, can only be understood and effectively managed at the level of concrete interaction *where moves and countermoves take many forms yet maintain some level of coherence, where interaction patterns tend to perpetuate themselves in destructive and constructive cycles,* and *where messages define and alter the relationships among group members.*

The *working habits* groups adopt, the *climate* established in the group, the use of *power* and the concern for *saving face* are four major forces that shape the nature of conflict interaction in a group or organization. In the next five chapters we explore these forces and the practical implications they hold for conflict management. In chapter 2 we examine conflict interaction and the development of *escalation and avoidance spirals.* We will explore the role of working habits, stress, and trained incapacities in the perpetuation of conflicts and their tendency to block participants' awareness of destructive interaction cycles. In chapters 3, 4, and 5 we will consider the roles of, respectively, *climate, power,* and *face-saving* in conflict interaction. We will review previous studies of these concepts and rethink them in terms of how they structure and are structured by conflict interaction. Finally, chapter 6 draws the various findings and insights into a diagnostic model of conflict and summarizes suggestions for successful *intervention* in group conflicts.

These chapters are, of course, concerned with conflict, but they are also concerned with *change.* Because conflicts are rooted in differences and incompatible interests, conflict always confronts participants with the possibility of change. Indeed, that differences arise at all is a flag indicating a need for adjustment of the group in response to members' difficulties or to an external problem. Once a conflict emerges, resolution of differences may require redefinition of policies or goals, reassignment of responsibilities, shifts in expectations for individual members, or even changes in the group's power and status structures. Members' recognition of these possible changes guides the forms conflict interaction takes. The active suppression of issues, the positive or negative evaluation of possible solutions, and the clarification of differences between members are all forms of conflict interaction which can be motivated and shaped by the participants' awareness of imminent change. In a very real sense, as a group manages its conflicts, so too, does it deal with the need to change in response to its environment or members' needs. Someone once said that "not to change is to die." The same can be said for failure to work through conflict.

REFERENCES

Adler, A. *The practice and theory of individual psychology.* New York: Harcourt, Brace and World, 1927.

Apfelbaum, E. On conflicts and bargaining. In L. Berkowitz (ed.) *Advances in experimental social psychology, 1.* New York: Academic Press, 1964.

Axelrod, R. *The conflict of interest.* Chicago: Markham, 1970.

Baker, P. M. Social coalitions. *American Behavioral Scientist,* 1981, *24,* 633–647.

Bartos, O. J. Determinants and consequences of toughness. In P. Swingle (Ed.), *The structure of conflict.* New York: Academic Press, 1970.

Bateson, G. *Naven* (2nd ed.). Stanford: Stanford University Press, 1958.

Billig, M. *Social psychology and intergroup relations.* New York: Academic Press, 1976.

Blake, R. R. & Mouton, J. S. *The managerial grid.* Houston: Gulf Publishing, 1964.

Blau, P. *Exchange and power in social life.* New York: John Wiley, 1964.

Brown, B. R. Face-saving and face-restoration in negotiation. In D. Druckman (Ed.), *Negotiations.* Beverly Hills: Sage, 1977.

Burke, K. *Permanence and change.* Indianapolis: Bobbs-Merrill, 1954.

Caplow, T. A theory of coalitions in the triad. *American Sociological Review,* 1956, *21,* 489–493.

Chertkoff, J. M., & Esser, J. K. A review of experiments in explicit bargaining. *Journal of Experimental Social Psychology,* 1976, *12,* 464–486.

Coser, L. *The functions of social conflict.* New York: Free Press, 1956.

Cosier, R. A., & Ruble, T. L. Research on conflict handling behavior: An experimental approach. *Academy of Management Journal,* 1981, *24,* 816–831.

Deutsch, M. *The resolution of conflict.* New Haven: Yale University Press, 1973.

Deutsch, M., & Krauss, R. M. *Theories in social psychology.* New York: Basic Books, 1965.

Ellis, D., & Fisher, B. A. Phases of conflict in small group development. *Human Communication Research,* 1975, *1,* 195–212.

Endler, N. S., & Magnusson, D. Toward an interactional psychology of personality. *Psychological Bulletin,* 1976, *83,* 956–974.

Erikson, E. H. *Childhood and society.* New York: W. W. Norton, 1950.

Filley, A. *Interpersonal conflict resolution.* Glenview, Ill.: Scott Foresman, 1975.

Freud, S. [*The interpretation of dreams*] (J. Strachey, trans.). London: Hogarth Press, 1953. (Originally published, 1900.)

Freud, S. [*The ego and the id*] (J. Strachey, trans.). London: Hogarth Press, 1947. (Originally published, 1923.)

Freud, S. [The unconscious] (J. Riviere, trans.). In *Collected papers.* London: Hogarth Press, 1925.

Freud, S. [*An outline of psychoanalysis*] (J. Strachey, trans.). New York: Norton, 1949.

Gamson, W. An experimental test of a theory of coalition formation. *American Sociological Review,* 1961, *26,* 565–573.

Gamson, W. Experimental studies of coalition formation. In L. Berkowitz (Ed.), *Advances in experimental social psychology.* New York: Academic Press, 1964, *1,* 81–110.

Gouran, D. S. *Making decisions in groups.* Glenview, Ill.: Scott Foresman, 1982.

Hall, C. S. *A primer of Freudian psychology* (2nd ed.). New York: World, 1979.

Hall, C. S. & Lindzey, G. *Theories of personality.* New York: John Wiley and Sons, 1970.

Hall, J. *Conflict management survey: A survey on one's characteristic reaction to and handling of conflicts between himself and others.* Conroe, Tex: Teleometrics International, 1969.

Hilgard, E., & Bower, G. *Theories of learning.* New York: Appleton-Century-Crofts, 1966.

Hill, W. A. Leadership style: Rigid or flexible? *Organizational Behavior and Human Performance,* 1973, *9,* 35–47.

Homans, G. C. *Social behavior: Its elementary forms.* New York: Harcourt, Brace, Jovanovich, 1961.

Janeway, E. *Powers of the weak.* New York: Morrow-Quill, 1980.

Janis, I., & Mann, L. *Decision making.* New York: Free Press, 1977.

Jones, R. E., & Melcher, B. H. Personality and preference for modes of conflict resolution. *Human Relations,* 1982, *35,* 649–658.

Karrass, C. L. *The negotiating game.* New York: Thomas Crowell, 1970.

Kelley, H. H., & Thibaut, J. *Interpersonal relations: A theory of interdependence.* New York: Wiley, 1978.

Kilmann, R. H., & Thomas, K. W. Developing a forced-choice measure of conflict-handling behavior: the "MODE" instrument. *Educational and Psychological Measurement,* 1977, *37,* 309–325.

Komorita, S., & Chertkoff, J. A bargaining theory of coalition formation. *Psychological Review,* 1973, *80,* 149–162.

Kriesberg, L. *The sociology of social conflicts.* Englewood Cliffs, N.J.: Prentice-Hall, 1973.

Lawler, E. J., & Youngs, G. Coalition formation: An integrative model. *Sociometry,* 1975, *38,* 1–17.

Lawrence, P. R. & Lorsch, J. W. *Organization and environment.* Homewood, Ill.: Irwin, 1967.

Leary, T. *Interpersonal diagnosis of personality.* New York: Ronald, 1957.

Lewin, K. *Field theory in social science.* New York: Harper and Brothers, 1951.

Marwell, G., & Schmitt, D. R. Dimensions of compliance-gaining behavior: An empirical analysis. *Sociometry,* 1967, *30,* 350–364.

Miller, G. R., Boster, F., Roloff, M., & Seibold, D. Compliance-gaining message strategies: A typology and some findings concerning effects of situational differences. *Communication Monographs,* 1977, *44,* 37–51.

Mischel, W. *Personality and assessment.* New York: John Wiley, 1968.

Morley, I. E., & Stephenson, G. M. *The social psychology of bargaining.* London: George Allen and Unwin, 1977.

Murnighan, J. K. Models of coalition behavior: Game theoretic, social psychological, and political perspectives. *Psychological Bulletin,* 1978, *85,* 1130–1135.

Neel, A. F. *Theories of psychology.* New York: Shenkman, 1977.

Phillips, E., & Cheston, R. Conflict resolution: What works? *California Management Review,* 1979, *21,* 76–83.

Poole, M. S. Decision development in small groups I: A comparison of two models. *Communication Monographs,* 1981, *48,* 1–25.

Pruitt, D. G., & Kimmel, M. J. Twenty years of experimental gaming: Critique, synthesis, and suggestions for the future. *Annual Review of Psychology,* 1977, *28,* 363–392.

Putnam, L., & Wilson, C. E. Development of an organizational communication conflict instrument. In M. Burgoon (Ed.), *Communication Yearbook* (Vol. 6). Beverly Hills: Sage, 1982.

Rapaport, D. *Organization and pathology of thought.* New York: Columbia University Press, 1951.

Roloff, M. E. Communication strategies, relationships, and relational changes. In G. R. Miller (Ed.), *Explorations in interpersonal communication.* Beverly Hills: Sage, 1976.

Roloff, M. E. *Interpersonal communication: The social exchange approach.* Beverly Hills: Sage, 1981

Rubin, J. Z., & Brown, B. *The social psychology of bargaining and negotiation.* New York: Academic Press, 1975.

Ruble, T. L., & Thomas, K. W. Support for a two-dimensional model of conflict behavior. *Organizational Behavior and Human Performance,* 1976, *16,* 143–155.

Rummel, R. J. *Understanding conflict and war* (Vol. 2). Beverly Hills: Sage, 1976.

Schaffer, D. Social psychology from a social developmental perspective. In C. Hendrick (Ed.), *Perspectives on social psychology.* New York: Lawrence Erlbaum Associates, 1970.

Sillars, A. Stranger and spouse as target persons for compliance gaining strategies. *Human Communication Research,* 1980, *6,* 265–279.

Simon, H. A. A behavioral model of rational choice. *Quarterly Journal of Economics,* 1955, *69,* 99–118.

Skidmore, W. *Theoretical thinking in sociology,* (2nd ed). Cambridge: Cambridge University Press, 1979.

Stogdill, R. *Handbook of leadership.* New York: Free Press, 1974.

Sullivan, H. S. *The interpersonal theory of psychiatry.* New York: W. W. Norton, 1953.

Tagiuri, R. The concept of organizational climate. In R. Tagiuri & G. Litwin (Eds.), *Organizational climate: Explorations of a concept.* Boston: Harvard University Press, 1968, 11–32.

Thibaut, J., & Kelley, H. H. *The social psychology of groups.* New York: John Wiley, 1959.

Thomas, K. Conflict and conflict management. In M. Dunnette (Ed.), *Handbook of Industrial Psychology.* Chicago: Rand McNally, 1975.

Von Neumann, J., & Morgenstern, O. *Theory of games and economic behavior.* Princeton, N.J.: Princeton University Press, 1947.

Walster, E., Walster, G. W., & Berscheid, E. *Equity theory and research.* Boston: Allyn and Bacon, 1978.

Walton, R. *Interpersonal peacemaking: Confrontations and third party consultation.* Reading, Mass.: Addison-Wesley, 1969.

Watzlawick, P., Beavin, J., & Jackson, D. *The pragmatics of human communication.* New York: Norton, 1967.

White, R., & Lippitt, R. Leader behavior and member reaction in three "social climates." In D. Cartwright & A. Zander (Eds.), *Group Dynamics,* (3rd Ed). New York: Harper and Row, 1968,

Wilmot, J. H., & Wilmot, W. W. *Interpersonal conflict.* Dubuque, Iowa: Wm. C. Brown, 1978.

CHAPTER 2

Seeing Escalation and Avoidance Cycles

Someone once said that the key to resolving almost any conflict lies in gaining a perspective on how we ourselves contribute to it. There is a lot of truth in this statement, but seeing our own contribution to a perplexing conflict is often difficult. As noted in chapter 1, the early stages of conflict emphasize differences between members; members focus on how their own needs and goals are not being met and on how other members stand in their way. Under these circumstances it is not easy for members to step back and see how the conflict works. They are focused on issues and people rather than on group processes or phases of interaction. What usually happens is that the group attempts to deal with the conflict as though it were "business as usual." Discussions proceed and motions are made in an effort to handle the disagreement through normal decision-making channels. Only when the conflict has escalated severely or come to a total impasse does the group acknowledge that different procedures may have to be used.

Sticking with "standard operating procedures" as long as possible has advantages. For one thing, it guarantees that members understand the basic rules for deciding the issue. For another, it may allow the group to resolve the conflict without ever admitting that it exists. This lack of acknowledgment may be particularly important in groups where members' commitment is weak and where there are long-standing tensions.

However, standard operating procedures also hide traps and dilemmas. They can blind members to others' viewpoints and bind them in cycles of uncontrolled escalation or avoidance. The effects of these procedures seem particularly insidious because these procedures are "second nature." Members rarely suspect that normally-helpful interaction strategies could actually be feeding the flames of conflict. This chapter tries to provide an explanation for why conflict easily runs out of control and how working habits contribute to this process. Its central point is that one key to *understanding conflict management lies in an examination of those destructive aspects of conflict interaction that persist despite participants' best intentions and best attempts to find a satisfactory solution.*

COPING WITH DIFFERENTIATION

Facing up to a conflict is not always prudent. Sometimes avoidance is the best policy. Avoidance is appropriate when the potential problems the group may encounter in addressing the issue outweigh the problems of leaving the conflict unresolved. Sometimes groups take (or are pushed into) an immediate and unreflective plunge, because one or more members believe that "there is no getting around this one." They focus on the effects of leaving the issue unresolved and give little consideration to the problems the group may face trying to work through the conflict. In other cases the decision to address a conflict is far more difficult. Parties may perceive the issue and recognize its current and potential consequences, but remain hesitant to confront it because they see clear "trade-offs" in doing so (for example, a small chance for a good solution vs. the tension of difficult meetings, the possibility that certain group members will leave, the risk of undercutting good working relationships). There is a balance of concerns to weigh and, as a result, the decision to avoid or confront is a difficult one. Although there are no surefire rules in these cases, three skills are crucial in determining whether avoidance is appropriate.

First, members must be able to *make a realistic assessment of the issue's significance*. Some conflict issues are simply not worth the group's time or effort; they are better handled by an individual decision rather than a careful consideration of alternatives (Boulding, 1964). Continual pursuit of differences of opinion on unimportant issues can exhaust members and can create an impression of greater disharmony than actually exists. The pitfall here, of course, lies in the possibility of an inaccurate assessment—in dismissing an issue as trivial when in fact it touches on vital concerns.

Second, productive avoidance hinges on an *acute sense of timing*. Groups using avoidance productively recognize that conflicts may need to be forestalled until a more propitious moment. Some relatively "simple" conflicts can explode or be mishandled if they are ignited at an inopportune time. The following conditions might warrant temporary avoidance of a conflict: some unrelated controversy is causing a great deal of tension in the group; members are under pressure to meet an important task deadline and the perceived conflict is unrelated to the task; people who are closely involved in the conflict issue are not present; members are discouraged and exhausted from recent attempts to resolve the issue; the tension of the moment makes clear thinking or creative discussion impossible. Although one or more of these conditions may be present, the need to avoid a conflict (at least temporarily) may only be recognized by one side. The following example illustrates how one member in a conflict may have to insist on avoidance when it is a clear necessity.

_____ **CASE 2.1** _____

Students in an upper division psychology of communication course were assigned a rather difficult five page "thought" paper on the role of imagery in the development of people's ideas. The assignment was to state and critique Rudolph Arnheim's view of visual thinking. One of the students in this class was a middle-aged woman who had just re-enrolled as an undergraduate after being away from school for about fifteen years. The woman was having difficulty in the course and had talked to her teaching assistant on several occasions about the adjustment problems she had in coming back to school. She said that she had the most difficulty with paper assignments. She received a 'C−' on the first paper in the class and had talked with the TA about her performance on that assignment.

When the TA read her paper on imagery, he was very disappointed; the woman's paper missed the point of the assignment entirely. Since he knew about the student's difficulties, he was apprehensive about how to respond to the paper and tried to think of an evaluation that would not discourage her further. He decided to make extensive comments on the paper, but not to put a grade on it. Instead, he said she could do it over, and he offered to talk with her in greater detail about why her paper strayed far from the point of the assignment.

On the day the essays were returned, the woman came to the TA's office with her paper in hand and "tore into him" verbally. She told the TA that he was too young to be teaching in a university and called him abusive names. Two of the TAs who shared the office space slipped out of the room—not knowing the details but eager to escape from an embarrassing and awkward situation. The TA was baffled by the woman's response and had all he could do to hold back from returning an angry assault. He felt he had been more than fair in giving the woman the option to do the paper over, and he was embarrassed by the woman's unrestrained attack on his credibility in front of his office mates. Although he started to defend his position, he soon realized that this was not the time to try to come to some understanding about the paper. The woman's attack was relentless and she was not dealing with the substantive issues of the assignment, so he decided to postpone discussion until both of them "cooled off." He asked her if she would come back during his office hours two days later to talk about the paper. The woman resisted the suggestion at first but eventually left the office and said she would "definitely be there when the office door opened on Wednesday."

About two hours after this discussion, the woman returned to the TA's office and, trying to hold back tears, said she had gotten another paper from a different course that same morning and had done poorly on it as well. She said that all her frustration with the semester seemed to hit at once and that she was sorry for the insults and attacks. Although the meeting was awkward for several minutes, the discussion soon turned to ways of improving the paper and the woman was eventually able to complete a successful second draft of the assignment.

Watching for conditions which make productive conflict interaction nearly impossible is important in learning how to use avoidance productively. A concern for these conditions can enable all parties in the conflict to recognize when avoidance is timely.

Third, a wise decision to avoid conflict rests on the *members' assessment of their own communication skills.* Resolving difficult conflict issues requires substantial interpersonal and group process skills. Members must be able to state viewpoints clearly and describe emotional reactions. The group must be able to establish and follow procedures that control interaction during intense discussions. Members in positions of leadership must be able to direct conflict interaction without predetermining the resolution. When these or other critical skills are not held by the group, avoidance may be appropriate until these skills are obtained or until a third party can be called in to compensate for the group's weaknesses.

Although avoidance may be appropriate under the conditions we have outlined, the critical factor is how each member *perceives* the incompatibility of positions and what significance is assigned to leaving the issue unsettled. If any member concludes that leaving an issue unresolved is more costly than the possible consequences of confronting it, avoidance becomes a potentially destructive way of dealing with conflict. For the person or persons who believe the issue needs to be addressed, further avoidance will create an air of falseness and inauthenticity. Participating in discussions that skirt the issue may seem pointless, frustrating and, in some ways, less than honest. Ultimately, continual withdrawal from the issue may fatally undermine productivity or social relationships in the group or organization. Seemingly innocuous issues develop into impasses as hidden agendas, defensiveness, and competition become prevalent. Repressing conflict can avoid short-term outbursts, but it can also muddle issues and heighten resentments, thereby making the problem more complicated than it originally was.

The negative consequences of sustained avoidance are clearly illustrated by the case of a small midwestern high school.

_____ CASE 2.2 _____

Midvale High has about 600 students with a faculty of twenty-five teachers, a principal, and two administrative secretaries. As in most small schools the principal was able to keep an eye on everyone's activity and had control of most decisions. This usually did not present a problem, because the faculty was very close; the principal described the school as "one big happy family" and saw himself as the "father" and head of the family. The principal and teachers nearly always agreed on matters of policy; decisions were rarely voted on because a consensus usually emerged.

However, a problem arose over the principal's unwillingness to adopt innovative course material advocated by several young teachers. This issue had been brewing for some time, but had not emerged, because the teachers tended to accept the family metaphor and generally agreed with the principal's views at faculty meetings. When one teacher finally did state her objections, the principal smoothed over the conflict by arguing that the faculty had to work together as a team to maintain high standards of education and improve last year's excellent record. Arguing over insignificant changes, he said, would only divide the faculty and make the school board believe they were dissatisfied.

Many other instructors privately agreed with the teacher's objections, but none expressed their feelings. In fact, some of them actually helped move the discussion to other issues. Although the group members avoided open conflict at this meeting, their dissatisfactions were not aired. Over the course of the academic year, teachers began bickering among each other about teaching styles and several of the newer teachers became discouraged and apathetic. The school began having employee turnover problems which were not remedied until the teachers openly expressed their objections to school policies, and formal moves were made to give instructors more control over curriculum.

People's reluctance to face conflict is understandable. Working through a conflict can lead to more serious consequences—strained interpersonal relationships, resentment, loss of commitment to group or organizational goals—than were ever anticipated or desired. When people experience one such blow up they are often reluctant to pursue other conflicts which may have the same explosive potential.

However, the inability to address important conflict issues can severely undermine the group's ability to work effectively.

Groups are thus faced with a dilemma: on the one hand, members must adequately engage in *differentiation; they must raise the conflict issue and spend sufficient time and energy clarifying positions, pursuing the reasons behind those positions and acknowledging the severity of their differences.* On the other hand, members rightly fear and often retreat from the process of differentiation, because it is here that conflict is most vulnerable to uncontrolled, hostile escalation. There is always the possibility that the interaction will not be able to move from differentiation to *integration,* to that phase of conflict where "parties appreciate their similarities, acknowledge their common goals, own up to positive aspects of their ambivalences, express warmth and respect and/or engage in other positive actions to manage their conflict." (Walton, 1969, p. 105) The *simultaneous need for and fear of differentiation* poses a difficult dilemma for groups that want to work through important conflicts. A closer examination of this dilemma reveals how it becomes the basis for members' inability to redirect their own destructive interaction.

Adequate differentiation is a critical prerequisite to constructive conflict resolution. Without a clear statement of each party's position, finding a problem-solving solution—one in which "the participants all are satisfied with their outcomes and feel they have gained as a result of the conflict"—is a hit-or-miss venture (Deutsch, 1973, p. 17). Without an appreciation of the severity of the differences and the consequences of leaving the conflict unaddressed, even a hit-or-miss attempt at resolution may not be made. Members may not be sufficiently motivated to deal with the problem.

_____ CASE (Introduction), continued _____

In the Women's Hotline case described in the Introduction, adequate differentiation did not occur until the group directly addressed the issue of Diane's performance at the meeting led by the outside party. During an intense hour and a half discussion at the outset of that meeting, the members confronted the basis of the problem they faced. The staff told Diane that they doubted her abilities as a staff person at the center even before the murder occurred. They thought she had more difficulty learning the job than other workers. Diane did not expect this general criticism although she knew her performance was less than adequate since the death of her client. After hearing this evaluation from several members, she became somewhat defensive and offered several specific instances when she felt unnecessarily rebuffed by other staff people and when a few helpful comments could have made a major difference in how she went about her work. Although she mentioned specific names of people present, she found it difficult to look at them as she spoke. Several staff members responded to the instances Diane cited and, in defense of their actions, explained why they were reluctant to help at the time.

This discussion was difficult for the group to get through. The staff was not sure how Diane was going to react to their criticism; this was, in part, why they withheld these comments for several months. Diane feared that her pointed remarks would ruin her working relationships with the other women at the center. If the members could not find a resolution they would be faced with a tense and uncomfortable work environment. Although this discussion raised the stakes of the conflict considerably, it was critically important that the group go through this differentiation process. Both sides had to acknowledge a set of reactions that they knew were risky to express. It was not until these positions were stated that the group began to construct a solution that would be satisfying to Diane and the staff. The exchange allowed the staff to state implicit evaluations that had been influencing their interaction at the center, and it allowed the group to see that any solution to the problem would have to focus, not on Diane's performance alone, but on the more general need for staff support at the center. Once this discussion was completed, the group was closer to an integration phase of conflict where all members recognized the need for assistance and acknowledged that some carefully defined policy might alleviate the problem.

Differentiation initially *personalizes* the conflict as individuals clarify their stands and people are identified with positions; however, it is not until these positions are articulated that the conflict can finally be depersonalized. Once individual positions are clarified, the groundwork has been laid for members to realize that the conflict lies in the *incompatibility* of positions and not in the needs or sentiments of one person or faction. Through differentiation members can obtain a depersonalized view of the conflict that sets it apart from any one member. If members can clarify the issues and air diverse positions without losing control (a difficult problem in its own right), they can recast the conflict as an external obstacle that all must overcome together. Once achieved, this depersonalized view provides a basis for commonality in the group. It often marks the beginning of an integrative phase, but by no means signifies the end of the conflict process. The parties must still generate ideas and choose a solution which, as Simmel (1955, p. 14) puts it, "resolves the tension between contrasts" in the group. From this point, however, the group can build on the accomplishments of differentiation.

DIFFERENTIATION AND ESCALATION

While differentiation is necessary for constructive conflict resolution, it can also nourish destructive tendencies. During differentiation, disagreements that members were previously afraid of, or unmotivated to deal with, take hold. The stakes seem higher because an unsuccessful attempt to resolve the issue means that members must live with a keener awareness of differences and a more vivid understanding of the negative consequences of leaving the issue unresolved.

In some cases, the group's decision-making *procedures* establish a framework for interaction that *heightens escalation* as the parties address the conflict during differentiation. Making a motion and having it seconded, for example, is a way for a group following Parliamentary Procedure to open discussion of an issue. The motion initiates differentiation. It also sets in place the expectation that, in all likelihood, there will either be an acceptance or rejection of the proposal before the group. Because the decision-making procedure calls for a vote on the proposal after a specified amount of time for discussion, the group's discussion presupposes the inevitability of a vote, of having to choose for or against the motion. Consequently, members who have reservations or concerns about the motion may believe they have to be adamant to prevent its adoption. Interaction becomes polarized and the option of delaying a decision until a more satisfactory solution emerges may never be considered.

Research from several areas points to several strains and pitfalls likely to ignite the process of differentiation into a spiralling escalation of "malevolent cycling" —highly personalized conflict that is turned away from issues and threatens interpersonal relationships (Walton, 1969).

(1) Research on *balance theory* (Swenson, 1973) suggests that relationships will become strained when group members disagree over important issues. Balance theory assumes people attempt to maintain consistency among their beliefs and feelings; for example, people tend to like people they agree with and dislike people they do not agree with. When a person finds out that someone he or she likes disagrees on an important issue, the inconsistency creates an uncomfortable strain in the person's thinking. Balance theorists argue that this strain is usually resolved either by a change in the person's beliefs about the issue or by a change in the person's liking for the other. These changes are assumed to follow the path of least resistance: feelings about whichever is less important—the issue or the person— will change most. Hence, the longer two members who like each other hold to opposing positions, and the more crucial these positions seem to them, the greater pressure they are under to feel hostility and lose respect for each other.

(2) Leary's (1957) classic research on *interpersonal reflexes* also points to likely sources of emotional escalation during this process. If a comment is made which is perceived as hostile, Leary's analysis predicts that it is likely to elicit further hostile responses. Similarly, Gibb's (1961) analysis of defensiveness indicates that *evaluative comments* (for example, "I don't think that proposal is any good because . . .") can easily elicit defensive responses because they seem threatening to the listener. Since differentiation calls for evaluation, defensiveness is likely.

(3) Research on the nature of *commitment* (Kiesler, 1971) suggests that making a position public or restating it several times can increase one's commitment to the position or behavior. When commitment to a position is high and that position is called into question by new information or arguments, people often intensify their stands in an effort to preserve their "good name" and self-image. Comments that attack others' positions run the risk of increasing polarization even further because parties may respond by taking more extreme stands than they originally held. Apfelbaum (1975) summarizes a number of experimental studies which indicate that once one side in conflict openly signals commitment to a position (and thus indicates they will be competitive rather than cooperative), the other side becomes more inflexible as well. Thus, the positions people take and their styles of interaction can become rigidified when members commit themselves to some position in front of the group. Since differentiation calls for statements of positions, the risk of escalation runs high during this phase of the conflict process.

Taken together, balance, interpersonal reflexes, and commitment generate potent forces toward destructive cycling. To break this cycling some means of counteracting these effects must be found.

DIFFERENTIATION AND AVOIDANCE

Although groups sometimes fall prey to the dangers of differentiation, they can also fall victim to an overly-zealous attempt to avoid these dangers. When parties try hard to avoid divisive issues, they may never realize their own potential for finding creative solutions to important problems (Pruitt and Lewis, 1977).

Indeed, the early acceptance of a solution which most members feel lukewarm about and dissatisfied with is often a sign of a group's retreat from the pressures of differentiation. Guetzkow and Gyr's (1954) study of seventy-two decision-making conferences illustrates this.

Guetzkow and Gyr compared interaction in groups with high levels of *substantive conflict* (conflict that is focused on the issues and on disagreements about possible solutions) to interaction in groups with high levels of *affective conflict* (interpersonal conflict characterized by extreme frustration—according to an outsider's observations). They were interested in the difference between substantive and affective conflicts because affective conflicts are more likely to exhibit spiralling escalation. Affective conflict is highly correlated with how critical and punishing members are to each other and how unpleasant the emotional atmosphere in the group is. In essence, affective conflict is a sign of differentiation gone awry. Guetzkow and Gyr's objective was to determine what conditions allowed both types of group to reach consensus about the issue they were attempting to resolve.

These researchers found very different behaviors contributing to each group's ability to reach consensus. Groups that were high in substantive conflict and were able to reach consensus sought three times as much factual information and relied upon that information more heavily in reaching a decision than groups not able to reach consensus. In other words, substantive conflict was resolved by a determined pursuit of the issue.

In contrast, groups high in affective conflict engaged mostly in flight or avoidance in order to reach consensus. Members withdrew from the problem by addressing simpler and less controversial agenda items, showed less interest in the discussion overall and talked to only a few members of the group. When consensus was achieved in the affective conflict groups, it was most often the result of ignoring the critical problem at hand and finding an issue members could *comfortably* reach agreement on. If the group or organization's goal is to reduce tension and discomfort at any cost then these flight behaviors serve it well. When members cannot easily ignore an issue, however, destructive tension can result from their inability to pursue the conflict.

DIFFERENTIATION AND RIGIDITY OF BEHAVIOR

Avoidance of an issue should be seen as one end point of members' unsuccessful attempt to deal with the demands of differentiation. Spiralling, hostile escalation, or the break up of a group is another possible outcome of members' inability to differentiate. The anxiety-producing nature of differentiation gives rise to a set of possible *intermediary* behaviors which can lead to either avoidance or radical escalation: *The most direct link between the stress of differentiation and either avoidance or escalation is the tendency for members to cling inflexibly to patterns of interaction that occur during differentiation.* Figure 6 summarizes the relationship among differentiation, inflexibility, and possible conflict resolution outcomes. The source of members' inflexibility can be found in the psychodynamic theories discussed in chapter 1. These developmental theories of maladaptive repetitive behavior (behavior that persists despite its destructive outcomes) trace the origin of these behaviors to a threatening or anxiety-inducing environment.

The psychoanalyst Alfred Adler, for example, maintains that running through

Figure 6

Possible responses to the demands of differentiation in conflict situations

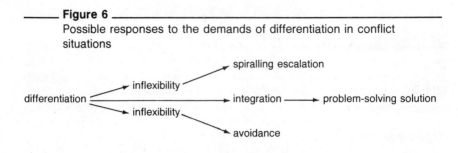

a normal person's life is a consistent pattern of responses, a way of reacting to the world. This orientation gives rise to the person's character and a set of guiding principles that are used to make decisions, to deal with people and, in general, to give meaning to the events of one's life. There are points in life, however, when a person's orientations clash with events in the world, when a guiding principle appears false. Adler offers an explanation for why, in some cases, individuals fasten to their orientations despite severe clashes with reality.

> The relatively normal person, when he realizes that his scheme is seriously in conflict with reality, is adaptable and modifies his orientation, abandoning what is patently false. But there are certain situations which work against flexibility and adaptability and favor rigid adherence to the guiding fictions. These are conditions in which the individual experiences exaggerated feelings of inferiority and psychological uncertainty, conditions that spell anxiety to him since anxiety is the sensation accompanying a strong uncompensated inferiority feeling. Under such conditions even a normal person may cling to his guiding fictions despite their conflict with reality. There are some individuals who live quite constantly under such anxiety-inducing conditions; and so rigidly do they adhere to their guiding fictions that these become accentuated and create a rigid, hardened lifestyle or character, an orientation out of tune with reality but nonetheless dogmatically maintained. (Luchins and Luchins, 1959, p. 19)

In much the same way that Adler describes the emergence of rigid individual behavior, groups and organizations are faced with anxiety-inducing conditions that work against flexibility and adaptability. These conditions are the result of the inherent demands of differentiation. The conditions which produce anxiety for members are those *pressures that work towards radical escalation:* (1) an initial personalization of the conflict, (2) the stress of acknowledging opposing stands, (3) hostile and emotional statements, (4) uncertainty about the outcomes of the conflict, and (5) heightened awareness of the consequences of not reaching a resolution (Holsti, 1971; Smart & Vertinsky, 1977).

Differentiation is a critically necessary but anxiety-provoking process that people face in any conflict or decision-making situation where major differences exist. If members pursue issues and work through the demands of differentiation without rigidly adhering to unworkable interaction patterns, there is a clear promise of innovation and of finding a problem-solving solution to the conflict. The pressures towards escalation are formidable, however, and the anxiety of differentiation can promote rigidity of behavior leading to either spiralling conflict or flight from the issue.

The standard operating procedures or *working habits* groups adopt as they make decisions and resolve points of disagreement are often forces which move conflict interaction towards escalation or avoidance. These habits are necessary and at times beneficial responses to the need for adequate differentiation, but they can become destructive when members rigidly cling to them in coping with the stress of differentiation. In the next section we describe several types of working habits that are normally functional but can become destructive during conflict interaction.

TRAINED INCAPACITIES AND CONFLICT

But, Wally, don't you see that comfort can be dangerous? I mean, you like to be comfortable, and I like to be comfortable too, but don't you see that comfort can lull you into a dangerous tranquillity? I mean, my mother knew a woman, Lady Hatfield, who was one of the richest women in the world, but she died of starvation because all she would eat was chicken. I mean, she just liked chicken, Wally, and that was all she would eat, and actually her body was starving, but she didn't know it, because she was quite happy eating her chicken, and so she finally died.

* * *

Roc used to practice certain exercises, like, for instance, if he were right-handed, all today he would do everything with his left hand. All day—writing, eating, everything—opening doors—in order to break the habits of living, because the great danger for him, he felt, was to fall into a trance, out of habit.

—Wallace Shawn and André Gregory, *My Dinner with André*

In his book *Permanence and Change,* Kenneth Burke (1954) used Thorsten Veblens' concept of trained incapacity to discuss "that state of affairs whereby one's very abilities can function as blindnesses." Burke offered two simple and somewhat outlandish examples as illustrations of this concept: a chicken can be taught to repeatedly come to a specific place to receive food when it hears a certain pitch of a bell. On one occasion, however, the chicken responds to the bell as it always has by coming to the same place in search of food. This time the chicken finds not food, but the threatening axe of its owner. In Burke's second example, a trout which has had a near miss with a fish hook on its way up stream avoids all food sources that even remotely resemble the color of the bait that nearly caught him. In both cases the animals' past training causes them to misjudge their present situation; their training has incapacitated them.

The concept of *trained incapacity* is useful in understanding behavioral strategies that result in unsuccessful differentiation. Certain *working habits* are adaptive and beneficial in the contexts in which they are learned; however, as conditions change and as conflicts deepen, they become maladaptive, harmful, and irrational. These behaviors are injurious, because they shape thinking and perception and therefore can prevent recognition of changed circumstances. When this happens, people continue to do "what has always worked," resulting either in no change or an actual worsening of the situation.

Trained incapacities play a crucial role in conflict sequences. Confronted with a real or imagined conflict, members tend toward habitual responses. As we have noted, the stress of differentiation can decrease individuals' ability to think clearly.

Several researchers (Beier, 1951; Holsti, 1971; Dill, 1968; Smart & Vertinsky, 1977) provide evidence that people under stress screen out essential environmental cues, distort incoming information, and are less flexible and creative problem-solvers. Habitual, preprogrammed responses provide excellent ways to cope under such circumstances; indeed, they are often all a person can think of in the heat of a crisis.

Because of cultural tendencies to repress and avoid conflict if at all possible, many people have not had much experience with conflict situations; fewer still have reflected at length on how to deal with conflicts. As a result, conflicts are novel, uncertain and often threatening situations for most people. Faced with such situations, individuals cling to habitual responses.

Some habitual patterns facilitate conflict management; others, although they may immediately improve the situation, also cause it to deteriorate over the long run. These patterns blind members to the negative consequences of their behaviors and can prevent people from changing their interaction when harmful escalation or avoidance cycles begin. People become locked in destructive cycles because they cannot recognize that behaviors which were once functional and beneficial are now worsening the problem. Since conflict interaction leans toward self-perpetuation, the functional behaviors can become the basis of an *unseen orientation* which defeats the members' own interests.

Because conflicts are, in effect, problems that a group must deal with, the trained incapacities most likely to worsen conflicts are those arising from work habits which facilitate group decision-making and problem-solving. Work habits become second nature to a group; the group comes to rely on them to complete work efficiently and solve problems. In order to understand these trained incapacities it is necessary to consider the essential requirements of the decision-making process (Scheidel and Crowell, 1979). To make decisions a group must do the following:

1. orient itself to the issue or problem at hand (in other words, obtain needed information to understand the issue, explore the causes and symptoms of a problem, examine what efforts have already been made to alleviate the problem, and so on)
2. come up with criteria for what a good solution should look like (in other words, determine what the decision must accomplish and what limitations any proposed solution is under)
3. generate possible solutions
4. evaluate the solutions and choose one as the group's decision

The first three requirements emerge from a group's need to *generate ideas.* The group must provide an accurate description of the problem, keep in mind what the solutions must accomplish in order for it to be effective, and be creative in generating possible solutions. The fourth requirement stems from a need to *select* an alternative as the group's decision. This decision-making function occurs as the group evaluates the proposed solutions and adopts one course of action to take. Although groups rarely follow these tasks sequentially, and they frequently underplay one or more of these functions, these four requirements are central aspects of any group decision. As an illustration, consider how one task group handled these functions.

_____ **CASE 2.3** _____

The student government association (SGA) at a large eastern campus established a task force committee of eight students to determine why one service arm of the organization was not working as planned. Although the SGA had funded a student-run career counseling office for two years, there was a general sense that it was not being used to its capacity. The task force was told to reach a decision about how the counseling office could be improved. The following is a brief overview of how the group proceeded through the main decision-making steps.

Orientation: The task force divided itself into three subgroups at its initial meeting. One group assessed the number of students that had been counseled by office staff over the past year, the second group examined the organization and staffing of the office, and the third conducted a campus-wide survey to determine what students currently knew about the office. Each of these groups compiled information and presented it at a meeting that was called by the chair of the committee.

Establishing criteria: Before suggesting possible solutions the group tried to determine what boundaries or limits their suggestions would have to meet. The committee noted that the SGA provided only $600 dollars per year for the office and because of a financial pinch, this figure would not be increased. The members also recognized that the university had strict regulations on the type of advertising any campus organization could use, and the group noted that students who volunteer to help at the counseling office usually have limited time because of heavy class loads.

Suggesting solutions: Six weeks after the task force began its work, the group brainstormed a list of thirty possible suggestions that might improve the office. These suggestions were diverse in scope and included such options as: sponsoring career workshops, hiring a full-time paid staff person, selling T-shirts with the office logo on them, renting sign space on the campus bus, staffing the office with students in counseling psychology who hold work-study jobs.

Choosing a solution: The task force was never able to make a final recommendation to the student government board because the semester ended before the suggested solutions could be adequately evaluated. The group gave an analysis of the problem, the results of their survey, and a list of possible suggestions to the student government board.

As groups make decisions members establish shared expectations about how ideas will be brought up for consideration and how problems will be defined. Groups come to rely on certain types of criteria for evaluating possible solutions, and they develop decision-making procedures to determine how and when an agreement on a solution is reached. In short, groups *establish and rely upon working habits* to reach acceptable decisions.

Since the major task in resolving conflict is to construct an acceptable and workable decision, a group's working habits usually come into play as the members confront the conflict issue. These working habits may be adaptive and beneficial, because they tend to facilitate group decision-making; however, they can also have corrosive effects on members' ability to manage and contain conflict, if the group relies upon them in situations where they need to be disregarded. *The benefits of these habits enhance their potential for harm precisely because it is so difficult to determine when the negative consequences begin to overwhelm the positive ones.* By the time the participants recognize they are in trouble, their interaction may have become so tangled that it is difficult for them to detect or correct their destructive tendencies. The group's working habits have become trained incapacities.

The first two trained incapacities we discuss (*goal-centeredness* and *destructive redefinition*) are working habits that can influence how the group *generates ideas* as it defines the problem, *comes up with criteria for evaluating solutions,* or *suggests possible solutions.*

GOAL-CENTEREDNESS

It is clear that a good deal of our behavior in everyday life leads towards achieving some goal or plan. As Miller, Galanter and Pribram (1960) argue in *Plans and the Structure of Behavior,* our activities are frequently organized in a sequence of moves that have some desired end point. Plans generate and control the sequence of behaviors we carry out. In everyday life, these goals range in type and in the number of behaviors required for their execution. Obviously, having plans or goals serves people well in a number of ways. Most importantly, they allow for the completion of critical activities and make it easy to direct and evaluate our actions, because each action can be assessed by determining whether it contributes to successful completion of the plan.

In conflict and decision-making situations, one set of goals are the solutions or outcomes members would like to see adopted. They are individuals' estimates of the best decision or course of action for the organization (or for their own interests). Entering a discussion with some solution to a problem or conflict in mind is a natural and in some ways useful response to the need for differentiation. It is natural because members often have explicit needs that they feel can only be met by the adoption of a particular solution. They may have thought about the problem for quite some time and have urged themselves to find a clear way out. Having a solution in mind can also be useful because it provides the members with clear guidance about the type of communicative behavior each should engage in during conflict interaction. The goal or solution can dictate the type of information the member should contribute and the arguments that should be made in support of a position. Each member can build a case for the solution he or she wants adopted. This focus on solutions can allow for differentiation to occur. If parties start the discussion of a conflict issue by arguing for alternative solutions, the information and arguments in favor of each solution will be aired and the points of difference between members can be clarified. People need to hear the pros and cons of suggested solutions in order to evaluate them and ultimately make a choice among them.

Goal-centeredness becomes an incapacity, however, when (1) it prevents parties from conducting an adequate assessment of the problem underlying the conflict (in other words, when it undercuts the group's attempt to orient itself to the problem), or (2) it becomes a way to quickly make a decision without a complete analysis of the chosen solution (in other words, when it prevents the group from establishing criteria for solutions or examining a solution in light of established criteria).

The tendency to be goal-centered can encourage people to begin the discussion of an issue with an evaluation of alternative solutions. There is, however, persuasive evidence to suggest that for successful problem-solving the group's attempt to define the problem (asking "what is wrong here?") should be separated from the search for solutions (asking "what should be done to alleviate the problem?") (Maier, 1967). More time should be spent on analysis of the problem than on evaluation of solutions. This approach to decision-making often succeeds because it is through an analysis of the symptoms and causes of the problem that the best solution—the one that comes closest to meeting all members' needs or all causes of the problem—is likely to surface. If members make statements about solutions they would like to see adopted at the very outset of the discussion, the process of differentiation cannot occur in a "problem analysis-solution evaluation" sequence. Any suggested solution is founded on some conception of the problem, but this conception may never be articulated if the solution is proposed first. The group may accept the assumed definition of the problem only because a solution has been proposed.

The experience of a twelve-person food distribution cooperative illustrates how excessive emphasis on goals can prevent members from making an adequate assessment of the problem. The conflict in question concerned whether or not to continue publishing the cooperative's newsletter.

_____ **CASE 2.4** _____

An umbrella organization that handled the publicity and some financial decisions for a number of food cooperatives had recently lost a member who published a monthly newsletter for the stores that belonged to the organization. The former member had journalism experience and was able to publish a successful periodical that reflected the values and sentiments of the cooperative movement and was, at the same time, a professional publication. After this member left, no one in the group had the experience or motivation to publish a periodical of similar quality. The group was faced with the issue of what to do about the dying newsletter.

The group had one discussion of the issue at a meeting, but no agreement was reached, and, in fact, the meeting became very tense because the newsletter was related to a number of issues which were as yet unresolved. A third party who was providing the group with a series of training sessions on meeting and decision-making skills was called in to facilitate the meeting at which the newsletter was to be discussed. When this agenda item arose, members almost immediately made statements about _what should be done_ about the newsletter. One solution some members proposed was to let the newsletter die because there was no one in the group who could successfully publish it. Another member soon responded by suggesting that the group as a whole try to publish the periodical. A third member suggested that the group hire a part-time worker. The discussion began with little direct attention to the underlying nature of the problem the group faced. Instead, the members entered the discussion with set ideas about what the solution should be. These solutions were debated before the group adequately assessed what functions the newsletter served, what needs prompted its publication, or what were the possible consequences of not publishing it. An examination of these issues would have given the members a clearer understanding of the problem they were trying to solve. Since these issues were not clarified, no criteria for what a good solution might look like emerged. Tension and hostile comments began to infect the second discussion of the issue and a stalemate seemed likely.

After the group was prodded towards a discussion of the problem itself, it became clear that there were two conceptions of the problem underlying the suggested solutions. One focused on the ability of an outsider, as editor, to remain responsive to the group and to reflect the group's values in the newsletter. There was a fear that the tone and character of the paper would change radically if it were handed over to someone who was not a member of the group. The other conception emphasized the critical need for communication with the member stores. This view emphasized that the newspaper served an important function in getting information about prices, staffing, and so on, to people who needed these updates periodically. Once these conceptions were clarified the group could view them as criteria that a satisfactory solution to the problem must meet. It allowed the group to assess any suggested solution by determining how well it would meet the various needs that members had expressed. Would the solution continue to get needed information to the stores? Would the solution remain true to the co-op's philosophy and image? Unearthing the implicit conceptions of the problem was critical in avoiding further impasses.

Goal-centeredness can also become an incapacity if it is used as a way out of the demands of differentiation. By suggesting solutions at the outset of a discussion, members can avoid any direct assault on controversial and potentially explosive issues that underlie the suggestion of a particular course of action. If the members feel that the emotional or divisive consequences of discussing an issue are worse than the adoption of a mediocre solution, then a quick vote, head nods, or uncommitted acceptance of a sub-optimum solution is an attractive alternative. An immediate choice may not be seen as avoidance, but as an accomplishment because a decision was reached without internal strife. In short, members can find that immediate suggestion and acceptance of solutions are beneficial and rely upon this tactic, ultimately defeating their own best interests in the long run.

DESTRUCTIVE REDEFINITION

The discussion of goal-centeredness suggests that people can change their goals and expectations as interaction unfolds. This is a natural result of the human need to make sense of situations, to explore the field of action. As unforeseen developments arise, members redefine the situation to take them into account. Redefinition is beneficial because it enables people to maintain a sense of continuity while adapting to the situation as it unfolds. It usually occurs more or less automatically, although individuals can control and change how they define what is occurring in the group. This is fortunate because redefinition is a critical determinant of the quality of interaction.

Successful differentiation often rests on the members' capacity to redefine conflict situations. As we have noted, integrative solutions emerge only after members move from a conception of the conflict based on their own positions and needs to one which centers on the incompatibility of these positions. When this redefinition occurs, members have a common ground that can serve as a basis for a joint attack on the problem.

If members do not achieve this common view, however, they may still need to redefine the conflict in order to give meaning to their behavior. When members fail to see the conflict as the incompatibility of issues and instead continue to push for their own positions, this tendency to redefine a conflict can become the basis for one of the most destructive forms of escalation. *Members can redefine the conflict so that winning the argument or beating the opponent is their major objective.*

Teger (1980) has suggested that there are critical points in conflict interaction where members feel they have invested more *in the fight* than could ever be justified by any resolution of the original issue. These critical points in conflict are similar, Teger says, to decisions people make when they have invested time, money, or effort in some activity over a period of time. Teger uses the example of watching old movies on late night TV as an illustration. Despite increasing fatigue, more frequent commercials and an obvious ending, there comes a point when late-night viewers have invested so much time in the movie that they have to see its conclusion. The goal becomes getting to the end of the movie even though continuing to watch it is counterproductive. In the same way, when members have invested heavily in conflict, but the issue seems less and less significant, the sides are likely to redefine the conflict so that the major goal becomes beating an opponent. In true Hatfield-McCoy style, the original issue may no longer be in sight.

Similarly, in dealing specifically with possible liabilities of problem-solving groups, Maier (1967) lists the urge to "win the argument" as one of the main obstacles to successful decision-making. He notes that the goal of winning rather than finding the best solution is a clear threat to the quality of the final decision.

Destructive redefinition arises from the same impulse that encourages people to center on goals; however, the conflict is redefined not in terms of other possible solutions to the problem, but strictly as an attempt to beat an "opponent" in the group. When members in conflict see the weaknesses of their own positions but still fight brutally for them, redefining the conflict gives meaning to members' behaviors at the cost of reason and hope for a constructive solution.

The next two trained incapacities (evaluative tendency and using objective standards) are working habits that influence how the group *assesses alternative solutions* or *adopts* one as its course of action.

EVALUATIVE TENDENCY

A third trained incapacity in conflict situations stems in part from the same need for a comfortable and guiding orientation that gives rise to goal-centeredness. As Osgood, Suci and Tannenbaum's (1957) research in the *Measurement of Meaning* and much subsequent work documented, people rely heavily upon a sense of values in making meaningful judgments of concepts. A value-based orientation guides the way we react to ideas, situations, and events in our lives. This evaluative orientation allows us to take stands, state preferences, and formulate decisions; it thereby becomes the basis for a large part of an individual's identity.

The process of differentiation is founded on *evaluation*. Any idea, decision, or outcome considered during a conflict interaction is assessed according to the values each member holds. An evaluative orientation allows for critical thinking and encourages pointed discussion of the issues. It is therefore a productive aspect of differentiation.

Janis' (1972) insightful analysis of *groupthink* (flawed decision-making that results from an overly cohesive and conforming group) demonstrates the consequences of preventing evaluation or critical thinking during decision-making sessions. Highly cohesive groups create pressures towards conformity among their members. These pressures stifle the evaluation of ideas and produce a shared illusion of invulnerability, a belief in the inherent morality of any decision the members make, an illusion of unanimity, and a false view of outsiders who offer a potential threat to the group. Having an evaluative orientation is critical for avoiding the pitfalls of groupthink and engaging in successful differentiation.

Although evaluative orientations are useful in making decisions, they can lead to destructive interaction patterns if members persist in making evaluative comments in contexts where judgments should be suspended. There are at least three contexts where evaluation can blind members to the need for suspended judgment (in other words, the need to withhold comments that offer positive or negative evaluations of ideas in front of the group).

First, at points in the process of differentiation *when evaluative comments have led to defensive and strong emotional responses, members may need to stress areas of agreement or commonality.* It may be important, for example, to allow people to see that they all still share the same general goal for the group even though they disagree about the means that should be used to achieve it. The objective of stressing points of commonality is not to deflect attention away from the issue, but to check a cycle of defensiveness.

Gibb (1961) identified evaluative comments as one of the main types of behavior that elicit defensive responses. When positions people hold are criticized, there is a strong likelihood that members will feel threatened by this criticism and respond defensively. If defensiveness does occur, further evaluative comments are likely to be taken as threats against the person rather than as productive discussion of the issue. The group is more likely to mark one person or faction as the source of the conflict rather than view the conflict as the incompatibility of positions. If a member makes a comment that summarizes the points of agreement and *links the criticism to the main issue,* the member can ward off further personal escalation of the conflict and help the group focus on the key issues. Frequently, these comments simply remind the members that there is basic agreement on values or goals, but this reminder can be a strong source of motivation for the members to tackle the issue wholeheartedly.

Second, at points in the interaction *when the organization needs to consider a broad array of alternatives, an evaluative orientation can stifle creativity.* There are times when members need to break away from a longstanding view of the conflict or from a limited set of solutions that have been endlessly debated. To toss off a slovenly or unimaginative mindset, the group may need to tap its own creative potential. Forestalling evaluation is critical in achieving this objective. When members believe that any suggestion they make will be immediately evaluated, a growing reluctance to contribute ideas may leave much creative potential unrealized. Several idea-generation techniques (like Osborn's (1957) brainstorming technique and Delbecq, Van de Ven, and D. Gustafsen's (1975) Nominal Group Process) were explicitly developed to forestall evaluative comments. (See also Gouran (1982) and Scheidel and Crowell (1979, pp. 256–268) for descriptions of these helpful decision-making techniques).

However, it is surprising how difficult it often is for people to follow the main rule of *brainstorming:* they have trouble withholding all verbal and nonverbal responses that could convey positive or negative sentiment. People immediately see the drawbacks, complications, or questionable side effects of suggested proposals and they find it difficult to withhold these reservations and objections.

At times, members fear that even the suggestion of a solution might make an undesirable change possible. Offering a negative comment immediately is seen as a way of preventing or at least reducing the chances that the change will be adopted.

A third context where an evaluation orientation can blind the group to the need for suspended judgment is at those points *when the group or organization lacks the critical information to make an intelligent assessment or decision.* At times, evaluation may prevent the members from recognizing the need for the information at all. In other instances, members may plunge ahead with an evaluation of alternative solutions despite a recognized need for further evidence. As a result, the information may never be sought or, once found, may carry less weight than it normally would have in the decision-making process. The pitfalls of premature evaluation recently emerged in the engineering unit of a major urban sanitation department.

____ **CASE 2.5** _____

The unit had to develop a means of moving hundreds of tons of treated sludge from a waste treatment facility to a highway construction project where it would be used as landfill for overpasses. An advertisement was put out for bids on this job and a number of trucking companies and engineering firms sent in proposals. Most called for the use of traditional earth-moving equipment and tractor trailor trucks to move the sludge from the plant to the construction site one load at a time. However, one plan took an innovative approach: it advocated a long conveyer belt to move sludge continuously over the three miles from the plant to the highway. This technique, the bid argued, would cost one third of what trucking would cost, and would also avoid road hazards and congestion caused by the trucks.

When the unit met to evaluate the bids, one member argued strongly for the conveyer scheme. His arguments were met by a barrage of criticisms: the scheme had never been tried before; there was no evidence it would work; it would require skilled technicians unavailable in this area; and the belt would break down too much. In the face of these protests, the member backed down. The unit dismissed the idea and refused to do any further research on it. The lowest bidder among the trucking proposals was given the job.

In fact, the conveyer idea did turn out to be feasible and is now being used in several locales. It was a good deal less expensive than trucking and has about the same breakdown record as trucks and earth-moving equipment do. By evaluating the conveyer idea immediately, the unit "shut it down." The group's immediate turn towards evaluating the options forestalled a fact-finding effort that could have tested rather than assumed the outcome.

At times, members do rescind or reevaluate decisions in the light of new evidence but in many cases the evaluation of alternatives leads naturally to the selection of one. People often comment on the need for information but then fail to assign someone the responsibility of obtaining it, or continue with a discussion that could unfold quite differently if the information were in hand. When necessary information is lacking, an evaluative orientation can blind members to the rather weak scaffolding that supports their decision.

USING OBJECTIVE STANDARDS

Moscovici's (1976) analysis of social influence processes in groups points to another trained incapacity that emerges in decision-making contexts. Moscovici has examined the *social norms* that determine the basis on which groups make judgments and reach consensus. These norms are the criteria a group employs to assess its own judgments and decisions. Members employ these criteria to persuade others to adopt new positions.

The objectivity norm is heavily relied upon in conflict and decision-making situations. This norm "concerns that need to test opinions and judgments according to the criterion of objective accuracy, so that decisions can be made on whether they may be universally accepted" (Moscovici, 1976, p. 153). When groups adopt this norm as a basis for judgment, the members believe that there are definite correct choices or responses for each issue in the conflict. The objectivity norm dictates that "in the course of social interaction, every person thinks and behaves with reference to the public reality—that reality which is open to inspection by all, which is the same for all and which is easily interpreted by all who have eyes to see and ears to hear" (Moscovici, 1976, p. 155). The objectivity norm stands in contrast to the preference norm where judgment is anchored in personal tastes; it presumes that differences of opinion can exist. It also differs from an originality norm where selection is assessed by both the degree of novelty of an alternative and its promise of practical innovation for the group.

People must rely upon some criterion or social norm to make judgments. If the decision is one that *can* be evaluated by *some objective standard,* then it is in the best interest of the organization to measure alternatives against that criterion. The use of objective criteria depersonalizes the conflict by allowing it to be decided on the basis of standards external to any party's preferences or prejudices. Objective standards are possible for such decisions as determining the amount of space needed for an organization, deciding on what type of training members may need to handle financial operations, or determining how many people are needed to complete a project. For these types of decisions, lengthy arguments can be costly and frustrating and are, for all practical purposes, counterproductive because objective standards can be used to determine them. They can be prevented by a clearer articulation of the standard and a more careful assessment of the possible solutions. Some bargaining texts also argue that negotiators should *always* link their offers to objective standards in order to reinforce their legitimacy in the eyes of the other party (Fisher & Ury, 1981).

This contention is not necessarily true, however. There are other types of decisions where there is no clear, objective standard for judging alternatives. The preferences of the members themselves determine the set of alternatives that the group can choose among. These decisions might include: reorganization of work space (Katz, 1979); assessing how much time, money, and energy members of a consulting firm should invest in a particular project; or deciding whether to increase the membership of a voluntary organization.

The process of differentiation is the same for both types of decisions; opinions and suggestions are stated, viewpoints are criticized and discussed, points of dissimilarity are clarified. It is the assumption members make about whether the decision can or cannot be assessed according to some objective standard that is critical. *The trap is set, however, because the demands of differentiation can encourage members to presume the existence of an objective standard in cases where there are none.* The assumption that some objective standard underlies one's position is a useful justification for arguing vehemently for a position, regardless of the nature of the decision itself. Consequently, in differentiation members can easily lose sight of the preferential nature of the decision before them: they mistakenly search for the *one right solution.*

One consequence of presuming that there is an objective standard is that the group may fail to treat its chosen solution in an appropriately *tentative* manner. If members recognize that the decision they face is not one that could be reached according to some objective standard, they can design a cautious implementation plan for the chosen solution. If they assume they have chosen the one right solution, they may see no need to implement the plan in steps, build in safeguards, or at least keep a watchful eye on the impact the solution is having.

In the previous example of the co-op attempting to decide the fate of its newsletter (Case 2.4), the early discussion of solutions was premised on the existence of an objective standard. There was a strong sense underlying the discussion that there would be only one right choice. As long as this norm prevailed, there was no consideration of provisional means to implement solutions. If the group decided to hire an outsider to publish the newsletter, for example, this solution could have been enacted on a one-month trial basis with a further stipulation that the editor give the final draft of any issue to some co-op member or committee for review before publication. As obvious as these modifications are, they were never discussed as long as the group held to its belief in the viability of only *one* solution.

The final trained incapacity we will describe can influence both the idea-generation and the selection process in group decision-making. It deals with decision-making procedures groups follow.

USING PROCEDURES

One of the primary characteristics of organizations and groups is their tendency to use *structured procedures* to help complete their tasks (Hall, 1972). Although rules are often adopted formally, many procedures evolve without being explicitly acknowledged. A procedure which works becomes institutionalized through repetitive use, as, for example, when a group spends the first fifteen minutes of its meetings socializing and eventually expects to do so at every session. Procedures become traditions. Members come to assume things should be done in a certain way and the organization's identity often becomes tied to its procedures (for example, "This is a democratic group—we vote on all major decisions").

Standardized procedures hold several advantages. If procedures are set *before* a decision is made, members have *sufficient knowledge about the process to participate and contribute.* They know, for example, when votes will be taken, how long they have to suggest alternative proposals, and who will end discussion of a topic. Chaotic or secret decision-making procedures discourage participation and may result in an inferior decision because some members feel lost during the meeting. Knowledge of set procedures like Parliamentary Procedure reduces members' uncertainty about how to behave in the group, and may therefore reduce stress for some members.

Procedural rules can also serve as *standards for deciding disputes* in the group. For example, a disagreement over whether a decision was made fairly might be settled by checking the rules on voting procedures. Since procedural rules are used and accepted by the group before the dispute, they may have a degree of legitimacy in the eyes of all, which allows the disagreement to be settled without arousing personal antipathies.

Finally, set procedures can often *equalize power among group members.* In the Nominal Group Technique, a structured decision-making method developed by Delbecq, Van de Ven and Gustafsen (1975), preliminary ideas are elicited by going around the group in order and having each member give one idea. This process is repeated until all members' ideas have been contributed. The Nominal Group Technique ensures that everyone contributes; it gives those members who are usually quiet or hesitant a formal opportunity to participate without being interrupted by more talkative or powerful members.

Procedures can become *incapacities,* however, when (1) they structure interaction so that confrontation and escalation are inevitable; or (2) they are used to suppress or avoid differentiation. Procedures which institutionalize controversy and opposition, such as the use of Robert's Rules of Order in meetings, serve a useful function for a group, because they insure that all sides of an issue are heard and they force members to make a definite choice among alternatives. The orderly, sharp debate of a well-run meeting under Robert's Rules often illustrates the benefits of Parliamentary-type methods. However, since the discussion of a motion begins with the expectation that a vote is inevitable if a serious conflict develops, Parliamentary Procedure may polarize opposing factions and cause competition and rifts among members.

_____ CASE 2.6 _____

In one labor union which used Robert's Rules, a major conflict erupted over whether or not to call a work stoppage in response to a grievance against plant administration. As debate ensued, it became clear that over two thirds of the membership did not favor the stoppage, although a large minority remained very much in favor of the move. The minority, however, was able to advocate its position long after it was evident the union would vote down the work stoppage by using parliamentary rules as tactics. Some members for example, attempted to add the work stoppage as an amendment to an unrelated proposal generally favored by the union. These tactics resulted in a polarization of union members: many of those opposed to the work stoppage were outraged at the minority's persistence; the longer members of the minority argued for the stoppage the more convinced they became of their positions. The end result was a major rift in the union. The minority—voted down—felt cut off from the rest of the membership, left the union, and attempted to form their own organization. In this case the easily-manipulated rules of Parliamentary Procedure certainly contributed to the problem, but just as important was the general climate Parliamentary methods can create in groups: an adversarial atmosphere that encourages stubborn adherence to one's own position in the face of opposition. Such a climate can be more conducive to factionalism than to common ownership of the problem and a united pursuit of a workable solution.

Procedures can also stifle differentiation by discouraging a direct assault on the issues. Voting on proposals is often used to avoid difficult situations (Hall & Watson, 1970). If two sides appear to be forming, the chairperson calls for a vote and assumes that once the vote is taken the issue is decided and the problem solved. This reasoning is flawed, however, because only the winning side gets what it wants in this case. The members who lose the vote may be dissatisfied and withdraw from the group or be much less committed to the decision. Disagreement can also be stifled by informal or implicit rules such as "let's get through our agenda as fast as possible." Such an attitude can make members feel they are imposing on the group by raising or complicating issues. As Janis (1972) has noted, decision-making groups often do not realize they have suppressed contributions or criticism and may even think they are doing an excellent job of decision-making.

SEEING DESTRUCTIVE CYCLES

Differentiation is an important part of conflict interaction. It allows people to exchange critical information and obtain a clear understanding of the problem. It frequently motivates members to deal with the issue because it makes the consequences of an unresolved conflict more apparent.

At the same time, differentiation is a major source of anxiety and tension in groups, because it is founded on a set of forces that can easily get out of hand and lead to uncontrolled escalation. In this chapter we have examined a number of behaviors that are important in achieving adequate differentiation and completing group tasks, but that can undermine interaction if members blindly cling to them. These behaviors become habitual because they are functional in many circumstances. Inflexible reliance on goals, evaluation, procedural rules, and so on, can contribute to *destructive cycles of escalation* or *encourage avoidance of the issue*. Because they are deeply ingrained habits, trained incapacities mold members' perceptions of the situation so that their negative consequences are not easily discovered. Members continue to believe their behavioral strategies are beneficial or defensible even when they undermine the conflict interaction. Trained incapacities promote interaction patterns that head towards escalation or avoidance.

Because escalation or avoidance cycles can stem from trained incapacities, these interaction cycles often go undetected until irreparable damage is done. *Seeing* that the group is in a protracted, destructive spiral is crucial because such insight is the first step in thwarting the trained incapacities that could be perpetuating the interaction. People in conflict must be aware of concrete symptoms that signal the possible onset of escalation or avoidance.

Figure 7 summarizes several symptoms that may emerge when the conflict is heading towards destructive escalation or avoidance of the issue. It should be emphasized that the mere appearance of the symptom is not an automatic cause for concern. Remember that constructive conflict interaction will pass through periods of escalation, avoidance, constructive work, and relaxation. Cycles only become threatening when they are *repetitive* and *prevent other forms of interaction from emerging*.

Once a destructive cycle is recognized, members (or third parties) can intervene to alter those behaviors that drive avoidance or escalation. A wide range of inter-

—— **Figure 7** ——
Interaction symptoms of escalation or avoidance cycles

Symptoms of avoidance	Symptoms of escalation
Marked decrease in the group's commitment to solving the problem ("why would we care?")	An issue takes much longer to deal with than was anticipated
Quick acceptance of a suggested solution	Members repeatedly offer the same argument in support of a position
Members stop themselves from raising controversial aspects of an issue	Members over-inflate the consequences of not reaching agreement
People "tune out" of the interaction	Threats are used to win arguments
Unresolved issues keep emerging in the same or different form	Mounting tension is felt in the group
Discussion centers on a safe aspect of a broader and more explosive issue	The group gets nowhere but seems to be working feverishly
Little sharing of information	Name-calling and personal arguments are used
Outspoken members are notably quiet	Immediate polarization on issues or the emergence of coalitions
No plans are made to implement a chosen solution	Hostile eye gaze or less-direct eye contact between members
No evaluation is made of evidence that is offered in support of claims	Sarcastic laughter or humor as a form of tension release
	Heated disagreements that seem pointless or are about trivial issues

vention techniques can be employed to deal with the dysfunctional habits (habits that impair normal functioning) discussed in this chapter. Some of these techniques establish formal rules of interaction. A rule establishing that no member can suggest a solution until a specified amount of time has been spent discussing the problem, can, for example, help counteract goal-centeredness. Other intervention techniques are far less formal. Simply making a comment that takes the group by surprise because it demonstrates how stilted or limited the interaction has become can often jolt the group and reverse a cycle. These and other practical intervention techniques will be the major focus of chapter 6 in this book. In the next three chapters we look beyond working habits to climate, power negotiation and face-saving as forces that also drive destructive interaction cycles.

—— **SUMMARY** ——

Destructive conflicts often result from people's inability to cope with the demands of productive conflict interaction. To be productive, conflict interaction must move successfully through a differentiation phase in which members state the nature of the problem, clarify points of disagreement, confront key differences, and acknowledge the consequences of not finding an acceptable solution. Behaviors necessary to complete successful differentiation can become destructive if members cling to these behaviors in changing circumstances. Working habits groups employ in making decisions can lead to radical escalation or avoidance of conflict when members act inflexibly and cling to these habits in situations which warrant change. Destructive interaction cycles can go unnoticed or unchecked in the group because members still view their behavior as functional. "Trained incapacities" are working habits gone awry. They are functional in some sense, but also prevent people from successfully monitoring their own conflict interaction. Goal-centeredness and destructive redefinition are trained incapacities that influence how members generate ideas or approach the problem at hand. Evaluative tendencies and over-reliance on objective standards influence how members evaluate and select a solution. Procedural incapacities are working habits that stem from established decision-making procedures in the group and can influence how ideas are generated in the group or how alternatives are evaluated.

_____ REFERENCES _____

Apfelbaum, E. On conflicts and bargaining. In L. Berkowitz (Ed.), *Advances in experimental social psychology.* New York: Academic Press, 1964.

Beier, E. G. The effect of induced anxiety on flexibility of intellectual functioning. *Psychological Monographs,* 1951, *65,* 3–26.

Boulding, E. Further reflections on conflict management. In R. Kahn & E. Boulding (Eds.), *Power and conflict in organizations.* New York: Basic Books, 1964.

Burke, K. *Permanence and change.* Indianapolis: Bobbs-Merrill, 1954.

Delbecq, A., Van de Ven, A., & Gustafsen, D. *Group techniques for program planning.* Glenview, Illinois: Scott, Foresman, 1975.

Deutsch, M. *The resolution of conflict.* New Haven: Yale University Press, 1973.

Dill, W. R. Business organizations. In J. G. March (Ed.), *Handbook of organizations.* Chicago: Rand McNally, 1968.

Fisher, R., & Ury, W. *Getting to yes: Negotiating agreement without giving in.* Boston: Houghton Mifflin, 1981.

Gibb, J. Defensive communication. *Journal of Communication,* 1961, *2,* 141–148.

Gouran, D. *Making decisions in groups.* Glenview, Ill.: Scott, Foresman, 1982.

Guetzkow, H., & Gyr, J. An analysis of conflict in decision-making groups. *Human Relations,* 1954, *7,* 367–381.

Hall, R. H. *Organizations: Structure and process.* Englewood Cliffs, N.J.: Prentice-Hall, 1972.

Hall, J., & Watson, W. H. The effects of a normative intervention on group decision-making performance. *Human Relations,* 1970, *23,* 299–317.

Holsti, O. R. Crisis, stress and decision-making. *International Social Science Journal,* 1971, *23,* 53–67.

Janis, I. *Victims of groupthink.* Boston: Houghton Mifflin, 1972.

Katz, R. Time and work: Toward an integrative perspective. *Research in Organizational Behavior,* 1979. *2,* 81–127.

Kiesler, C. *The psychology of commitment.* New York: Academic Press, 1971.

Leary, T. *Interpersonal diagnosis of personality.* New York: Ronald, 1957.

Luchins, A., & Luchins, E. *Rigidity of behavior.* Eugene, Oregon: University of Oregon Books, 1959.

Maier, N. Assets and liabilities in group problem solving: The need for an integrative function. *Psychological Review,* 1967, *74,* 239–249.

Miller, G., Galanter, E., & Pribram, K. *Plans and the structure of behavior.* New York: Holt, Rinehart and Winston, 1960.

Moscovici, S. *Social influence and social change.* New York: Academic Press, 1976.

Osborn, A. *Applied imagination.* New York: Scribner's Sons, 1957.

Osgood, C., Suci, G. & Tannenbaum, P. *The measurement of meaning.* Urbana: University of Illinois Press, 1957.

Pruitt, D., & Lewis, S. The psychology of integrative bargaining. In D. Druckman (Ed.), *Negotiations.* Beverly Hills: Sage, 1977.

Scheidel, T., & Crowell, L. *Discussing and deciding.* New York: Macmillan, 1979.

Simmel, C. *Conflict.* New York: Free Press, 1955.

Smart, C., & Vertinsky, I. Designs for crisis decision units. *Administrative Science Quarterly,* 1977, *22,* 640–657.

Swensen, C. *Introduction to interpersonal relations.* Glenview, Ill.: Scott, Foresman, 1973.

Teger, A. *Too much invested to quit.* New York: Pergamon Press, 1980.

Walton, R. *Interpersonal peacemaking: Confrontations and third party consultation.* Reading, Mass.: Addison-Wesley, 1969.

Climate and Conflict Interaction

Perhaps because we live in the scientific age, most of us prefer well-defined, straightforward explanations for the way things are. Ideally we should be able to isolate the forces that shape conflict, and then define, measure, and study these forces to come up with a fairly complete explanation. Unfortunately, however, the world seldom lives up to our ideals. There is simply more there than is dreamed of in this simple scientific philosophy. Conflict behavior cannot be reduced to responses to a set of well-specified variables or processes. People also act on the basis of their general "feelings" about a situation, feelings which often cannot be precisely defined, boiled down to a simple explanation, or reduced to a set of conditions.

Experienced members of organizations and groups often speak of "getting the feel of" a situation or "learning the ropes." Managers, labor leaders, and politicians observe an "air of conflict" or "a mood of compromise" among their employees, colleagues or opponents. Planners and consultants assess the "climate for change" in the organizations or groups they try to influence. All of these people are responding to the general, global character of their groups and organizations, to what has been called the *climate* of the situation. Climate represents the *prevailing temper, attitudes, and outlook* of the group and, as the meteorological name implies, it is just as diffuse and pervasive as the weather.

Climate is of critical importance for understanding both groups in general, and conflict in particular, because it provides *continuity and coherence* to group activities. As a general sense of the group, climate enables members to ascertain the group's general direction, what it means to be part of the group, what is appropriate in the group, how fellow members are likely to react, and other information necessary to guide their behavior and help them understand the group. In the brown-bag session discussed in the overview of climate in Chapter 1 (see Case 1.1), the open and relaxed climate encouraged participants to exercise their curiosity and to be receptive to each others' comments. Questions, answers, and discussion flowed freely and spontaneously for most of the session. When the newspaper columnist was challenged, the atmosphere grew tense, and members became hesitant and defensive.

The challenge seemed out of place, given the openness of previous discussion; it introduced great uncertainty, as well as some hostility into the proceedings. Members reacted to the challenge as a violation of appropriate behavior, and subsequent interaction was colored by this reaction. Eventually, rather than risk escalation of the challenge and permanent collapse of free, relaxed exchange, group leaders chose to terminate the session. By evoking certain types of behavior and discouraging others, the open climate gave the discussion direction and held it together. It united the diverse styles and concerns of individual members by providing a common ground for acting together and for reacting to a "crisis."

Implicit in any group's climate is an attitude toward conflict and how it should be handled. Climate constrains and channels conflict behavior; it lends a definite tenor to interchanges that can accelerate destructive cycles or preserve a productive approach. In the brown-bag session the questioner's challenge was hastily cut off because the group was in "guest speaker mode," which implied a respectful and friendly attitude toward the editor. The challenge raised the specter of open and prolonged disagreement and potential embarrassment of the speaker. The group's open, nonevaluative climate made the challenge seem inappropriate and, rather than allow such a disagreement to ripen, those in charge were eager to end the session. Interestingly, the reaction of other members to the challenge contributed to the sudden shift from an open climate to a tense and evaluative one, even though this is the last thing they would have wanted. The *interplay of concrete, specific interactions and generalized climate* is a critical force determining the direction of conflicts. We will spend a large part of this chapter exploring just this relationship.

At first glance, climate is an uncomfortably vague concept. In order to get a handle on it, it is tempting to define a set of variables or properties that "make up" climate and classify different sorts of climates (for example, cooperative versus competitive climates) on the basis of whether they have various combinations of properties. Most social scientists have tried to do just this (see, for example Deutsch, 1973, or James & Jones, 1974). We believe this approach is mistaken. Climates are extremely complex and diffuse. As a result, it is difficult, if not impossible, to isolate a few defining variables that can capture all the varied forms and nuances of climates. More importantly, the concepts we use to explain and understand human behavior should be equivalent to those used by people as they act. To reduce climate to a simple set of variables is to do violence to the concept. Climate is a diffuse, generalized conception for people in groups, and our explorations of it should take this into account. Therefore, while we will try to tease out some properties of climates in order to help people analyze their own groups, we will always operate from the assumption that climate is a holistic, general characteristic of groups. We will emphasize *how it comes to be,* because we believe climate can best be understood and controlled if we can clarify how it is produced, maintained, and changed by group activities.

DEFINING CLIMATE

To get a grasp on this elusive concept it will be helpful to consider a specific case that provides a good example of how climate develops and operates in a work group. This case was reported by a third party who was called in to mediate a difficult situation.

_____ CASE 3.1 _____

Riverdale Halfway House is a correctional institution designed to provide low-level security confinement and counseling for male youth offenders. It houses about twenty-five second- and third-time offenders and for all practical purposes represents the last stop before prison for its inhabitants. Residents are required to work or look for work and are on restricted hours. Counseling and other life-adjustment services are provided and counselors' reports on a prisoner can make an important difference in both the length of his incarceration and the conditions of his release. Since the counselors are also authority figures, relationships between staff and prisoners are delicate and touchy. Staff members are subject to a great deal of stress because prisoners attempt to manipulate them to gain favors or to induce punishments for their enemies.

The staff of Riverdale consists of a director who handles funding, general administration, and external relations with other agencies (notably the courts and law enforcement offices); an assistant director who concentrates on external administration of the staff and the halfway house; three counselors; two night caretakers; and an administrative assistant who handles the books and paperwork. The director, George, was the newest staff member at the time of the conflict. The assistant director—who had also applied for the director's slot that George filled—and the three counselors had been at Riverdale for at least a year longer than George. They described George's predecessor as a very "charismatic" person. Prior to George's arrival relations among the staff were very cordial. Morale was high and there was a great deal of informal contact among the staff which made their jobs easier and relaxed tension significantly. The staff reported a high level of respect for all workers under the previous director. Workers felt engaged by an important, if difficult, task that all would work on as a team.

With George's arrival, the climate at Riverdale changed. Right before George started on the job, the staff all chose new offices and rearranged furniture, leaving the shoddiest pieces for George's use. George regarded this as a sign of rejection. He believed the staff had "worked around him," and had tried to undermine his authority by rearranging things without consulting him. He was hurt and somewhat angry despite the staff's attempts to explain that no harm was meant; he remained suspicious. Added to this was George's belief that Carole, the assistant director, resented his being director and wanted his job. Carole claimed she did not resent George, although she did fear that he might have her fired. She tended to withdraw from George in order to avoid conflict. Her withdrawal was interpreted by George as a sign of further rejection, and so this withdrawal also reinforced his suspicion.

The previous director left pretty big shoes for George to fill, and this showed especially in George's working relationship with the staff. The staff felt he was not open with them, and that he quizzed them about their work in a way that seemed manipulative. Several staff members, including Carole, complained that George swore at them and ordered them around; they considered this behavior an affront to their professionalism. George's attempts to assert his authority also angered the staff. In one case which led to a major conflict, George investigated a disciplinary problem with two staff members without consulting Carole who was ordinarily in charge of such matters. George's investigation did not find any problems, but it embarrassed the two staff members (who had been manipulated by prisoners) and made Carole feel George did not respect her. George admitted his mistake and hoped the incident would blow over.

Ten months after George arrived at Riverdale, the climate had changed drastically. Whereas Riverdale had been a supportive, cohesive work group, now it was filled with tension. Interaction between George and the staff, particularly Carole, was formal and distant. The staff had to some degree pulled together in response to George, but their cohesiveness was gone. Informal communication was down, and staff members received much less support from each other. As the third-party mediator observed, the staff members expected disrespect from each other. They felt stuck with their problems and believed there was no way out of their dilemma. There was no trust and no sense of safety in the group. Members felt they had to change others to improve the situation, and did not consider changing themselves or living with others' quirks. The staff wanted George to become less authoritarian and more open to them. George wanted the staff to let him blow up and shout and then forget about it. There was little flexibility or willingness to negotiate. As Carole observed, each contact between herself and George just seemed to make things worse, "so what point was there in trying to talk things out?" The consultant noted that members seemed to be unable to forget previous fights. They interpreted what others said as continuations of old conflicts and assumed a hostile attitude even when one was not present.

The third party tried to get the group to meet and iron out its problems, but the group wanted to avoid confrontation—on several occasions, scheduled meetings were postponed because of other "pressing" problems. Finally, George found another job and left Riverdale, as did one of the counselors. Since then, the staff reports that conditions have improved considerably.

Based on an analysis of this and other cases, as well as previous research on climate, we will offer the following definition: *Climate is the relatively enduring quality of the group situation that (a) is experienced in common by group members, and (b) arises from and influences their interaction and behavior.* Several aspects of this definition require explanation and illustration from the case.

First, climate is not psychological—it is not an intangible belief or feeling in members' minds. Climate is a quality of the group itself because it arises from interaction among group members. For this reason *it is greater than the beliefs or feelings of any single individual.* The climate of Riverdale was hostile and suspicious not because any particular member had suspicions about or disliked another, but because of how the group as a whole interacted. Members were hostile and suspicious toward each other, and these interchanges built on themselves until most group activities were premised on hostility.

This is not to say that individual members' perceptions of climate are not important. People's perceptions play an important role in the creation and maintenance of climate, because these perceptions *mediate* the effects of climate on people's actions. However, climate cannot be *reduced* to the beliefs or feelings of individual members. Various individuals in the Riverdale case had different perceptions of the hostile situation. George thought the group was hostile because Carole wanted his job and the staff resented him. Carole felt the hostility was because George cursed at her and went around her in making decisions. It is clear that neither George nor Carole had the "correct" or complete view, but they were reacting to a common situation. Their beliefs and feelings represent a particular sample and interpretation of experiences in the group.

These perceptions are strongly influenced by the individual members' position in the group, as a study by Albrecht (1979) illustrates. Albrecht compared the perceptions of organizational climate by "key" communicators (active communicators who link large groups of people) with those of "non-key" communicators (those who were more isolated from the communication flow). She found that key communicators identified more with their jobs and were more satisfied with their communication with superiors than did non-key communicators. Albrecht explained these differences as a function of greater frequency of communication (greater activity leads to a more positive image of the organization) and greater amount of information obtained by the key communicators (more information creates greater involvement on the job). Numerous other studies have also shown different perceptions of organization climate depending on the members' position in the authority hierarchy (Schneider & Bartlett, 1970), the type of work done (Powell & Butterfield, 1978), and how long the member had belonged to the group or organization (Johnston, 1976). Clearly, different experiences and different day-to-day interaction patterns create different perceptions of climate. Hence, George, as a new manager, and Carole, as his "old-hand" assistant, had somewhat different views of Riverdale's climate. These different perceptions were one reason George and Carole reacted differently in the conflict.

Because group activities and interaction create and are influenced by climate, George and Carole's perspectives reflected Riverdale's climate. They can be viewed as individual interpretations of the group's climate, which is "experienced in common" by group members. However, individual perceptions provide only a partial picture of the climate itself. The group's climate is greater than any individual's perceptions and can only be identified and understood if the group's interaction as a whole is considered. As we will see below, the individual member's perceptions of climate play an important role in maintaining or changing climates, but they are *different* from climate at the most fundamental level.

A second feature of the definition is its characterization of climate as *experienced in common* by group members. As the preceding paragraph suggests, since climate emerges from interaction, it is a shared experience for the interactors. This implies that there should be some common elements in members' interpretations and descriptions of the group, even though there will be differences in specific details and concerns. Thus the staff at Riverdale all agreed that the group was tense, hostile, and hard to manage. Although each person focused on different evidence —George on the furniture incident, Carole on George's cursing—and had somewhat different interpretations, a common theme emerged, and the consultant was able to construct a unified picture of the climate from the various members' stories. Common experiences do not mean identical interpretations, but they do mean a unifying theme.

Third, climate arises from *interaction*. Because climate is a product of interaction, no one person is responsible for it. In the Riverdale case it would be easy to blame George for creating the hostile atmosphere but closer consideration shows that all the other members contributed too. The counselors rearranged the furniture without considering that George might be insecure in his first days on the job. Carole withdrew whenever George confronted her, which prevented an airing of the issues and may have increased his suspicions. The hostile atmosphere at Riverdale was so pervasive because most members acted in accordance with it. Their actions reinforced each other and created an expectation of hostility in most interchanges.

Climates are also *relatively enduring*, that is, they persist for extended spans of time and do not change with every change in interaction (Tagiuri, 1968). In some groups the same climate may hold for months or years. At Riverdale, for example, the hostile climate built for ten months before a mediator was called in. Members of a community consulting group reported a consistent atmosphere of support and cooperation extending for several years; although many disagreements and controversies arose during this time, they were worked out in a constructive and cooperative manner. Furthermore, employees of some corporations have observed a consistent "tone," "flavor," or "attitude" in their work environment which has evolved over months or years and seems likely to persist into the future (Roy, 1960; Kanter, 1977; Dalton, 1959). In other cases a group's climate has a shorter life, as in the brown-bag discussion, where a challenging, hostile climate supplanted the generally relaxed climate after only an hour.

Both long- and short-lived climates represent periods where definite themes and directions predominate in the group's interaction and both are relatively enduring in the sense that they occupy a chunk of the group's time. The difference between them lies in the relative stability of their themes, and this in turn depends on whether the themes are reinforced in day-to-day group interaction (Poole & McPhee, 1983). In some groups the climate is firmly established in fundamental assumptions of group operation, and, therefore, changes very slowly. For example, in the community consulting group, cooperative means of decision-making were built into the group's meeting procedures, and cooperative activity was therefore reinforced whenever conflicts arose. In other groups, interaction remains more unstable; there is little consensus on basic assumptions, and the overall sense of the group shifts relatively easily. Shifts in group interaction can shift the underlying assumptions of the group rather quickly. The brown-bag discussion, which brought together a group of relative strangers, is one such case. Because climate *reinforces* the patterns of interaction it arises from, the longer a climate holds for a group, the more entrenched and enduring it is likely to become (Poole & McPhee, 1983). Climates are changed by changes in interaction that "break the spell" and reroute the group.

HOW CLIMATE AFFECTS CONFLICT INTERACTION

The link between climate and interaction is reciprocal. Climate affects interaction, and the interaction, in turn, defines and alters the climate in a group. Both sides of this relationship need close examination in order to understand the role climate plays in conflicts. This section expands on our definition of climate by exploring how climate constrains and channels conflict interaction, and it suggests how group members can diagnose climates.

THE USES OF CLIMATE

In all interaction, and particularly in conflicts, one of the key problems group members face is their *uncertainty* about how to act and about what the consequences of their actions will be. Uncertainty is natural in conflict because most people are not as accustomed to conflict as they are to other sorts of interaction. Perhaps due to a cultural tendency toward avoiding or ignoring undesirable situations, many people simply do not think or learn very much about conflicts. Even for those members who are accustomed to conflict, every situation is novel; each conflict presents specific problems and choices the member has never faced before and invites the member to react in ways he or she has never acted before. Even if it is a dreary rehash of a long-standing argument, each conflict holds the potential for change, for better or worse.

There are two ways in which group members can respond to this uncertainty. Some members reduce their uncertainty by becoming *rigid,* that is, by responding to all conflicts in the same way regardless of circumstances. Rigid behavior can take many forms, but two of the most striking examples provide good illustrations. Most of us have seen people who get defensive and lash out at anyone in their way. We also see others who try to ignore or avoid all conflicts regardless of how important they are. Both forms of behavior tend to perpetuate themselves and they can be maddening for those who have to deal with them, but rigidity has definite benefits in both cases. There are numerous ways that an attacker can intimidate potential opposition into giving in or never registering a complaint (Donahue, 1981). In the same vein, the avoider can often stifle issues that are threatening to him or her. Like the working habits discussed in chapter 2, rigid responses also have the psychological benefits of reducing internal tension and enabling the member to mount some response to a potentially paralyzing situation. However, like permanently-fixed working habits, rigidity can result in destructive escalation or avoidance cycles, because it encourages stereotyped, repetitive responses. If the counterattacker cannot intimidate others or if the avoider cannot successfully stifle issues, their rigid behavior quickly accelerates negative spirals of conflict interaction. (Interestingly, Rubin and Brown (1975) summarize evidence suggesting that men are more likely to fall prey to this type of rigidity than are women. They believe this is because women are more responsive to others' interpersonal cues than men and, therefore, tend to be more flexible—they call it "interpersonally oriented." Men, on the other hand, tend to interpret conflicts in win-lose terms and therefore approach all conflicts with whatever strategies usually win for them. Although these explanations are somewhat debatable, they are certainly thought-provoking.)

More numerous—and also more effective—are those members who *attempt to cope with their uncertainty by diagnosing the situation and reacting in a manner appropriate to it.* Because exact prediction is impossible, members must project their actions and estimate how others will respond to them. This projection can occur consciously (as when a member plots out a strategy for the conflict), or it can be unconscious (as when a member takes a reactive stance and only looks ahead to the next act), but it always involves *estimations* and *guesswork* about the future. Climate is indispensible in this process. Members use their sense of the group's climate to gauge the appropriateness, effectiveness, or likely consequences of their behavior. *The prevailing climate of the group is projected into its future and sets a standard for behavior in the conflict.* At Riverdale, for example, the firmly-entrenched climate of hostility and suspicion led Carole to expect hostile interactions with George, and therefore she came into the situation with her guard up, tended to interpret most of George's actions in an unfavorable light, and tended to act in a hostile or defensive manner toward George. Unable to predict the specifics of a conflict, members use their general impressions of a situation (in other words, of its climate) to generate specific expectations about how things should or will go. Because climate is so diffuse and generalized, it is difficult to trace the particular reasoning involved in these projections; for this reason, they are often called "intuition."

In the preceding paragraph we concentrated on members' projections of their own behaviors, but equally important is their understanding of others' behavior. Here again, climate plays a major role. Especially critical are members' attempts to deduce the intentions of other members, because these in turn affect their own actions. For example, at some point early in the conflict Carole decided George intended to undermine her authority and maybe even force her to leave Riverdale. As a result, she was uncooperative and withdrew whenever George confronted her, answering what she perceived as hostility with hostility. Carole may have been right or wrong in her conclusions about George. That she drew conclusions at all was enough to stimulate her hostile behavior.

Psychologists have called the process by which people draw conclusions about others from their words or deeds *attribution,* and have focused on the biases that creep into such judgments (Sillars, 1980). A particularly important bias has been found in conflict situations, and climate plays a critical role in promoting it. In a thought-provoking article, Thomas and Pondy (1977) report that when people in business describe conflicts, they tend to exaggerate their own cooperativeness while at the same time exaggerating their opponent's competitiveness, (in other words, his or her responsibility for the conflict). In a study of communication strategies in college roommate conflicts Sillars (1980) found a similar tendency. These findings imply a bias toward overestimating others' competitive tendencies (see also Deutsch, 1973, chap. 8). This bias can have important effects on conflict interaction. Sillars found that subjects who attributed responsibility for the conflict to the other were more likely to use avoidance and competitive strategies and less likely to use collaborative strategies than were those who did not make this attribution. However, the bias reported by Thomas and Pondy does not show up in some situations. In particular, studies of trust have found a bias toward assuming cooperativeness on the part of others once trust has been established (Zand, 1972; Deutsch, 1973, chap. 8).

These different outcomes can be understood if climate is taken into account. In the Thomas and Pondy study the business workers were asked to talk about a recent conflict, and it is likely they chose instances where there was open controversy, in line with the common conception of conflicts as fights. In such cases the climate is very likely to be competitive and at least somewhat hostile, and the participants are thus primed to see others as competitive. The studies on trust specifically tried to induce a climate of cooperation, by instructing participants to be concerned about how the outcome of a game affected their opponents. Therefore it is not surprising people perceived each other as friendly and cooperative. In both cases the direction of the bias towards attribution of either competition or cooperation was determined by the climate of the situation. Interestingly, the studies of trust also postulate that members' perceptions of others as cooperative caused them to behave more cooperatively and reinforced the trusting atmosphere. The same cycling effect is also presumed for situations where distrust and competition prevail: perceptions of competition breed competitive behavior and reinforce hostile reactions (Sillars, 1980). The prevailing climate of a conflict situation colors members' interpretations of one another, thereby encouraging certain types of behavior and reinforcing the situational climate.

To this point we have spoken primarily of the uses of climate for individual members. But members' actions, each guided by climate, combine and build on one another to impart a momentum to the group as a whole. At Riverdale, for example, individual members picked up on the hostile climate and their defensive and unfriendly actions thrust the group into a tense spiral of hostile exchanges. This process can also work to the benefit of groups. Friendly and responsive actions encouraged by an open climate also tend to create a chain reaction and give the conflict a positive momentum. The influence climate exerts on individual member's behavior translates into a more *encompassing influence on the direction of the group as a whole.*

THEMES

But just what is the "content" of climates? What do climates tell members that helps them make specific projections? Climate can best be described as the general *themes* running through group interaction. At Riverdale, for example, one theme was the lack of respect members had for one another. This theme was clearly reflected in the behaviors of Riverdale's staff: George cursed at people and worked around Carole's authority; staff members excluded George from their office improvements and talked about him behind his back. Identifying this theme permitted the consultant to understand some of the dynamics at Riverdale.

The problem facing any attempt to identify climates is the amazing diversity of themes. If we observe a hundred groups, we will probably find a hundred different sets of themes. In some groups we might find a cooperative atmosphere based on dedication to a common task or mission and in others cooperation based on warm and supportive friendships. At Riverdale hostility and mistrust were grounded in suspicions about the possible misuse of authority, while in another group hostility might be grounded in competition for scarce rewards, such as raises or promotions. The variations are endless. However, within the many specific variations it is possible to identify general categories of concerns addressed by group themes. The four general themes we will discuss arise from "universal" features of human relationships which have been identified by a number of previous studies (Foa, 1961; Wish & Kaplan, 1977; Bales & Cohen, 1979). These themes, shown in Table 3, emerge repeatedly because they relate to problems and concerns faced by every group. Although they certainly do not cover every theme, we believe they offer useful guideposts for the identification of climates.

One category of themes revolves around *dominance or authority relations.* These themes are concerned with a set of questions concerning how members ordinarily deal with the distribution of power and respect. Is power concentrated in the hands of a few leaders, or is it accessible to most or all members? How important is power in decisions: to what extent is power and influence used to mandate decisions or resolve disagreements, as opposed to open discussion and argument about the issues? How rigid is the group's power structure: can members readily shift roles and assume authority, or are the same members always in control? Related to this, what does leadership mean in the group: are the differences in power, status, and respect accorded to leaders greatly different from those accorded to followers? Answers to these and related questions are important in understanding how members are differentiated in a group and how they act together.

At Riverdale, for example, power was part of the day-to-day interaction. George used his directorship to berate staff members. His attempts to circumvent Carole and her opposition created a climate in which the use of power and opposition were taken for granted, with predictable consequences for the group's interaction. Dominance themes are important determinants of conflict behavior because they enable members to draw conclusions as to how differentiation will be handled by other members and how differences will be resolved. If, for example, a member perceives

TABLE 3. Four Important Categories of Climate Themes

Type of Theme	Examples of Issues Associated with Each Type of Theme
1. Dominance and Authority Relations	Is power concentrated in the hands of a few leaders or is it shared? How important is power in group decisions? How rigid is the group's power structure: do members shift roles? How is power and respect distributed among members?
2. Degree of Supportiveness	Are members friendly or intimate with one another? Can members trust one another? Can members safely express emotions in the group? Does the group tolerate disagreements among members? To what degree does the group emphasize task versus socioemotional concerns?
3. Sense of Group Identity	Does the group have a definite identity? Do members feel ownership of group accomplishments? How great is member commitment to the group? Do members share responsibility for decisions?
4. Interdependence	Can members all gain if they cooperate, or will one's gain be another's loss? Are members pitted against one another?

domination of the group by a few members and these members disagree with his or her position, it is logical to assume they will try to force their own views on the group. This reasoning may lead the member to avoid conflict because there is too much to lose, or to state his or her case in extremely forceful terms in an attempt to fight the dominant members. Just such an assumption about George kept Carole from confronting him about the issues that were undermining their relationship.

A second category of themes concerns the *degree of supportiveness in the group*. This category covers a cluster of related issues: are members friendly toward each other? Can members trust one another? Can members safely express their emotions in the group? Does the group tolerate disagreements and different points of view among members? What is the degree to which the group emphasizes concern with its tasks over the socioemotional needs of the members? Answers to these and related questions give members an idea of their safety in the group and level of commitment members have to one another. At Riverdale there was very little emotional safety. Members distrusted one another, and there was little tolerance for disagreement. Members dug into their positions and assumed they were right, that it was up to others to mend their ways. People protected themselves and showed little concern for others' feelings. Although emotions were expressed to some extent (at least by George), they were perceived as weapons and not as a means for deeper understanding. Emotionality themes are important in conflict because they allow members to draw conclusions about whether needs and feelings should and will be addressed in managing the conflict. In groups where emotional expression is not safe, there will often be a tendency to conceal needs or address them indirectly. This veiling can make successful conflict management much more difficult.

Consider the following example of the impact concerns about supportiveness can have on emotional conflicts. The organization in question is a small cooperative bakery with seven staff members. Although bakery workers were generally congenial with one another, they did not have sufficient intimacy or trust to air an emotional crisis, and this lack of trust made the conflict much worse than it should have been.

_____ CASE 3.2 _____

A group of seven people had established and run a bakery for two years when a severe conflict emerged and threatened the store's existence. Two workers had been in a committed intimate relationship for several years, but were now going through a difficult breakup. During this time, neither the man nor the woman could stand being around one another, but neither could afford to quit their jobs. The store needed both members' skills and experience to survive financially.

For over three months the climate in the work place grew more and more unbearable. Workers had to deal with the tension between the couple while working under daily time pressures and the constraints of having a minimum of staff. Many believed that they could not be effective workers if the situation got much worse. Important information about bakery orders and deliveries was not being exchanged as workers talked less and less to each other. The group decided to call in a third party to help improve the situation. In discussing the problem with individual staff members, the third party realized that the workers strongly resented having to deal with the "relationship problem" at the bakery. They felt they were being forced to choose sides in the conflict or risk losing both people's friendship. At the same time, they were personally hurt by seeing two people they liked go through a very difficult emotional trauma. Although the staff members were eager to share these feelings with the third party, almost nothing had been said to the man or woman about these reactions. The staff was not willing to discuss these emotional issues because they seemed highly volatile and might lead to an eventual breakdown of the work group. The climate in the group deterred people from expressing emotional reactions critical to helping the couple understand how their actions at the store were affecting the entire staff. As a result, tension heightened, and the bakery was about to go under. The presence of the third party increased members' feelings of safety, and eventually they were able to talk about their problems. It was finally decided that the man would train his successor and leave the bakery within three months, while the woman would stay on.

A third category of themes concerns *members' sense of group identity* (Wilson, 1978). It covers questions such as the following: does the group have an identity of its own or is it just a collection of individuals? Do members feel ownership of the group's accomplishments? How great is their commitment to the group? Do members know about and trust in one another's commitment? Themes relevant to these and related questions give members information that allows them to project the consequences of conflict for the group itself. For example, if the group does not have a definite identity, and member commitment is low, the group may fracture into subgroups if conflict comes into the open. Members with an interest in preserving the group might try to hide conflict in order to prevent this. An important reason the staff at Riverdale was unable to manage its conflict was because members believed raising the issues again "wasn't worth the hassle" and would only worsen an already unpleasant situation. The group's cohesiveness had been so disrupted by its problems that members feared they would not be able to do their job if the conflict advanced any further.

A final category of themes concerns *the type of interdependence among group members.* These themes address what motivates members: Can all members gain if they cooperate, or will one member's gain be another's loss? Do members normally take a competitive attitude toward each other? The themes in this category are closely related to the climates discussed by Deutsch (1973). (See chapter 1, p. 17.) As we noted in chapter 1, at least three types of interdependence can be identified—cooperative, competitive, and individualistic—and these have quite different effects on group interaction.

For example, at Riverdale interaction among many members was premised on a competitive assumption. George and Carole were each trying to protect his or her own "turf" from the other. The other staff members were resistant to George and regarded him as an opponent who would try to defeat them by browbeating and using his authority. Answers to questions revolving around motivational interdependence are important in conflicts because they influence whether, as noted in chapter 2, working habits in groups already predispose members toward destructive redefinition of conflicts into win-lose terms. A "competitive" climate can encourage this tendency, while a "cooperative" climate can discourage it.

We have advanced these four categories in order to illustrate common climate themes, and not as a complete description. Although these themes capture important aspects of climates, climates are much more complex and dynamic than the categories themselves imply. The categories represent general types of themes in climates and, taken in isolation, give only a "frozen" picture of climate; they cannot mark the ways in which climate is constantly being renewed in a group's interaction. Moreover, the four categories *omit* many features of climates. To adequately understand a group's climate, it is necessary to identify the *specific combinations of themes in the particular group under consideration.* Even if all themes in a group happen to fall in the four categories, the specific combinations of themes will very likely be unique to the group in question. It is important to understand the *unique* themes of a group in order to understand the particular patterns of conflict which emerge in the group.

In addition, the four categories of themes are *not independent.* The same theme can cross more than one category, as the Riverdale case shows. The suspicious and hostile relationship between George and the rest of the staff (notably Carole) had consequences related to *both* the dominance and supportiveness categories. As this also implies, not all the categories of themes will be important in every group. In some groups one theme may dominate all others. For example, in one office, the boss was so authoritarian and angered his employees so much that they organized against him. When the boss was not around they ridiculed him and fantasized about revenge. They slowed down their work and covered for each other so the boss would not find out. The office was preoccupied with authority relations; other concerns were less of an influence over members' behavior.

Thus far we have focused on the influence climates exert on conflict interaction. In order to complete our picture it is necessary to consider the other side of the coin, the reciprocal influence of interaction on climates.

HOW CONFLICT INTERACTION AFFECTS CLIMATE

In our definition of climate, we pointed to the critical role of interaction in creating and sustaining climates. Members' immediate experience of climate comes from interaction; by observing how others act and react, a member picks up cues about others' sense of the group's climate. Since each member acts on an interpretation of climate based on observations of the other members (and their reactions to him or her), the prevailing climate has a "multiplier" effect in the group: it tends to reproduce itself because all members orient themselves to each other and each orients to the climate in projecting his or her own acts. For example, in a group with a history of cordial and cooperative relationships, members tend to be friendly and cooperative because they assume that is "the way things should be" in the group. When a member sees others being friendly and cooperative, this reaffirms the group's climate and probably strengthens the member's inclination toward cooperativeness. Because this is happening for all members, the effect multiplies itself and becomes quite strong.

However, this multiplier effect can also change a group's climate under some conditions. If a member deviates in a way which "breaks" the prevailing climate, and other members follow his or her lead, the direction of the group's interaction can be changed. If the change is profound and holds on long enough, it can result in a shift in the overall climate of the group. Take the cooperative group we just mentioned. If one member selfishly starts to press his or her interests, others may conclude that they must do the same. Once a number of members begin to act only for themselves, the assumptions underlying action in the group may shift to emphasize competition and taking advantage of others. This reflects a radical shift in the group's climate, the result of *a single member's shift multiplied through the actions of other members*. As we will show below, this is obviously a very complicated process.

To illustrate how conflict interaction both reflects and reproduces a group's climate, we will explore how a psychological evaluation unit at a large hospital responded to several controversies and disagreements surrounding an important decision.

_____ **CASE 3.3** _____

The unit is composed of three psychiatrists, a psychologist, and two social workers and is charged with diagnosing disturbed patients and with running a training program for newly-graduated doctors interning at the hospital. The climate of this group can best be described as "quietly suppressed." The psychiatrist who heads the committee, Jerry, is a "take-charge" person, and the psychologist and social workers are intimidated by his forceful style. Jerry tries hard to be open and include them, but, partly due to Jerry's strength, and partly due to uncertainty about their own status, the three have relatively little input into group discussions. The other two psychiatrists, John and Laura, sometimes provide a balance, but they are not as aggressive as Jerry and therefore tend to be overshadowed. John and Laura are aware of Jerry's take-charge tendencies and have tried to encourage the psychologist and social workers. However, all tend to hang back in the face of Jerry's initiatives.

Three themes set the climate of this group. The first pertains to *dominance and authority relations* and can best be described as a dilemma. On the one hand, operation of the group is premised on Jerry's dominance. He is the formal head of the unit; he chairs most meetings and represents the unit in the hospital bureaucracy. Partly as a result of his leadership, Jerry has evolved a forceful, take-charge style, and members of the group seem to expect this of him. On the other hand, full, relatively equal, participation by all members is necessary for the unit to be effective. The unit was purposely designed as a multidisciplinary cross section, with competent professionals from all "helping" areas: psychiatry, psychology, and social work. Each profession must exert its influence if the unit is to function properly. However, Jerry's dominance discourages participation by the social workers and psychologist in the group decision-making process. This aspect creates a paradox. If all members insist on a strong voice in the group, the group will be less effective because the power Jerry needs to negotiate with the bureaucracy is undercut and because Jerry may resist sharing power and disrupt the group. But if weaker members do not assert themselves the group will also be less effective because people whose expertise is needed are not contributing. A large portion of members' behavior is colored by their responses to this dilemma.

The second theme pertains to *supportiveness* and is related to the first. It concerns the safety of being open in the group. The unit emphasizes a high level of professionalism for its members and, because of this, presentation of oneself as a professional is very important. In some areas this code implies that members should hold back: for example, expression of anger is seen as unprofessional, as is making a "half-baked" suggestion in a decision-making discussion. In other areas this implies full openness: for example, when researchers come in to present new therapeutic ideas to the group, members are encouraged to ask questions as part of the learning process. Thus, whether it is safe to be open with the group is determined by whether openness is "professional" or not. For most of the duration of the meeting we will examine, openness is not considered to be professional.

The third theme concerns the group's identity, and can be described as *the problem of survival.* The psychological evaluation unit was created at a time of budget surplus for the hospital. The services it provides were originally provided by the staff psychiatrists, but the unit was created to consolidate diagnostic techniques in one unit and leave the staff psychiatrists free for therapy. However, a budget crunch set in the last year and the hospital board is looking for services and units to cut. Since the evaluation unit is new, it is high on the list of departments that will be scrutinized. Members are worried about the unit's survival and most decisions are made with an eye toward making the unit look good, or, at least, not look questionable to outside observers. Members are concerned with legitimating the functions of the unit to the hospital.

These themes were identified from observation of a number of group meetings and form the backdrop for the controversy we will consider. In the meeting we will discuss, the unit is evaluating a psychiatric intern who has repeatedly missed his turns of duty at evaluation clinics. In the ensuing discussion a number of disagreements emerge which the group must negotiate on its way to a decision.

_____ **CASE 3.3, continued** _____

Jerry, who chairs all meetings, introduces the issue. Talking for about five minutes, he gives a brief history of the intern's problems and summarizes his own attempts to talk to the intern. In particular, Jerry asked the intern what a proper attendance rate should be. The intern ventured a 10 percent absentee rate as an adequate figure. Jerry introduces this figure as a standard and then asks people "what they think." The psychologist and one social worker, Megan, asks what the intern's excuse is, and Jerry responds with a lengthy answer detailing the excuses and offering commentary on them. [One thing Jerry does here which reinforces his position of strength is to talk at length when he introduces the problem. The amount of time spent talking in a group has been shown to be both an indicator and a determinant of dominance in the group (Folger & Sillars, 1980; Folger, 1980; Hayes & Meltzer, 1972). Moreover, Jerry defines the problem based on his own perceptions and opinions, therefore keeping any conflict that might arise on his own turf. Laura, who also knows about the problem, does not introduce it; although Jerry asks Laura if he is presenting the case accurately, he dominates the floor when the discussion is set up.]

Laura then speaks, arguing that once every two months is more than enough. Megan, one of the two social workers, jumps in, and the following exchange results:

Megan:You shouldn't even give him that (once every two months) . . . I mean, if an emergency comes up that's one thing. If you say you're gonna get off . . .

Jerry: (interrupting) This is not . . . This is not time that we expect him to take. This is how often we expect emergencies to occur.

Megan:But he's going to interpret it as if we're gonna give him a day every two months if we say it . . .

Jerry: (nodding "no" as Megan speaks and speaking immediately on her last word) It depends on how we want to say it, but what we had in mind was, if you look at how often he's here or not here—it's sort of a gross way to do an evaluation, but it's one possibility. And one could say, "if emergencies come up with more frequency, you need more time to attend to your emergencies, and we could make an exception." How you word it might vary, but I think what we need is some kind of sense for what's tolerable.

Frank: (the other social worker) What about the things that he has done when he shows up—expectations as far as staying or leaving early. Which is . . . I think one of many things. After his last patients, five or ten minutes later he's gone. And yesterday that happened and five minutes later we had a walk-in who really needed medical help, and I was the only one there. I could've used (help) . . . that was, you know, it was like 11:15 and he didn't show up. Don't we expect the interns to check to see if there are any walk-ins before they leave?

Jerry: (interrupting) We can talk about that as another issue . . .

Frank: (interrupting) Well, it's another expectation that needs to be addressed . . .

At this point Laura clarifies her position on the intern's attendance, and the issue raised by Frank is dropped. In both cases Jerry cuts off the social workers, redefines the issues they raise, and turns the discussion back in the direction he has defined. That the other two psychiatrists tacitly support his approach reinforces the social workers' uncertainty and hesitancy. In effect, Jerry and the others are reproducing the suppressed climate of the group. This also allows Jerry to use the presumption of his dominance to "win" the argument.

Laura and Jerry then pursue a long exchange in which they try to define an acceptable level of participation for interns. Jerry's participation in this interchange is marked by his attempts to define criteria for evaluating the intern. For example:

Laura: (after a long speech) . . . to vanish from sight (when patients need him), I just don't find that acceptable. (pause)

Jerry: On the other hand, if it's 11:15, and you don't have any patients . . .

Laura: (interrupting) That's a different issue.

Jerry: We don't have to provide any options. We can say that we recognize that over a year and a half your participation has been mitigated because of unusual circumstances, and that's the end. I mean, we don't have to make a deal at all . . .

[In this sequence Jerry attempts to help by raising another option available to the group. As group decision-making research has shown, the more options a group considers, the better its decision is likely to be. However, notice that Jerry still controls the definition of the issue. He does not respond to Laura's disagreement, but shifts the discussion to another alternative, an alternative that he dismissed as a legitimate topic for discussion earlier. Since other members generally respond to these shifts, Jerry unwittingly maintains control. Moreover, since the way in which issues are defined is in line with Jerry's style of thinking and his particular concerns, other members of the group are caught off balance in discussions. They are not as prepared to work issues through to their conclusions as Jerry is, and so they come across as less competent or as having little to say. This is especially likely to be true of the social workers, who have very different backgrounds and less administrative experience than Jerry. The other two psychiatrists and, to a lesser extent, the psychologist raise their own issues, but these issues are usually redefined and commented on by Jerry. When Jerry raises an issue he has the advantage of forethought; he can think things through before the discussion because he dictates when it will begin.]

As the discussion progresses, the group tries to set an acceptable number of absences for the intern. After arguing back and forth, the group determines that setting an ideal attendance rate is impossible. Rather, members decide to talk to the intern in order to make him aware of the problem, and then to reevaluate the situation in two months. Throughout this process Jerry moderates the discussion. He is responsive to concerns of the members, but still sets the tone of the decision, as the following excerpts from the discussion suggest.

Laura: I guess I agree. I want to give him time off . . . But if he's gonna be there, then he has to be there.

Jerry: But we have to come up with some kind of sense that if he exceeds we have to say "thank you, but no thank you."

Laura: I'd say more than once in two months, or maybe twice in two months more than an hour late. Nobody else does that . . . that I know of . . . in terms of missing times.

Megan: (talking over Laura's last sentences) Rather than just specifically making a
case for him maybe we should decide what's appropriate—what the expectations are for all the residents . . .

Jerry: (interrupting) I think we are. I think you're right that the kind of sense we're
generating is not necessarily specific . . . It turns out that he's going to be
the one for whom it's an issue . . . And we also have to acknowledge that there
will be individual circumstances that . . . change. We may need to face that.
But I need to have some type of sense of what we expect of him and at what
point we should acknowledge that he should or should not participate. And
one way—it's sort of simple and artificial—is to do attendance, to say "How
many hours are you late? How many times are you late?" That avoids in part
coming to grips with, you know, an overall kind of evaluation, and maybe
we don't want to use a numerical scale. I'm open to lots of different suggestions. The one that I wasn't willing to accept was that if others in the
subspecialties used their own internal sets I wasn't going to ask them to
change (i.e., other departments could evaluate the intern according to their
own criteria) . . .

[Jerry continued to elaborate this position for another minute. Note that he interrupted
Megan and gave a summary of how he sees the issues and what he is willing to accept.
Note also that he spoke much longer than Megan.]

John: I think there's a double-barreled threat (from the intern's absences). If Dr.
Jacobs (director of the hospital) is coming and casual conversation says (the
intern) is OK when he's here, but he's never here, then clearly that's another,
that's a threat—

Jerry: (interrupting) That's been defined. That one seems clear and has been
addressed.

[Jerry here attempted to move the group on to another issue. He did so by interrupting
John to tell him his first (of two) concerns has been addressed. John never raised the
second concern. The discussion moved on to another topic after Jerry's interruption.]

Jerry: (summarizing the group's decision) I'm comfortable if what the group wants
to do, then, is take it back to (the intern) and say we have a set of expectations
—they include your participation—your full participation—in this program.
That we will reassess our impression of that participation—and we hope you
will assess it—on a monthly basis or something and that if we need to—
because there's some question of whether or not your participation is complete
—then we'll meet and we'll need to talk about it.

[This is a fair summary of the group's decision, but it is cast in terms of what *Jerry* is
comfortable with. He personalizes and takes charge of the group's decision.]

The inhibited climate of the group is not a result of total control over group
decisions by Jerry: Jerry eventually gives in to the arguments of others and shifts
his position away from setting a figure for absences. The group's climate results

from the way in which the group manages its decision-making process, particularly actual or potential disagreements. Jerry's attempts to lead the group to an effective, efficient decision, end up controlling the discussion. By persistently stepping in to restate, redefine, summarize, and comment, Jerry channels the discussion. The other members, with few exceptions, respond by following Jerry's lines of thought and thereby reinforce his control over the discussion and his resolutions of disagreements. The end result of this process is to create a sense that Jerry can and will jump in and redirect the discussion at any time, that he is an arbiter of opinions and suggestions in the group, and that lower-status members do not have as good a grasp of the priorities of the group as Jerry does. The social workers and the psychologist are hesitant and tense during meetings, and outside of meetings they complain to each other and spend a good deal of time planning how to "get heard" in meetings.

Another striking feature of this decision is how much disagreement and frustration there is, yet how little of this actually emerges in the discussion. Members, especially the weaker ones, are very restrained and try to speak in "reasoned, measured tones." Disagreements are rarely admitted, much less sharpened. Instead Jerry (and to a lesser extent Laura) incorporates dissenting ideas into the final solution insofar as they fit. If dissenting opinions do not fit, they are cut off. Other members of the group do not seem to play an active role in changing the original proposal; they introduce ideas and passively allow them to be incorporated, relying on Jerry's willingness to cooperate. This pattern is in part due to the professionalized climate of the group, which worked against strong expressions of disagreement, and in part due to members' acceptance of dominance relations in the group. But members' subdued behavior also reinforces these qualities of the group's climate: by assenting to "professionalism" and Jerry's leadership they are reproducing it.

None of these effects are necessarily intentional. Jerry makes honest attempts to be open to others' suggestions and often changes his stand in response. He asks others for their ideas and uses a lot of open questions (for example, "What should we do here?") in an attempt to elicit their participation. However, Jerry's style—even when he is only seeking to clarify—translates ideas into his own terms and tends to stifle different points of view. His interruptions and lengthy answers prevent others from taking the initiative—they "disenfranchise" members with less forcefulness or less skill at managing interaction. Members' reactions to Jerry do little to counteract these tendencies and, in some cases, even reinforce them. Although the excerpts do not show it, when members speak, they direct most of their comments to Jerry. As we have noted, they also pick up on Jerry's comments and defer to him when he interrupts. Members are generally unaware (or only marginally aware) of these tendencies. They see themselves as trying to contribute—and perceive Jerry as trying to cut them off—without recognizing their own complicity in the process. The entire group "works together" to create and sustain the suppressed, hesitant, uncomfortable atmosphere.

In this example we have focused on how a climate is reproduced in interaction. However, interaction can also change climates. One bit of advice often given to lower-status members is simply to be more assertive, to speak up when issues concern them, and not let themselves be interrupted. We believe this advice is sound, for the most part. To shift the climate of their group in a less suppressed direction members could, for example, make Jerry aware of his tendency to interrupt; they might also support each other when they attempt to redefine the problems facing the group. If Jerry is sincere about opening up the group, he will not resist these moves. This lack of resistance should, in turn, encourage further moves which will open up the group even more and reproduce the open climate. This opening up should not, however, be done in a fashion that threatens Jerry's authority. In the face of an openly divisive challenge Jerry is likely to strike back in order to save face and this could promote bitter, open conflict. In chapters 4 and 5, where we discuss the dynamics of power and face saving, there will be some important qualifications of this analysis.

Moves that depart from the patterns implied in the prevailing climate function as "bids" for change in the group. If members follow up on these bids, they become institutionalized and have the potential to alter the group's climate. More often, however, bids are rejected by the group. Sometimes members simply fail to support an action which departs from accepted patterns, while in other cases dominant members actively suppress a bid for change. When members look back at successful bids for change, they often identify them as *critical incidents* (or turning points) in the life of the group. Critical incidents break up climates, either because they make members more aware of themselves or simply because they are so striking that members unconsciously pick up on them and perpetuate new patterns. Once interaction patterns are changed, they generalize to climates, and if they change for a long enough period, the *prevailing climate changes*. Unfortunately, we do not know enough about critical incidents to specify what allows a bid to become a turning point. In general, however, the bid must catch the attention and imagination of members, it must address some deep-seated problem in the group, and it must not move powerful members to organize against it.

The interaction-climate relationship is a complex one, and works on several levels. Obviously, *climates are maintained and changed through specific actions that are relevant to particular issues and concerns*. Jerry's tendency to jump on people implicitly told members who wished to enter into the discussion that the group (specifically, Jerry) was judgmental and therefore likely to criticize or reject their contributions.

Donald Roy's famous case study of a factory work group, "Banana Time," provides another good example (Roy, 1959). In this study Roy took a job in a factory assembling plastic raincoats so that he could observe how workers dealt with boring and repetitive work. He was assigned to a work unit with three other workers who soon "taught him the ropes" and included him in their social circle. Games, jokes, and teasing provided the major escape for Roy's comrades. Usually all would participate with enthusiasm in these incidents, but Roy observed one instance when a joke backfired and disrupted the group's congenial atmosphere. When one member (Ike) teased another member with higher status (George) about his son-in-law (who was a college professor), George blew up and withdrew from Ike. George would not speak to Ike, with whom he had formerly been very close, and Ike's apologies were ignored. The normally-pleasant atmosphere of the group was poisoned. The group gradually returned to normal, but George's message was clear: there were limits on teasing in the group. George's outburst defined (and perhaps narrowed) the latitude members had in their relationships with one another, and thereafter the group was more restrained for some time.

Because climates are generalized, interaction influences climate on a second level: *changes in one theme can generalize to other related themes.* In the psychiatric unit, Jerry's controlling moves in group discussions directly maintained dominance relationships. However, they also influenced members' sense of the safety and supportiveness of the group. If one's contributions are likely to be overruled or ignored, one is unlikely to feel highly regarded or safe in a group. George's reactions to Ike pertained not only to emotional relationships in the group, but indirectly to the group's sense of its own identity. Roy commented that the work group fell apart for all practical purposes when George refused to speak to Ike. The lack of supportiveness threatened the group's effectiveness and called the group's sense of itself into question.

At a third level, *interaction can create a climate that temporarily overshadows more enduring qualities of a group.* In the psychological evaluation unit, a meeting several weeks after the one examined above exhibited a much more relaxed atmosphere. The group discussed a schedule of in-service meetings members would present over the next year. Interaction was relatively uninhibited, and both social workers contributed freely on topics that fell in their areas of expertise. Jerry talked no more than any other member, and the other two psychiatrists facilitated the meeting in a noncontrolling manner. For this one meeting, the tensions in the group dissolved. Perhaps due to differences in topic, perhaps to a fortunate conjunction of moods, the group's interaction cast an altogether different spell. For the time being, a more spontaneous, open atmosphere prevailed, and the joking and excitement evident in the meeting reflected this more fraternal attitude. At the next meeting members were more inhibited, though not as tense as before. The previous climate, marked by quandaries about power relations and safety, had reasserted itself.

Because they are sustained by interaction, climates are vulnerable to temporary shifts due to temporary alterations of interaction patterns. These shifts can be beneficial, as in the evaluation unit, or they can present problems, for example, when a normally harmonious group is disrupted by a "no holds barred" fight between two members. The shifts, however, are also vulnerable to the reassertion of the former climate. The longer the group has sustained a climate, the deeper its grooves are worn, and the more likely the traditional quality of the group is to reassert itself. It is only by hard work that a temporary improvement in climate can be institutionalized.

As we have shown, climates are created and maintained by particular events in group interaction. However, because climates are generalized and diffuse, it is easy for group members to forget this. Members are often aware of a change in the tone of the group soon after a critical incident occurs. It is hard, for example, to miss the connection between an insult and increased tension in the group. However, if the tension persists and becomes a part of the group's prevailing climate, the climate tends to become second nature to the group. Members forget that climate depends on how they interact and assume the group is "just that way," that the enduring qualities of the group are independent of what people do. When this happens, it becomes a *trained incapacity.* In failing to realize that they themselves hold the key to maintaining or changing their group's atmosphere, members are thereby controlled by the atmosphere. Like the social workers in the psychological evaluation unit, members may assume they have to keep acting as they do because there are no other alternatives. This assumption, more than any other force, is responsible for the tendency of climates to reproduce themselves rather than change.

In closing this section, it is necessary to introduce an important qualification: throughout this discussion we have spoken as though every group has a well-defined climate. This is not always the case. Climates are generalizations from group interaction, and they can only emerge insofar as group interaction has at least some consistent, characteristic patterns. Most groups exhibit such patterns, however sketchy. Even though most members of the brown-bag group in chapter 1 (see Case 1.1) had never met, the group developed a definite atmosphere, because participants freely entered into the exploratory, question-and-answer format. The group evolved a pleasant climate that was threatened by the challenge to the speaker.

However, if a group's interaction patterns vary frequently and unpredictably, there is no basis for a coherent climate. Groups of people thrown together for an "exercise" in a class or workshop are often chaotic, because members have no knowledge of each other and no commitment to future interaction. As a result, they act only for themselves and the group as a whole develops no coherent themes. Even more difficult are groups which are beset by disaster, often in the form of an unexpected and bitter fight between two important members. In conflicts of this type members often feel their group is falling apart; they lose their bearings because the situation gives them no clues for predicting what will happen next. This is in part because the conflict introduces a whole new situation to the group, one which is incompatible with the traditional climate, but not clear enough to institute a new climate.

How definite a group's climate is depends largely on how structured the group is. Since groups range on a continuum from very rigid and structured to almost chaotic, climates may range accordingly. This should not imply, however, that change in a group is synonymous with lack of structure. In fact, most changes use existing structures of the group and do not require a radical break in the prevailing climate. Even fundamental alterations in climate often occur gradually and result in relatively little disruption. Only when change calls the whole existing basis of the group into question at once does it throw the group into chaos. This does not happen often, but it is important to recognize that it can happen, and that when it does, all bets are off so far as climate is concerned.

IDENTIFYING CLIMATES

Because climates are so diffuse, yet so important, it is critical for members to be able to identify them. Unless members can detect and work on their group's climate, it will remain a nebulous, "untamed" force, always liable to "get away" from members and impart a harmful momentum to the group. Our discussion implies several guidelines for the diagnosis of climates:

(1) Climate themes can only be identified by *observing the entire group* for an extended period. Although exchanges between key members—for example, George and Carole at Riverdale—may play an important role in the group, they must be generalized and influence other members' interchanges to become part of the group's climate. To become a "relatively enduring" feature of a group, interchanges "with the same feel" must occur repeatedly and be recognized as charac-

teristic of the group by members. This implies that climate themes should permeate group interaction and that those which are most enduring and significant will tend to emerge most frequently over time.

(2) It is necessary to focus on group interaction to diagnose a group's climate. *Talking with members* is a critical part of diagnosis. The consultant got most of her initial ideas about Riverdale by interviewing the staff members involved in the conflict. However, members' ideas about their group will always be somewhat biased. One member may be angry at another and therefore attempt to cast that person in a negative light by calling him or her the source of all the group's problems. In other cases, members will bias their accounts in order to make themselves look good. Thomas and Pondy (1977) interpreted their finding that business employees reported their own conflict behavior as generally cooperative to be a tendency on the part of their subjects to perceive themselves more favorably than they perceived others. In some cases, members' reports will be biased because they are unaware of their own behavior and therefore do not see themselves as part of the group's problems. In the Riverdale case neither George nor Carole was aware that their own behavior contributed to the conflict; each blamed the other and believed the other had to change to resolve the conflict. Because individual oral or written accounts are thus "contaminated," they cannot be the sole source of evidence on climate. Accounts can give us initial insights, but these must be checked by *observing how members interact.* If observations based on interaction are consistent with reports, then the conclusions in the reports can be trusted, at least to some extent.

However, if the group's interaction is inconsistent with reports, the inconsistency itself can be an important source of information about the group. One of the authors was working with a city-wide charitable group to try to resolve arguments that broke out whenever the group tried to set its yearly appropriations budget. The secretary of the charitable group had confided that he believed the president always favored funding proposals by groups she had special interests in. However, on observing several meetings, the consultant noted that the president was fairly objective, whereas the secretary pushed his own interests very strongly. This suggested the secretary had trouble monitoring his own behavior and had projected his personal tensions and biases onto the President, who was threatening because she stood in the way of his priorities. The consultant took the secretary aside in a confrontational manner to discuss the problem, and, for a while, the secretary was able to take his biases into account. (The group later reverted to its old bickering, however, because of problems in following the third party's advice.)

Only by *cross-checking individual's oral or written accounts, minutes of meetings, other historical records, and actual observations* can an accurate estimate of climate be made. This need for cross-checking has a particularly important implication for members trying to diagnose their own groups: you will need to talk to other members (and to outside observers, if available) to get their views on the group. Your own views represent only one perspective and may bias your perceptions of interaction. There is no privileged vantage point; even the external observer can be subject to misperceptions: all views must be cross-checked to identify climates accurately.

(3) The four categories discussed above (see Table 3) supply some ideas of the types of themes likely to emerge in climates. Most of these themes can be interpreted as answers to questions of concern in these categories—for instance, is power

TABLE 4. Suggestions for Diagnosing Climate

---

1 Observe the group for a long period of time
2 Interview members
3 Check members' accounts by observations
4 Look at minutes, archives, and other historical data
5 Analyze group metaphors and other figurative language

---

evenly distributed? *Metaphors* used by group members are a particularly fertile source of themes. Often they contain unconscious associations capable of telling us more about the group's sense of itself than any member's account. For example, one college department we are acquainted with described itself with a "family" metaphor. Members repeatedly referred to the department "family," and people being interviewed for faculty positions were told the department was like a "big family." In line with this metaphor several faculty members filled the slots reserved for father, mother, uncle, and aunt. Even the problems and conflicts in the faculty related to issues of authority and independence often associated with parent-child or parent-parent relationships. Patterns of conflict behavior in the department reflected the family metaphor to some extent: the "father" tried to take charge of the situation, and the "mother" tried to soothe those involved and sympathized with them. The "children" were rebellious, but unsure of themselves and tended to knuckle under when the "father" applied pressure. Of course, the family metaphor should not be carried too far in this case, because it was not the only force affecting conflict behavior. However it did give some insights into the workings of the department that could not have been gleaned from direct questioning of the faculty. Because the precise details of meaning are only *implicit* in a metaphor, groups will often use them readily, whereas they wouldn't accept an *explicit* description (like the departmental example) carrying similar meaning. This makes them very valuable as an "in" to understanding a group.

In some cases a metaphor or theme will be expanded considerably, into an entire fantasy for the group. Bormann (1972) has discussed the dynamics of fantasy themes and their roles in holding a group together. In particular he argues that fantasy themes often develop as a drama, with a definite plot, scene, and distinguishable heroes and villains. These dramas provide a deeper meaning for group life and help members understand their world and guide their actions. Building on his work, Cragan and Shields (1981, pp. 235–270) analyzed fantasy themes in a fire station in St. Paul, Minnesota. The fire fighters saw themselves as heroic, courageous professionals acting in a dangerous situation. In order to do so, they needed to be dedicated, competent team players, able to get along with others and get the job done. They emphasized self-confidence and "were willing to let their actions do the talking." An integral part of the fire station's climate was also the belief that the public thought of fire fighters as having a soft job, being reckless in fighting fires, and being undependable and slow. So the vision emerges of courageous, professional men performing heroic and hazardous duty, but who are misunderstood and disliked by the very people they save. This interpretation of their world is likely to promote the supportiveness necessary to carry the fire fighters through their hazardous duties. It also promotes a sense of the fire company as a misunderstood and badly treated group, setting fire fighters off against an ignorant and ungrateful public. Clearly this may have important effects both on how fire fighters interact with each other in conflicts and how open they are to the public when citizens have complaints. Very likely their perception of distance from the ungrateful public would cause fire fighters to use avoidance strategies and "stonewall" any citizen complaints.

Of course, not all themes will be as well developed as those in this firehouse. Many climates are much more literal and consist of themes or ideas devoted to the particular group itself with little dramatization or exaggeration. Nonetheless, *metaphors and dramatic self-descriptions* are one of our best sources of clues about a group's climate.

(4) *Intuition* (our verbalized knowledge) can and does play an important role in the diagnosis of climates. Because most of us have spent considerable time in groups, we have experienced climates first hand and, therefore, know at least what some climates "feel" like. The problem is developing our intuitions to the point where we can verbalize and work with them. This chapter is designed to help in this process, but *practice* in becoming attuned to climates as we experience them is the real key.

SUMMARY

On almost every piece of music, composers describe the emotional tenor of the piece they have written in a short phrase above the first measure. Phrases like "allegro agitato," "appasionato," or "tenderly" are instructions that tell the performer what mood the piece should convey to an audience. In some ways, climates are like these musical instructions. They do not specify the "notes," the specific behaviors members undertake. Instead they give an indication of the expected tone or temper for group interaction. Climates reduce members' uncertainty about how to act and about how to interpret others' actions by providing a simple, general idea—a "feel"—of the group and of whether things are right or wrong, appropriate or out of place. This is particularly important in the uneasy uncertainty of conflict; the general temper of a group in conflict is a critical determinant of whether the conflict takes a productive or destructive direction. A hostile, tense climate can make escalation inevitable; a cooperative climate can turn the same situation toward problem-solving.

Climates are composed of general themes expressing members' beliefs and feelings about the group and the leading problems or concerns of the group. We discussed four major categories of themes, those that (1) concern dominance and authority relations, (2) relate to the supportiveness group members show toward one another, (3) express the group's sense of its own identity, and (4) concern the type of interdependence among group members. These general categories do not exhaust the variety of possible conflict themes, but they do represent the areas most commonly found in climate analyses.

Climates are the product of group interaction. Climatic themes shape conflict interaction, and conflict interaction moves in a cyclical fashion to reproduce (and sometimes to change) climates. This cycle leaves an opening for those who would like to change their group's climate. Changes in interaction and critical incidents can alter climates by creating new behavioral precedents and by making members aware of undesirable ruts their group may have fallen into. Changes in interaction set up new expectations for the future and raise new issues that may persist and change the climate if sustained by members' actions. As the "composer" of its own interaction, a group changes the instructions on how behaviors will be played out and interpreted. These shifts in climate come as the group hears its own changes in emotional pitch; they become a strong influence on the forms conflict interaction takes.

REFERENCES

Albrecht, T. L. The role of communication in perceptions of organizational climate. In D. Nimmo (Ed.), *Communication yearbook* (Vol. 3). New Brunswick, N.J.: Transaction, 1979.

Bales, R. F., & Cohen, S. *SYMLOG: A system for multiple level observation of groups.* New York: Free Press, 1979.

Bormann, E. G. Fantasy and rhetorical vision: The rhetorical criticism of social reality. *Quarterly Journal of Speech,* 1972, *58,* 396–407.

Cragan, J. F., & Shields, D. C. *Applied communication research: A dramatistic approach.* Prospect Heights, Ill.: Waveland, 1981.

Dalton, M. *Men who manage.* New York: Wiley, 1959.

Deutsch, M. *The resolution of conflict.* New Haven: Yale University Press, 1973.

Donahue, W. A. Development of a model of rule use in negotiation interaction. *Communication Monographs,* 1981, *48,* 106–120.

Foa, U. G. Convergencies in the analysis of the structure of interpersonal behavior. *Psychological Review,* 1961, *68,* 341–363.

Folger, J. P. The effects of vocal participant questioning behavior on perceptions of dominance. *Social Behavior and Personality,* 1980, *8,* 203–207.

Folger, J. P., & Sillars, A. Relational coding and perceptions of dominance. In B. Morse & L. Phelps (Eds.), *Interpersonal communication: A relational perspective.* Minneapolis: Burgess, 1980.

Hayes, D. P., & Meltzer, L., Interpersonal judgments based on talkativeness I: Fact or artifact? *Sociometry,* 1972, *35*(4) 538–561.

James, L. R., & Jones, A. P. Organizational climate: A review of theory and research. *Psychological Bulletin,* 1974, *81,* 1086–1112.

Johnston, H. R. A new conceptualization of source of organizational climate. *Administrative Science Quarterly,* 1976, *21,* 95–103.

Kanter, R. M. *Men and women of the corporation.* New York: Basic Books, 1977.

Poole, M. S., & McPhee, R. D. Bring intersubjectivity in: A structurational analysis of climate. In M. Pacanowsky & L. Putnam (Eds.) *Communication and organizations: an interpretive approach.* Beverly Hills: Sage, 1984.

Powell, G. N., & Butterfield, D. A. The case for subsystem climate in organizations. *Academy of Management Review,* 1978, *3,* 151–157.

Roy, D. F. "Banana Time": Job satisfaction and informal interaction. *Human Organization,* 1959, *18,* 158–168.

Rubin, J. Z., & Brown, B. *The social psychology of bargaining and negotiation.* New York: Academic Press, 1975.

Schneider, B., & Bartlett, C. J. Individual differences and organizational climate II: Measurement of organizational climate by the multi-trait, multi-rater matrix. *Personnel Psychology,* 1970, *23,* 493–512.

Sillars, A. Attributions and communication in roommate conflicts. *Communication Monographs,* 1980, *47,* 180–200.

Tagiuri, R. The concept of organizational climate. In R. Tagiuri & G. Litwin (Eds.), *Organizational climate: Explorations of a concept.* Boston: Harvard University Press, 1968.

Thomas, K. W., & Pondy, L. R. Toward an 'intent' model of conflict management among principle parties. *Human Relations,* 1977, *30,* 1089–1102.

Wilson, S. *Informal Groups.* Englewood Cliffs, N.J.: Prentice Hall, 1978.

Wish, M., & Kaplan, S. Toward an implicit theory of interpersonal communication. *Sociometry,* 1977, *40,* 234–246.

Zand, D. E. Trust and managerial problem-solving. *Administrative Science Quarterly,* 1972, *17,* 229–239.

Power: The Architecture of Conflict

THE ROLE OF POWER IN CONFLICT

POWER AND THE EMERGENCE OF CONFLICT

The third principle of conflict interaction we outlined in chapter 1 noted that *conflict is sustained by the moves and countermoves of the participants and that moves are dependent upon the power people exert.* Those who have power in a conflict have the resources to act and influence others and the skill to use these resources effectively. In order to understand how power becomes the basis for moves in a conflict, it is necessary to examine the emergence of conflict interaction: the turn conflict takes from a latent awareness of differences to actions and reactions that shape the direction and outcomes of conflict interaction.

When conflict emerges in a group or organization, it is rarely a surprise. In any setting where people work together, reach decisions jointly, or are in some way dependent upon one another, people usually become aware of important differences before any conflict-related interaction occurs. We noted in chapter 1 that Rummel (1976) identified a series of steps in the emergence of conflicts. He found that before any observable conflict surfaces, there is usually a "latent conflict phase" in which participants become increasingly aware of opposing viewpoints, attitudes, or goals. A "consciousness of opposition" precedes conflict interaction and lays the groundwork for it. During this latent conflict phase, people may become aware of differences that actually exist in the group, or they may incorrectly *assume* there are differences when none exist. In this phase, however, people do not attempt to move towards their objectives or interfere with each other's behavior. There is an awareness of differences, but no stimulus to react to it.

Knowledge of real or assumed differences stems largely from members' *experience* with each other. In groups or organizations that have a history, members know the stands others have taken on various issues and the alternatives people supported during previous decisions. They come to expect certain members to push for cautious or conservative choices and others to suggest or encourage major innovations. They know which members are allies and which enemies. Each member's stand provides a general sense of where he or she would like to see the group head and how it should get there. In assessing and planning their own stands, members try to forecast likely positions and anticipate where support or opposition will arise. This creates a consciousness of opposition when members foresee disagreement or incompatible goals.

——— CASE 4.1 ———

As an illustration of how this consciousness emerges, consider this example of an academic department in a major university. Traditionally, departments' faculty members have made decisions about a wide variety of issues. In smaller subcommittees or as a whole group, they discuss and decide how the yearly budget should be spent, who should be hired when new positions become available, what the curriculum requirements should be for students, what graduate programs should be offered, which students should be admitted to the graduate programs, and so on. As these issues are discussed, faculty members learn how each of their colleagues would like to shape the department. In most cases, each faculty member covers some "subfield" within the broader discipline the department represents (for example, in an English department —British literature, American poetry, writing and composition). These subfields can become the basis for the partisan stands faculty take; they can influence preferences about who should be hired when a position is being filled, where research money or teaching assistants should be allocated within the department, and so on. Faculty members often argue that their subfield is underrepresented within the program and that it needs to be buttressed in order to maintain the department's reputation.

In our case, the university faces severe budget cutbacks and the department's chairperson has told several people informally that he thinks each department may be asked to eliminate two faculty positions for the next academic year. As this information travels through the grapevine, informal discussions occur between faculty members concerning how the department should handle the cutbacks. Some members may state their positions explicitly as they discuss the consequences of eliminating someone from the current faculty. Through these discussions and through recollections of how various faculty members have felt in the past, members may garner sufficient knowledge to anticipate the areas people are likely to suggest for elimination. If preferences differ, an awareness of opposition can mount as the department considers what it would mean to lose two teaching positions. The untenured faculty who may be asked to leave obviously have the greatest stake in the outcome of the decision and are likely to assess how much support they (or their area) has in the department and who are their potential advocates and opponents.

In this oversimplified example, the faculty has a prevailing sense of an issue arising, they recognize likely differences in viewpoints on this issue, and they share an uncertainty about whether these differences will need to be addressed. There is, in other words, *a perception of potential incompatibility of goals or objectives.* However, at this point the conflict remains *latent,* because there is no immediate stimulus for the professors to act on their positions.

What might make the department members act on their expectations in this situation? In examining phases of conflict interaction, Rummel (1976), Walton (1969), and others have suggested that some critical event activates latent conflict.

This *triggering event* turns a "consciousness of opposition" into *acknowledged conflict*. Obviously there are any number of events that could become triggers in the case described above: the dean could notify each department that two positions must be eliminated; an untenured faculty member who wants to start looking for another position if he is going to be terminated could request an early decision on the issue; or a faculty member could send a formal letter to the chair which argues strongly for the elimination of two positions in contemporary poetry if the cutbacks materialize.

Any of these incidents could be triggering events for conflict interaction, by stimulating parties who perceive incompatible goals *to move toward obtaining their objectives and to anticipate and elicit countermoves by those who hold opposing stands*. Once there is a recognition that members are acting in behalf of their positions, the conflict interaction can move through cycles of withdrawal, joking, problem-solving, heated arguments, proposals and counterproposals, and so on, in all their many forms. The triggering event signals a transition in the way people think and act about the conflict: *While latent conflict is sustained by perceptions of differences, conflict interaction is sustained by the moves and countermoves of the participants*. In the latent phase, people think in terms of *possibilities*, while conflict interaction confronts them with *real* threats and constraints. Just as a critical incident changes the general tenor of the group's climate, a triggering event alters the group's response to differences and shapes the particular form conflict takes.

It is easy to think of triggering events in negative terms, as "the straw that breaks the camel's back." However, a triggering event also carries with it an important *opportunity*. As we noted in Chapter 2, a critical requirement of constructive conflict management is *thorough and successful differentiation of conflicting positions*. Members must raise the conflict issue and spend sufficient time and energy clarifying positions, pursuing the reasons behind those positions, and acknowledging their differences before they can move to an integrative solution. By bringing the conflict out, a triggering event sets the stage for constructive resolution. It opens the possibility of clearing away problems and tensions that keep the group from functioning as effectively as it could. There is, of course, no guarantee that a constructive resolution will happen. As we observed in Chapter 2, uncontrolled escalation and destructive avoidance can also develop during differentiation. *How* the group handles differentiation is the key to whether it becomes destructive or constructive. In part, how the group handles it depends on members' *ability to recognize and escape their trained incapacities and to diagnose and alter negative features of their group's climate*. It also depends on *members' specific responses to the triggering event*, which are shaped by their access to and use of power.

A letter from a faculty member advocating the elimination of two positions in contemporary poetry could be a triggering move in the latent conflict situation described above. The response it elicits depends upon how the move is perceived in the situation. In one possible scenario, the faculty might believe that the letter will fall on "deaf ears." They might predict that the chairperson is likely to read the letter, perhaps acknowledge its receipt, and say that it will be kept on hand for later use. In this case the response or countermove to the letter is essentially the chairperson's appeasing comments to its author, accompanied by inaction by other faculty members. In a second scenario, the letter might be sent to a faculty member who is a good friend of two associate deans, has made "end runs" around the chairperson to the dean on previous decisions, and usually carries considerable weight in shaping departmental policy. In response to the letter, those who are concerned about the proposal might ask the chair to call a meeting to discuss the whole array of options for dealing with the potential cutbacks. Some faculty may write their own letters to put other positions on the matter "on paper." Others may confront the member who wrote the letter and ask why such a proposal was offered when no requests for cutbacks had yet been made. Any of these responses would in turn be likely to elicit further moves, as people recognize that individuals are acting on their attitudes about how the department should handle staff reductions.

In both cases, the letter was a move that fractured the latent conflict phase; one person acted in behalf of his or her own goals and others responded to the move. Once the faculty *recognized and acted upon the latent issue* the conflict entered a new phase of open engagement. *How* they reacted to this trigger set the stage for how the conflict was played out. In the first scenario, others did not believe the letter presented much of a threat. As a result, it did not elicit a strong reaction and it did not begin a chain of reactions and countermoves aimed at settling the issues. Members recognized an issue had been raised, but there were no drastic countermoves because its consequences were neither immediate nor threatening. The letter "set the agenda" for future discussions. In the second case, the letter began a lengthy series of moves and countermoves which would not only determine how the department would handle the cutbacks but perhaps change the relationships among the faculty members and alter the long-term climate of the department.

Once a conflict is triggered, the moves members make depend on the power they can marshall and exert. *Members' ability and willingness to use power and their skills at employing it determine the moves and countermoves that sustain the conflict.* People's power establishes the set of actions they can employ to reach their goals and sets limits on the effectiveness of any move others can make. Each move reveals to others how willing a party is to *use* power and what kinds of power they have. The response to the move reveals whether the use of power will go unchallenged.

The most important difference between the two scenarios described above is the difference in power held by the faculty members who wrote the letters. In both cases the letter could easily be construed as an attempt to sway the attitudes of the chairperson and other faculty by getting a "jump" on others. Laying out one set of arguments before other positions or proposals are developed or stated could give the writer a great advantage. Despite their common objective, only the second letter was perceived to have the potential to influence the outcome of the cutback decision. The second faculty member was perceived to hold power and had been known to use it on previous occasions: other faculty knew that this individual had strong persuasive abilities, was a good friend of two deans, and was willing to discuss departmental issues with the deans before raising them with the chair or colleagues in the department. In responding to the letter, other faculty had to rely on their own sources of power (for example, the right to request a faculty meeting about an issue, the ability to build faculty alliances, and so on) to prevent the letter from firmly setting attitudes before a full discussion of the issue occurred.

The shift from latent conflict to the emergence of conflict interaction inevitably *confronts the participants with the issue of power.* In latent conflict, members may have a sense of the sources of power in the group and they may make estimates of how likely it will be for members to use power if the conflict surfaces. Once conflict interaction begins, however, each move and countermove confirms or challenges the assessments of power members had previously made. Members are caught up in an active process of *testing and determining* the role and limits of power in the conflict. But how, exactly, does this happen? In the next section we will examine the nature of power more closely and point to several defining characteristics that make power a major influence on the direction conflict interaction takes.

A RELATIONAL VIEW OF POWER

The everyday use of the term "power" often clouds or misrepresents its nature (Bacharach & Baratz, 1970; Deutsch, 1973; Janeway, 1980). Expressions like "He holds enormous power," or "The purchasing department's manager has lost the power she once had" imply that power is a possession, something that belongs to an individual, that can be increased or lost and that, by implication, can be carried away from a group or organization. In this view power is a quality of the strong or dominant, and something the weak lack. This view is dangerously misleading. The social philosopher Hannah Arendt (1969) points to the problem with this view when she states that: "Power is never the property of an individual; it belongs to a group and remains in existence only so long as the group keeps together" (p. 44).

In Chapter 1 we defined power as the *ability to influence or control events*. What does it mean to say this ability "belongs to the group"? For one thing, it means recognizing that social power stems from *relationships* among members. Members have power in a group when they have access to *resources* that can be used to *persuade or convince* other members, to *change* the group's course of action, or to *prevent* others from moving toward their goals in conflict situations. These resources (which give power if used effectively) are controlled by individuals; it is easy to assume the resources themselves equal power and that their owner therefore possesses power. However, this conclusion ignores the fact that any resource serving as a basis for power is only effective because other members *endorse* this resource (Jewell & Reitz, 1981). The member's resource only imparts power because it carries some weight in the *context of relationships where it is used*. The young child who throws a temper tantrum has power over his parents only if they are bothered (or touched) by his raucous fits and are willing to appease the child because his behavior is annoying (or heartbreaking). The boss who threatens to fire a worker, can only influence a worker who *values* the job and *believes* the boss will carry out the threat. In both cases the second party must "endorse" the first's resources for them to become a basis for power.

The range of resources group members can employ to exert power is broad (French & Raven, 1959; Wilmot & Wilmot, 1978). Potential resources include the member's *special skills or abilities, expertise about the task at hand, personal attractiveness or likability, control over rewards and/or punishments, formal position in a group or organization, loyal allies, persuasive skills,* and *control over critical group possessions* (for instance, the treasury), to name a few. *Anything which enables members to move toward their own goals or interfere with another's actions is a resource* that can be used in conflicts. However, in order for a move to have an impact on others' moves or on the outcome of the conflict, the resources it uses must be given some credence by the group—*either consciously or unconsciously group members must endorse them.*

At first glance, it would seem that the need for endorsement leaves an easy way out for weaker members in conflict. Isn't it always possible to undermine the use of power by withholding an endorsement of some resource? In one sense, weaker members always have this option in principle. But the claim is misleading, because the tendency to endorse power is deep-seated and based in powerful and pervasive social processes. At the most superficial level, we endorse power because the resources it is based on enable others to grant or deny things that are valuable. As Richard Emerson (1962) states: "[The] power to control or influence the other resides in control over the things he values, which may range all the way from oil resources to ego-support" (p. 11). This is an important, if obvious point, and it leads to a more fundamental issue. *This control is exerted in interaction;* therefore, both the would-be controller and the controlled have a part in playing it out. One person makes a control bid based on real or potential use of resources, and the other accepts or rejects it.

Perhaps the most critical aspect of this process is the second person's acceptance or rejection of the legitimacy or force of the bid, in other words, the second person's endorsement (or lack of endorsement) of the others' resources and his or her ability to use them. This social process of endorsement is what underlies members' perceptions of others' behavior as attempts to influence or control. If someone imitates the shape of a gun with their fingers, points them at someone else, and says, "Hand me your wallet," the "target" person may laugh at the joke, but they would not see this as a power move. If that same person picks up a gun and does the same thing, nearly everyone would see it as an attempt to influence or control. A person's endorsement of a gun as an instrument of force is a product of years of experience (education, television shows, first-hand encounters) which give him or her an idea of its power and of how someone could handle it. The influential powers of intangible social resources, such as a good reputation or persuasive abilities, are built in much the same way: group members must endorse them if they are to carry any weight. People's tendencies and willingness to endorse power stems from several sources.

(1) The *social categorization* process (Tajfel, 1981) creates strong preconceptions about what types of people are usually powerful and what types are generally weak. These preconceptions set the stage for certain endorsements. Starting in early childhood and continuing throughout adult life, a major factor in the definition of personal identity is the individual's perceptions of the social groups or categories he or she belongs to ("I am an American"; "I am a Texan"; "I am a baseball player"). Moreover, people's identities are defined not only by the groups they belong to, but by groups they do not belong to. So, for example, many Americans define themselves both as being Americans and as *not* being Russians or Mexicans or some other nationality. Members of labor unions can draw their sense of identity as much from being opposed to management as from belonging to the union. As a result, every organization and society can be described as a network of complementary and opposing groups. For example, in a typical American factory we would find groups divided between labor and management, line workers and staff, male and female, white collar and blue collar, to name just a few. Each group is defined not only in its own terms, but also with reference to its complementary or opposite group. Social categorization is the process by which we determine what groups we and others belong to; it creates identifications and opposition among people.

Erica Apfelbaum (1979) investigated the relation of social categorization to people's sense of their own and others' power. She notes that different resources and the ability to use them are associated with different social categories. Ranking executives, for example, are assumed by society to be wealthy, have connections, and be skillful at negotiation. Welfare mothers, on the other hand, are assumed to be poor and have little ability to get ahead in the world. An aura of competence and power attaches itself to the executive that the welfare mother does not have. So it is, argues Apfelbaum, with all social categories: each is associated with a definite degree of power, with certain resources, and with certain abilities to use the resources available to them. These associations set up expectations that work in favor of or against endorsement of power moves by people from various categories—we endorse those we expect to be powerful and do not endorse those we expect to be weak.

These associations have several consequences. For one thing, they make the use of power easier for certain members and more difficult for others. In the 1960s sociologists conducted a number of studies on the effects of members' status outside decision-making groups on member behavior (Wilson, 1978). Consistently, members with higher status in society (doctors, lawyers, university students) were more influential than those with lower status (laborers, high school students), even if both members had exactly the same resources.

For example, a study by Moore (1968) had junior college students work in pairs to estimate the number of rectangles in an optical illusion. The experimenter led the students to believe that their partner was either a Stanford University student or a high school student. There was no difference in the ability of the students to estimate squares, but those who thought they worked with university students changed their estimates significantly more often than those who thought they worked with high school students—in other words, they allowed themselves to be influenced by "university" students and exercised influence over the high school students. The junior college students expected university students to be brighter and therefore to be better at the task. This assumption led the junior college students to endorse the university students' resources; the opposite assumption encouraged them to give less weight to the high school students' attempts to use their own resources. Whenever people from different social categories work together, similar preconceptions about their respective powers will strengthen endorsement for some and weaken it for others.

Expectations about social categories not only shape members' perceptions of others' resources and abilities, but also influence their perceptions of themselves. People who belong to a social category generally expected to be powerful and who regularly receive endorsement for power moves (for instance, corporate executives) will tend to see themselves as powerful and effective. They will be confident when making future moves, and their confidence, in turn, is likely to lead to effective use of power which reinforces their self-concepts. The same is true for those belonging to "powerless" categories. They expect to be ineffective and therefore give way before the powerful. Janeway (1980) argues that this is one of the major reasons women, minorities, and other low-power groups often take weak roles in conflict situations: they see themselves as having fewer resources than dominant groups, as being spectators rather than actors. Even though these groups have resources, including intelligence, social skills, and even sheer numbers, they do not realize their potential power. They believe they are weak and isolated and have little chance of competing with the "powers that be." In groups, such members often do not assert themselves and, when they do their efforts are not given the same weight of endorsement members from powerful categories receive. Once again, there is a self-reinforcing cycle that serves to prove the weak are powerless and further strengthens other members' tendency to refuse endorsement.

Apfelbaum calls the socialization process that creates these perceptions of weakness "degrouping"; she argues it is the most important mechanism by which the powerful maintain their position. Here also is one of the roots of the common idea of power as a *possession:* if certain social groups are assumed to be consistently powerful, it takes only a small step to assume power is theirs by right, in other words, it is a possession. Since the process of learning social categorizations is very gradual and extends over years, it is easy to lose sight of their flexibility and forget that all social groups are, to a great extent, created by those in and out of them. If the social definition of *who* is powerful changes, patterns of endorsement and, therefore, of who can exert power effectively can change radically.

(2) The use of power also carries a *mystique* that reinforces endorsement of moves by powerful members. Janeway (1980) explores the childhood and adolescent experiences through which people learn to use and understand power. The actions of adults are incomprehensible to children and so, Janeway argues, children attribute to adults mysterious, unfathomable powers. As the rich fantasy life of childhood gives way to the mastery of adulthood, people learn how power works, but the aura persists, dimmed, perhaps, but never extinguished.

In addition to childhood experiences, the historical connection between kings and queens and the divine also contributes to power's magical aura, Janeway observes. As a result, "Even today, it seems, the governed are ready to accept the idea that the powerful are different from you and me, and not simply because they have more power. We grant them a *different kind of power* that contains some element of the supernatural" (p. 77). This mystique functions to reinforce existing power relations: "For the powerful the magic aura offers a validation of dominance over and above the consent of the governed; for the weak, a defensive shield against feelings of inferiority and ineffectiveness" (p. 126). After all, if power is a magical, unattainable possession, the strong must have special qualities and the weak cannot handle it and should not try. The magical aura about power inspires a certain awe that facilitates its endorsement. It also tends to perpetuate power and weakness in the same hands over time. In groups, more experienced, "older" members are often attributed with this aura or mystique. Although they at first may have more knowledge and information because of their longer stay in the group, the mystique assigned to them by newer members can linger and keep certain members in unwarranted influential positions.

(3) *Interaction* in the immediate group situation also plays a part in the endorsement of power; it is the primary means through which endorsement is achieved. The response of other members to a power move has a strong influence on a member's endorsement. If, for example, the foreman of a painting crew gives an order, and all members of the crew follow it without question, they are reinforcing one another's endorsement of the foreman's authority. Each worker observes the others obeying, and this lends additional weight to his or her own respect for the foreman's authority. Assume, on the other hand, that the foreman has been unfair in the past and that workers have doubts about whether he deserves his authority. If one worker refuses to go along with the foreman's order, it may very well

undermine other members' endorsement of the foreman's moves. Members see that others do not accept the foreman unquestioningly, and their respect for his authority and ability to use it may subsequently decrease.

The *way* in which a member executes a power move will also influence its endorsement. Power involves the use of resources; *successful* power moves require *skillful and appropriate* use of resources. For example, when a leader or supervisor gives feedback and criticism to subordinates, it is more effective when (a) it is done privately rather than in front of co-workers, (b) positive points and improvements are discussed in addition to problems, and (c) raises or compensation increases are not tied to criticisms or the subordinate's attempts to solve his or her problems (Downs, Smeyak, & Martin, 1980, chap. 9; Meyer, Kay, & French, 1965). A supervisor who follows these rules is more likely to elicit cooperation from subordinates, partly because they offer a positive method of giving feedback, but also because they allow the subordinate to save face and do not push him or her into challenging the supervisor's authority. A boss who berates a worker in front of his or her co-workers is likely to face a challenge or, at least, create resentment that may emerge later on. Exerting power in a socially-appropriate manner that follows the path of least resistance is conducive to present and future endorsement by the group.

Exactly what constitutes "appropriate and skillful" use of power varies from case to case. Research offers a few general principles, but they are sketchy at best and do not add up to a systematic theory. Later in this chapter we will discuss several examples of power tactics and how they might be used effectively.

(4) To this point we have emphasized what might be called the "unconscious" bases of endorsement. However, endorsements are often openly discussed and decided upon by groups. In these cases, *the group values certain abilities, knowledge, or personal characteristics* and explicitly supports the legitimacy of the resource. A group might, for example, pride itself on always having sufficient information before reaching any final decision and compliment those who are most persistent in gathering and evaluating background material. One member could use this knowledge of the group's conception of itself as a basis for a move in a decision-making conflict. He or she could attempt to stop the group from adopting a solution by making the members feel guilty about not conducting an adequate search for information. In this instance the "powerful" individual uses a resource the group willingly endorses as a basis for a move. The move may or may not be successful and may or may not be intended for the good of the group, but it appeals to a resource that, as Arendt says, "belongs to the group."

Recognizing the *relational nature of power* forces us to acknowledge the status of resources in a group. Regardless of how tight a hold someone has on any resource, the resource is always *used* in the context of a relationship. It is the *other's view* of the resource that makes it a basis for influence. If this view is altered during the conflict interaction, the bases of power shift, and the possibilities for moves in the interaction are redefined. Because power is inherently relational, it is never entirely under one's control. The *response* to the use of power determines whether the resource that has been employed to attempt influence will remain a source of power as the conflict unfolds.

As members use resources, their moves renew, maintain, or reduce the weight a resource has in the group. A clumsy move can weaken endorsement of a resource and credibility in the abilities of the user. A well-executed move can enhance endorsement of a resource. The *skills of the user, the response of other members, the eventual course the conflict takes,* all determine whether a resource maintains or loses its endorsement. Even the nature of the resource itself is important, because some resources (for example, money or favors) can be "used up," and others (for example, physical force) allow no turning back once employed. The use of resources is an extremely complex process, and we will return to it throughout the rest of this chapter.

POWER AND CONFLICT INTERACTION

The use of power in conflict interaction imposes constraints on the other person involved. When one person successfully exerts power, the move usually brings about a reduction of options for his or her opponent, by limiting the forms of interaction the other person can engage in, by eliminating a possible resolution to the conflict, or by restricting the opponent's ability to employ countervailing power. These constraints influence the direction the conflict takes. They make certain behaviors or styles desirable or, alternatively, unthinkable. They shape people's perceptions of each other. They kindle hope or desperation, cooperation or competition. As the conflict evolves and changes, so do the constraints the participants operate under. The other person's responses to moves set further constraints, the responses to the countermoves set still further constraints, and so on, until the conflict is no longer wholly controlled by either party, but is a collective product. It is greater than—and in a real sense out of the control of—any single member.

To illustrate the relational nature of power, the influence of power on conflict interaction, and the multiplication of constraints, consider the following case of a research and development committee in a large corporation.

_____ CASE 4.2 _____

Tom was manager of three research and development laboratories for a large chemical and materials corporation. He supervised general operations, budgeting, personnel, and proposal development for the labs. Each lab had several projects going, and each project team was headed by a project director, who was usually a scientist or an engineer working on the problem. Tom had been a project director for ten years in another of the corporation's labs and had been promoted to Lab Manager four years ago. Although he had had to transfer across the country to take this job, he felt he had earned the respect of his subordinates. He had been regarded as an outsider at first, but he worked hard to be accepted and the Labs' productivity had gone up over the last two years. Tom's major worry was keeping track of everything. His busy schedule kept him from close supervision over projects.

As in most labs, each project generally went its own way. As long as it produced results, a project enjoyed a high degree of autonomy. Morale was usually high among the research staff. They knew they were on the leading edge of the corporation's success and they enjoyed it. The visibility and importance of research was shown by the fact that project directors were regularly promoted upward—in fact, the presiding officer of the Board had once been a project director. Because of this, scientists with an interest in management were drawn to project directorships. Although not necessarily the best researchers, they were the most ambitious. Playing their political cards right was very important for project directors. A negative evaluation from the "man upstairs" could be the kiss of death for their aspirations. At the same time, it was also important to produce. A record of innovative successes was invaluable in gaining promotions.

It was in this milieu that Tom decided to try to increase productivity still further by introducing procedures to enhance research creativity. Research teams often met to discuss ideas and decide on future directions. In these meetings ideas were often improved, but they could also be killed or cut off. Tom had studied research on decision-making showing that groups often suppress good ideas without a hearing; the research suggested ways of preventing this suppression and enhancing group creativity. Tom hoped to harness these findings to increase productivity. He wanted to develop standard procedures for making decisions in research meetings, procedures that would enhance rather than hinder idea development.

Tom decided to form a committee of some project directors and himself, with the purpose of developing procedures suitable for the project teams. He asked four project directors who had been at the lab for several years if they were willing to review the research and meet regularly over the summer to help decide on appropriate procedures. The four agreed to take on the task and the group began its work enthusiastically.

During the first six weeks of the summer the group met on a weekly basis to discuss articles and books they had read and consultants they had talked to. The group was able to narrow down a set of about fifteen procedures and programs to four prime possibilities that were reviewed by all five people. Eventually two programs emerged as possibilities. However, as the list was narrowed from four to two there was a clear split on how the group felt.

One procedure was strongly favored by three of the project directors. The fourth project director liked the procedure better than the other option, but was less vocal in showing her support for it. In general, the project directors felt the procedure they favored was far more consistent with what project teams were currently doing and with the problems faced by the corporation. They believed the second program, which involved a lot of writing and the use of special voting procedures, was too abstract for working research scientists to accept. It would be difficult, they said, to use this procedure because everyone would have to fill out forms and explain ideas in writing before a meeting could be held. Because of already heavy work loads, their people would not go along with the program. Researchers would ridicule the program and be prejudiced against future attempts to stimulate creativity.

Tom argued that the second program was more comprehensive, had a broader conception of problems, and would help contribute to the development of more far-reaching ideas than the first, which was a fairly conservative "brainstorming" process. Although discussion focused on the substantive nature of each program and its relation to the objective of creativity, the project directors knew that the program Tom favored was one he had been trained in at his former lab. Tom was a good friend of the consultant who had developed it. The project directors talked outside of the meetings about this friendship and questioned whether that link was shaping Tom's attitudes. The climate of the group, which had initially been positive and enthusiastic, became increasingly tense, as issues connected to the power relations between the manager and project directors surfaced.

Although the project directors knew the manager could choose the program he wanted, the way in which a final choice would be made was never clarified at the beginning of the summer. The time that the project directors spent reading and evaluating the programs gave rise to an implicit expectation that they would have an equal say in the final choice. At the same time, the project directors had all worked at the lab for at least four years and had experienced firsthand the relative power of managers and project directors. They heard horror stories of project directors who had gotten on the manager's "wrong side" and been denied promotion or fired. When push came to shove, they expected the manager to have greater power and to be willing to use it.

At its final meeting the group discussed the two programs for quite some time but there seemed to be little movement in people's evaluations of the alternatives. The climate became somewhat uncomfortable at the meeting as the group began to wonder how the final choice would be made. Somewhat hesitantly, the manager turned to each project director individually and asked the same question. Tom asked each person, "How upset would you be if I choose the program I prefer?" The project directors gave a number of different responses to the question. One said he was uncomfortable answering. Two indicated that they felt they would have difficulty using the creativity program as it was currently designed. The fourth said she thought she could live with it. After these answers were given, Tom told the project directors he would leave a memo in their mailboxes informing them of the final decision.

Two weeks after this discussion, the project directors were told that the second program, the one the manager preferred, would be ordered. The memo also said that the other program would be used, on an experimental basis, by one of the eighteen projects.

The decision caused considerable resentment. The project directors felt "used." They saw little reason to have spent so much time discussing programs if Tom was just going to choose the program he wanted, regardless of their preferences. When the program began in the fall, one of the project directors told his team that the program would be recommended rather than required, and he explained that it might have to be adapted extensively to fit the unit's style. He made this decision without telling the manager. While the move was in clear violation of Tom's authority, he knew Tom could not visit the teams often and was therefore unlikely to find out about it. Another project director instituted the program, but commented afterwards that he felt he had not integrated it into his unit well. He questioned how much effort he had actually invested in making the program "work."

The incident also caused the manager's stock to fall in the eyes of the project directors. Several commented that they had lost their respect for Tom as a result. They saw Tom as someone who was willing to manipulate people for his own purposes. This opinion filtered to other project directors and scientists through the "grapevine," and caused Tom considerable difficulties in a labor grievance during the following year. In this dispute several researchers banded together and defied the manager, because they believed he would eventually back down. The lack of respect generated in the creativity committee undermined Tom's authority with his subordinates. In addition, the project director who made the program optional for his workers served as a model for similar defiance by others. Once the directors saw that "optional" use of the program would go unpunished, they felt free to do it themselves, and Tom's control was further reduced. Tom eventually transferred to another division of the corporation.

This case is set in a corporate lab, but it could just as easily have occurred in other situations, such as a committee developing an advertising campaign, a team developing new software for a computer company, or a textbook selection committee in a university department. The case offers a clear illustration of the role of power in conflict interaction. During the early meetings members offered their reactions to various programs and tried to move steadily towards a final choice. Although there were differences of opinion about the programs in these early meetings, *expertise and knowledge* (the resources used by members to exert influence and shape attitudes about the programs) were implicitly endorsed by the whole group. Members tried to articulate criteria for assessing the programs and to apply the criteria to the programs being considered. The moves people made to keep a particular program under consideration were arguments based on knowledge and experience they had as researchers. Reasoned argument was the operating norm for the group, and as members worked together to make decisions through rational argument, they were, in effect, reinforcing the group's endorsement of expertise.

Once the list was narrowed to two programs and a consensus did not emerge through reasoned argument, members began to use other resources. In turning to each project director and asking them, "How upset would you be if I choose the other program?" the manager gave a strong indication that he might be willing to use his *formal authority* to force selection of the program he preferred. This move was significantly different than any move that participants had made before, and it broadened the scope of the conflict considerably. The assumption that influence would rest on logical argument and expertise was now overturned. The project directors anticipated that Tom's right to choose the program might be exercised. Although Tom's question was not the actual exercise of his right, it signalled the potential use of this power base to "resolve" the group's conflict. Tom was testing what impact the move might have if he disregarded the project directors' arguments and chose the program he wanted.

Tom's move marked a turning point in the conflict because it *altered the resources* members used. *Tom moved from the use of expertise and knowledge, resources common to all members, to invoking his formal authority, a resource exclusively his.* The project directors' response to Tom's move also invoked a new resource, their ability not to cooperate with their superior. The ability to run their projects independently was an "ace in the hole" for the project directors. Tom was responsible for productivity in all projects, and if his actions in this committee undermined the project directors' motivation or ability to work effectively, the outcome might reflect poorly on his ability to direct the labs. If projects were not productive, it would undoubtedly reflect on the project directors, but the reputation of the labs in the corporation ultimately rested with Tom. This reputation would be threatened if word got out that several project teams were unproductive and unruly.

In suggesting that he might use his power, the manager *elicited* the threat of a similar use of power by the project directors. The project directors signalled their potential willingness to act on their own power in responding to Tom's move; Tom's move elicited *a reciprocal use of power* in the conflict interaction.

It is instructive to stop for a moment and reflect on what this countermove meant to the project directors. They were well aware of the power their manager could exert, because they had all been in the corporation for many years. They held the manager-project director dichotomy firmly in mind and were well *aware that they held few resources in comparison to Tom.* Moreover, because they themselves aspired to rise in the corporation, greatly admired the intellectual and political prowess of higher officers, and saw Tom's station as well beyond reach for the time being, Tom's acts did hold a certain *magical aura* for the project directors. The way in which the group worked also reinforced the project directors' endorsement of Tom's moves, because the group operated in a fairly equal and congenial manner. Each project director saw the others going along with the process in apparent satisfaction, so there seemed little reason to question Tom's moves. However, when Tom threw over the rational basis of influence and invoked the authority of his position, the project directors were jolted into considering counter-measures. They raised the argument of difficulty in using the program, but implicit in it was the threat of ineffectiveness. This threat was probably *not consciously planned.* Their response was fairly weak because of the considerable endorsement they accorded to Tom's power. However, it carried the germ of an idea, and later, when their respect for Tom had waned even further, at least some of them would act against him.

The question-response exchange between Tom and the project directors illus-trates how the use of power (or in this case, the indication of a willingness to use power) imposes constraints and thereby directs future moves in the conflict. When Tom asked for a response to the unilateral choice he might make, *it reduced the range of appropriate moves his subordinates could make* at that point in the interac-tion. It would not have been appropriate, for example, for them to comment on the relative academic merits of the two programs in responding to Tom's "How upset would you be . . . ?" question. This question *sought* an indication of how willing the project directors were *to employ the power they had.* If, in response to the question, one of them had said "I think the program we want has the following strengths . . ." the statement would not have been an appropriate response to the question (although it might have been effective as a strategy to change the subject and avoid the question altogether). The question—along with Tom's direct focus —created a subtle, but strong pressure to respond on the manager's grounds.

The question moved the discussion away from a consideration of the relative merits of the two programs; information and expertise were no longer a basis for influence at that point in the exchange. Tom's move *constrained* the project direc-tors' options in the interaction and actually *directed* them toward a reciprocal use of power. Any statement that would have been a conversationally appropriate response to the question (for instance, "I'll walk out of the meeting," "I'll be very angry and notify your supervisor," "I'd get over it") is a comment about the project directors' ability or willingness to use their own bases of power. Tom's remark interrupted the group's present direction and turned the interaction towards a series of moves based on *alternative resources*—it was a classic triggering event.

Tom's final decision to choose the program he preferred and the response of the project directors to this move illustrate the importance of endorsement. In moving away from a form of influence that the group as a whole endorsed, Tom relied upon the right he had as manager of the labs to choose the program he wanted. Although the right was a "given" in the situation (in other words, the project directors recognized that the final choice could be made without their consent), it did not necessarily have to be endorsed or accepted once that power was exercised. A bid for influence may not be successful if the other members do not endorse the basis for the move. The project director who decided to recommend rather than require the program and the director who said he did not use the program effectively did not fully endorse Tom's right to decide what program would be used. Although the project directors may or may not have been intentionally challenging Tom's power, in effect, their response was based on a belief that they had a greater say in how their projects were run than was previously assumed. The project directors' decision questioned Tom's authority—his right to enforce the use of a program in the labs.

This does not mean that the project director did not fear reprisals by the manager. If Tom found out about this decision, he would either have to reestablish his power by imposing sanctions on the errant director or have to accept his diminished managerial role. It is likely he would have done the former. The project director was aware of this and gave credence to Tom's power, but he did so to a much lesser extent than he might have. After Tom's move, the project director saw him as unworthy of respect; he saw a way around Tom's power. The project director's original high endorsement of Tom began to ebb.

The decline in endorsement of Tom's authority begun by this incident continued through the labor dispute. Other subordinates saw that Tom could be defied successfully and heard disparaging remarks about him. They gossiped about "stupid" things they had seen Tom do and about his lack of respect for other project directors. The firm base of managerial respect was eroded and the project directors became more and more confident of their own resources vis-à-vis their manager. Tom's loss of endorsement clearly points to the dangers of using strength.

MOVES AND COUNTERMOVES IN CONFLICT

The previous section analyzed the use of power in conflicts in terms of the continuous ebb and flow of endorsement. This section focuses on *specific moves and countermoves that may be used in conflicts and on the role power plays in these moves*. In essence, moves and countermoves are the *vehicles* of power; they constitute "power-in-action." How appropriate and skillful a member's moves are determines the member's effective power in the group. This section will look at moves from two perspectives. First, we will consider individual conflict tactics—single moves a member might choose—and their possible consequences. Although an analysis of single moves is useful, conflicts are always interchanges composed of multiple moves and countermoves. So we will consider, second, some strategies members might employ to "choreograph" *whole sequences of moves*. In particular we will focus on strategies designed to *elicit cooperation* from the other individual.

THE USE OF POWER IN CONFLICT TACTICS

Several researchers have developed extensive lists or typologies of conflict tactics (see chapter 1: Tables 1 and 2, Exchange Theory; Wilmot & Wilmot, 1978; Roloff, 1976; Sharp, 1973; Walton, 1969). A number of these tactics are listed and briefly explained in Table 5. The variety and range of these tactics clearly shows the many guises power can take in conflicts. Within this diversity, however, four distinct modes of power can be discerned: (1) Some tactics operate through the *direct* application of power: they are intended to compel the other to respond regardless of what the other wants. These tactics bring physical, economic, and political resources directly to bear in order to force the other to comply. (2) Other tactics involve a *direct and virtual* use of power: they attempt to elicit the others' compliance by communicating the *potential* use of direct force. In direct, virtual uses of power, a member openly displays his or her resources and ability to employ them. Threats are probably the purest example of this tactic, but the chart shows numerous other cases. (3) Third, tactics may employ power in an *indirect* mode: a member may attempt to employ his or her power to shape interaction without ever making the use of power explicit. In the indirect mode, power or the potential

TABLE 5. Conflict Tactics and Power Modes

		Power Mode Used in Tactic			
Tactic	Definition	Direct	Direct, Virtual	Indirect	Hidden
Postponement (Wilmot & Wilmot, 1978)	Putting the conflict off to a more opportune movement. For example, A says "I do not have time to talk about this now. Let's wait until tomorrow."			✓	
Refusal to Recognize Conflict (Wilmot & Wilmot, 1978)	Party does not acknowledge that a conflict exists. For example, in response to B's disagreement, A says, "I really don't think we disagree on this."				✓
Precueing (Wilmot & Wilmot, 1978)	Giving information about one's reaction to the conflict prior to openly dealing with it. E.g., when A nonverbally indicates disgust at B's mention of the conflict.		✓		
Gunnysacking (Wilmot & Wilmot, 1978)	Attacking the other by dumping a number of accusations and problems on him or her at once. Often the whole group gangs up on the person. Also called "dumptrucking."	✓			
Fogging (Wilmot & Wilmot, 1978)	Turning aside a criticism or attack by only acknowledging part of it. Assume A criticizes B: "You have ruined this report. You are always so late with things!" B fogs when he says: "Yes, the report was less than perfect." B fogs by not recognizing the accusation of lateness.			✓	✓
Labeling (Wilmot & Wilmot, 1978)	Attaching a name, often unfavorable, to the other's behavior in conflict. For example, A says to B, "You don't have to be so hostile!"			✓	
Issue Expansion (Wilmot & Wilmot, 1978)	Party purposefully adds issues to conflict in order to strengthen his or her case. Also referred to as "bundling boards" (Walton, 1969).		✓	✓	
Coalition Formation (Wilmot & Wilmot, 1978)	Two or more parties form an alliance against another member.	✓	✓		

| | | Power Mode Used in Tactic | | | |
| | | Direct | Direct, Virtual | Indirect | Hidden |
Tactic	Definition				
Threats and Promises (Wilmot & Wilmot, 1978)	Statements that specify what party X wants party Y to do and the consequences if Y complies. For a threat the consequences are negative. For a promise the consequences are rewards.		✓		
Quid pro quo (Wilmot & Wilmot, 1978)	Getting "something for something." Each party gives the other something in exchange for granting something. For example, party A does not shout at B in exchange for B's being more attentive to A's grievances.			✓	
Negative Inquiry (Wilmot & Wilmot, 1978)	When party B accuses or attacks A, A responds by asking for more information. For example, B charges A with doing an ineffective job, A asks exactly what B means, what A could do differently, and so on. This often clarifies issues and, by so doing, reduces conflict.			✓	
Umbrellas (Walton, 1969)	Issues introduced to legitimate anger or grievance resulting from another less legitimate issue. For example, A may resent B because of an insult. This is not a legitimate excuse to argue. However, if B has made a mistake, A may use this as an umbrella to take his anger out on B.		✓	✓	
Altercasting (Positive) (Marwell & Schmitt, 1967)	A tells B to comply with his request because a person with "good" qualities would comply. For example, A tells B that B should be accommodating because a "wise" person would go along.			✓	✓
Altercasting (Negative) (Marwell & Schmitt, 1967)	A tells B to comply with his request because only a person with "bad" qualities would not comply. For example, A tells B that only a "petty" person would not go along.			✓	✓
Fractionation (Fisher, 1969)	Breaking a conflict down into individual issues which can then be handled separately.			✓	✓

use of power remains implicit and tacit. (4) Finally, tactics may constitute a *hidden use of power*: in this mode, tactics use power to hide or suppress potential issues. The actual consequences of power are hidden, because the issue is decided before it even develops or emerges.

As Table 5 illustrates, some tactics employ *more than one mode of power*. The particular mode or modes involved determine how open or explicit the influence attempt can be, the conditions it must meet in order to be effective, and the member's general orientation and attitudes toward the other. As we will see below, the modes in which a tactic operates indicate several important things about the tactic. First, they determine what skills and styles of behavior are necessary to use the tactic effectively. Making a threat, which involves direct, virtual power, re-quires a fundamentally different approach than does postponement, which utilizes the power indirectly. Second, power modes shape the type of resistance the tactic is likely to meet. Different measures are necessary to counteract different modes of power. Finally, each mode has different effects on the endorsement of power underlying the tactic. For example, direct uses of power are much more likely to undermine endorsement than are hidden uses.

We will illustrate the fundamental principles and processes involved in the "nondirect" power modes by considering in detail three important and common tactics: *threats and promises* (direct, virtual power), *relational control* (indirect power) and *issue control* (hidden power). For each we will outline how the tactic can be used, the conditions governing its effectiveness, and the likely points of resistance it can meet. Because the three tactics are "pure" examples of each category, the principles and problems enumerated here can be generalized to other tactics employing the same power mode.

   Threats and promises.   In one form or another, threats and promises appear in almost every conflict described in this book. Formally, we will define a *threat* as *an individual's expressed intention to behave in a way that appears detri-mental to the interests of another, if that other does not comply with the individual's request or terms* and a *promise* as *an individual's expressed intention to behave in a way that appears beneficial to another, if the other complies with the individual's request or terms.* Threats and promises, then, are two sides of the same coin, one negative and the other positive (Bowers, 1974; Deutsch, 1973; Kelley, 1965).

Threats and promises are important not only because they are so common, but also because they are clear examples of the *direct, virtual* use of power to influence interaction. Threats and promises directly link resources—rewards and punish-ments—with influence attempts and therefore offer a clear illustration of the essential features of the implied use of power. Perhaps because of this, threats and promises have been researched more than any other conflict tactics (Rubin & Brown, 1975, pp. 278–288; Tedeschi, 1970; Bowers, 1974). Although this research is fragmented, sometimes contradictory, and often hard to grasp, it can be put into perspective by considering threats and promises as aspects of power—*as moves involving the skilled application of resources with an impact dependent upon the endorsement of the influenced individuals.*

It is obvious that effective promising or threatening depends upon one person's control over resources the other person values. A manager in a large corporation can hardly threaten an employee with dismissal if the employee knows the manager has no authority to hire or fire; nor will employees believe the manager's promise of a raise if they know the manager has no clout "upstairs." However, effective influence does not necessarily stem from the person's *actual* control, but rather the other's *perception* that the person controls an important resource. A person's actual control over a resource becomes critical only if he or she has to carry out the threat or deliver the promise. The effectiveness of threats and promises is thus dependent on the individual's skill at convincing others that he or she has the resources and willingness to use them.

In an insightful essay Burgess (1973) argues that threats of violence are effective not because of the violence itself, but because the threatener is able to create in the other a vivid picture of the consequences of noncompliance, a picture so vivid it is itself a virtual form of violence. In this view the vividness and effectiveness of threats and promises depends on at least five factors—their *specificity,* the *person's credibility,* their *immediacy,* their *equity,* and the *climate in which they are presented.*

If threats and promises operate by constraining another's behavior, then the more *specific* the behavior requested, the more effective the threat or promise is likely to be. Because threats and promises involve the *virtual* use of power, they constrain the other's behavior only by the instructions they give, and the more specific the instructions, the tighter the constraint (Tedeschi, 1970). This line of reasoning is also supported by the finding that threats generally elicit more compliance than promises in bargaining experiments (Rubin & Brown, 1975, pp. 283–285), because threats are normally much more specific than promises. Consider the case where one member wants to get another to choose one of four possible behaviors. A promise of the form "If you do X, I will reward you," gives the other a constraint, namely a reward if he or she does X. A threat, "If you do not do X, I will punish you," carries more constraints, because it threatens punishment for *three of four choices.* In general, the more specific the constraints, the more likely the threat or promise is to prove effective.

The *credibility* of the person making a threat or promise is strongly related to its effectiveness (Rubin & Brown, 1975, pp. 283–284), although the dynamics of credibility differ for the two tactics. In the case of threats credibility is established by demonstrating the ability and willingness to carry out the threat, in other words, by a show of determination. Accounts of the Cuban Missile Crisis, for example, detail a number of specific "tough" moves the Kennedy Administration made— such as mobilizing armed forces, mounting air patrols, and stirring up public opinion—to demonstrate to the Russians that it meant business (Allison, 1969). Promises, on the other hand, depend much more on the person's being perceived as trustworthy and having good intentions toward the other, as well as being able to "deliver the goods." Indeed, the very act of making a promise tends to make others feel friendlier and more trusting toward the promiser and so may set up a cycle reinforcing the person's credibility still further as long as promises can be delivered (Evans, 1964; Heilman, 1974; Rubin & Brown, 1975).

Burgess argues that violent threats are effective because they "collapse time," that is, they require the other to make an immediate choice and therefore heighten the impression of constraint still further. Faced with an urgent choice, the man with a gun at his head complies because there seems to be no safe alternative (although, given time to reflect, he may find several). To the extent that threats or promises can be made *immediate*—for example, by imposing time limits, exhibiting a sample of the reward or punishment to come, or giving a "hard sell"—they are more likely to be effective.

A fourth consideration influencing the effectiveness of promises or threats is the degree to which the promise or threat is perceived as *equitable* by those being influenced. In an excellent study on compliance to threats, Kaplowitz (1973) showed that a subject's compliance depended on whether he or she perceived the threatener's request to be equitable or not. This result suggests that threats are more likely to be rejected (with an accompanying decrease in endorsement) if they are perceived as inequitable, and that effective use of threats depends on the threatener's ability to make the required behavior seem fair, reasonable, justifiable, or beneficial to the other. Given the positive value generally placed on equality and fairness in our culture (Walster, Berscheid, & Walster, 1973), it seems safe to predict that equity will also enhance the effectiveness of promises: a promise which does not cost the promiser unfairly should elicit more compliance than one which does.

Finally, the effectiveness of threats and promises depends on the group's *climate.* Friedland (1976) found that threats were viewed differently by subjects in a bargaining experiment, depending on whether they were cooperatively or competitively interdependent. In a *cooperative* climate, threats were seen as attempts by the person to *influence* the other for the other's own good. In a *competitive* situation, threats were seen as attempts to *coerce.* Given these different perceptions, the effectiveness of the threat depends on different factors in the two climates. In the cooperative climate, compliance with the threat depended on the other's belief that the person really does know what is best for both of them. In the competitive climate, compliance depended on the other's belief in the person's willingness and ability to punish them. It is quite likely that other climate themes, especially supportiveness, may influence how threats are perceived. In the same vein, a *promise* given in a competitive climate is likely to be perceived quite differently than one in a cooperative climate. In general, different climates will influence what makes a threat or promise effective.

Skilled use of threats and promises requires *the ability to recognize, adapt to, and sometimes alter these five factors.* As with all power processes the very act of threatening or promising can create or dissipate others' endorsement of the resources being used. If a threat or promise is not carried out, it can suggest to others that the person does not have the necessary resources or the will to use them; this suggestion may in turn make others less likely to respond in the future and less likely to give credence to the person's resources. This development is particularly true of intangible resources, such as authority. If the manager of a working group cannot carry out his or her promise to get a raise for his or her workers, they may lose respect for the manager and refuse to go along with future attempts to motivate or guide them (Pelz, 1952; Stogdill, 1974, chap. 25).

Carrying out threats or promises also has consequences for their endorsement. As might be expected, actually carrying out threats may cause others to resent that person and may ultimately undermine his or her resources. Promises have a unique advantage over threats in that carrying them out actually enhances others' endorsement of the person's power. As we noted above, the use of promises tends to make the party seem more likable, trustworthy, and considerate in the eyes of others. These perceptions reinforce the very credibility needed to pull off a promise effectively. In an effort to combine the greater compliance created by threats with the credibility reinforcement of promises, Bowers (1974) has suggested that most people use "thromises"—messages which convey both rewards and punishments simultaneously. If a manager says "We really can't take Friday off unless we finish this report today," she is conveying a rewarding offer in language often used for threats. By doing this, she may be able to enhance her employees' liking for her by indirectly offering a reward, yet constrain their behavior effectively. In addition, by indirectly indicating that *she* wants Friday off, she may increase the workers' identification with her and further strengthen her credibility and their endorsement of her authority.

In closing we should not overlook one additional function of promises and threats. In addition to influencing others, they also convey *information* about the person's preferences and determination and can be used strategically to communicate toughness or the willingness to compromise. If a small child defies her father at bedtime, and he threatens her with a spanking, he conveys that her going to bed is important to him and that he is unwilling to compromise. If he promises to read her a story if she'll go to bed, he is still conveying the importance of the issue, although more "softly," but he is offering a deal—she can stay up for the story if she'll sleep afterwards. Threats and promises also convey important information about the person's perceptions of the other. In our father-daughter example, a threat implies that the father thinks his daughter can be intimidated (or that nothing less than the threat of punishment will get her into bed). A promise implies a more easygoing relationship in which both are working for the same ends. Raven and Kruglanski (1970) point out that making too small a threat can imply that the other can be easily intimidated, while making a large threat may be seen as a sign of respect for the opponent.

By carefully observing another's threats and promises (especially those which are implicit or indirect) and how they are carried out, members can learn about others' values, intentions, and determination. Conversely, of course, the other may use promises and threats to mislead. A common labor negotiation tactic is to make threatening gestures about a minor issue—say, the number of paid vacation days given employees—in order to get the employees to focus on that issue and draw their attention away from more important issues like retirement benefits. Skillful threats and promises can misdirect the other's attention and are often as strategically important for what they do *not* say, as for what they communicate.

The basic properties of threats and promises apply for all *direct, virtual tactics*. Most important, they depend upon the person's ability to project to the other the potential consequences of a direct move. This requirement makes the person's credibility critical. It also implies that a vivid or salient presentation is likely to make direct, virtual moves more effective. How well the tactic fits with existing norms, such as equity, and with the group's climate are also important determinants of the tactic's effectiveness. Norms and climate play an important role in members' interpretation of a person's move and, hence, in its effectiveness.

Relational control. During any face-to-face interaction, people constantly *define and redefine their relationships.* In describing how this process occurs, Watzlawick, Beavin, and Jackson (1967) have noted that every message carries two levels of meaning. Messages have a *report* aspect that conveys the content of the statement (in other words, the meanings people understand because they know the semantics of the language) and a *command* aspect that carries relational messages.

A relational message is a verbal expression that indicates how people regard each other, their relationship, or regard themselves within the context of the relationship (Burgoon & Saine, 1978). In effect, a relational message says "I see us as having this type of relationship." Relational messages are always bids. They attempt to define a certain type of relationship but may or may not be successful depending upon the response they receive from a listener.

There are as many possible relational messages as there are different types of relationships. These messages can convey implicitly that someone feels inferior or superior to another person, that they are irritated, that they like someone, or that they see the relationship as one where it is all right to discuss very personal feelings. Any of these relational statements sends information to a listener about the way the speaker wants the relationship defined. If the listener responds with relational messages which accept the bids that are offered by the speaker, the speaker controls the definition of the relationship. A group member who continuously refuses to take stands on important issues could be sending a relational message which says, "Don't see me as someone who will share responsibility for decisions that get made in this group." If other members allow the person to remain in this position, they have accepted the relationship that the recalcitrant person has bid for. Alternatively, people who "guilt-trip" others are also bidding for a certain definition of the relationship. They want to induce a feeling of indebtedness in the other person and establish a relationship where the other is motivated to act because he or she is in some sense obligated to do so. The other's response to the guilt trip is what determines whether the relationship bid is successful.

Having one's definition of the relationship accepted in interaction is an indirect use of power that can gain considerable control in a conflict. Relational control is indirect because it sets expectations about what can and cannot be said in future interactions without any *explicit* statements or directives to other people. Relational messages are, by their very nature, implicit messages. We generally know or have a good sense of what our relationships with others are like (in other words, whether someone likes or dislikes us, treats us as inferiors, equals or superiors, and so on) without them having to tell us explicitly. Although there are instances when people overtly discuss and define their relationships, even these discussions carry implicit relational messages about what the relationship is like now that the participants have decided that talking about the relationship is permissable or necessary. A relationship between two close friends, for example, often is changed dramatically when they talk about whether they love each other. The mere occurrence of such a discussion, regardless of where the actual content of the conversation heads, says something about what the relationship is currently like; the discussion is a turning point in the relationship because, on a relational level, the friends have said to one another that these types of discussions are now possible (or impossible).

Relational control is an important form of influence because people often accept previously defined relationships without questioning them. Their understanding of a relationship sets a frame or context which defines what can or cannot be said in a conflict as long as that frame is in place. If the relationship remains in place, it can prevent certain strategies from being used or arguments from being raised because they are not considered or, if considered, because they seem inappropriate. The relationship itself would have to be renegotiated in order for the behaviors to come to mind. If the relationship goes unquestioned, the interaction is likely to remain unchanged as well.

Since relational messages are implicit, they are often problematic. First, *they can easily be denied, misinterpreted, or reinterpreted after an interaction.* Comments that seem condescending or demeaning to one member may be viewed as helpful or assisting to others. Second, *conflicts that escalate over trivial or inconsequential issues are often fights over the implicit relational messages and definitions that these issues carry.* Fights over who will do a trivial task that must be done regularly by someone in the group often reflect an unsettled relationship issue. Typically, the relationship issue centers implicitly around who has the *right* to assign such tasks. As long as the relational issue goes unacknowledged, escalation over the minor problem is likely to continue. Finally, *the implicit nature of relational messages often masks the interactive nature of relational control.* Like any use of power, relational control requires the endorsement of others in the interaction. A relationship is not established until a relational bid has been accepted. Because relational messages are implicit, people often fail to recognize the ways in which they contribute to the definition of their own relationships. The example of the hospital workers in chapter 3 (Case 3.3) clearly illustrates how the workers *endorsed* the relationship that Jerry bid for and thereby set expectations for what could and could not be said at decision-making meetings.

Like other indirect tactics, relational control requires that the use of power remain undetected. If someone sees that there is an attempt being made to manipulate a relationship, the attempted control can be undermined. Indirect tactics, on the other hand, are often particularly effective as a means of control because they go unnoticed—they gain their advantage before they are seen. Relationships are defined and redefined with every message that speakers send. As a result, they become second nature; we do not reflect on whether we are accepting or rejecting a certain definition of a relationship each time one is offered. We do act and react based on the type of relationship that has been negotiated.

Issue control.   In an effort to clarify several power-related issues, Bachrach and Baratz (1962; 1970) criticized the available sociological and political studies of power. They argued that power researchers were blinded to the most important and insidious use of power by their emphasis on *observing the behavior* of parties in conflict. This emphasis constrained them to study only direct, virtual, and indirect uses of power to control decisions and prevented them from considering hidden uses of power, which resulted in what they called "nondecisions." A *decision* is a "choice among alternative modes of action" (1970, p. 39); it is arrived at through interaction among the parties and hence is shaped by moves involving the direct, virtual, and indirect use of power. A *nondecision* is suppression or avoidance of a potential issue which might challenge or threaten the values or interests of one of the parties. It is a "nonevent," which never surfaces and results from the hidden use of power by one or more members. *Power is hidden in this case because there is no opportunity to observe its operation;* if an issue never even materializes and nothing happens, it seems as though power has never come into play when in fact it is responsible for the lack of action.

Crenson (1971) illustrates nondecision-making in a study of air pollution control in Gary, Indiana. He marshalls impressive evidence that U.S. Steel prevented the adoption of air pollution standards not by directly opposing them, but by controlling the political agenda of the city. Because U.S. Steel was responsible for Gary's prosperity and had a reputation for being powerful, the issue simply was not raised for a number of years, and when the issue did finally come up the company was evasive. It did not take a strong stand for or against the issue and most of the opposition was done by community leaders with little connection to and no direction from U.S. Steel. As Crenson reports:

> Gary's anti-pollution activists were long unable to get U.S. Steel to take a clear stand. One of them, looking back on the bleak days of the dirty air debate, cited the evasiveness of the town's largest industrial corporation as a decisive factor in frustrating early efforts to enact a pollution control ordinance. The company executives, he said, would just nod sympathetically "and agree that air pollution was terrible, and pat you on the head. But they never *did* anything one way or the other. If only there had been a fight, then something might have been accomplished." What U.S. Steel did not do was probably more important to the career of Gary's air pollution issue than what it did do. (pp. 76–77)

Its reputation for power and for benefitting Gary was sufficient to protect U.S. Steel from having to face the pollution issue for quite some time. Lukes (1974) and Bachrach and Baratz maintain that the hidden use of power is one of the most important and potentially dangerous precisely because it often goes totally undetected.

Issue control frequently occurs in face-to-face interaction. The psychological evaluation unit described in chapter 3 (see Case 3.3) provides an excellent example of this. Recall that Jerry (the psychiatrist who headed the unit) dominated the group, whereas Megan and Frank (the two social workers) were in weak and subordinate positions. From our analysis of the unit it was clear that Jerry's dominance presented a major problem for Megan and Frank, as well as for other members of the group. In a highly professional organization, staff members want to have input on issues relevant to their areas of expertise and Jerry's style prevented this input; both Megan and Frank expressed irritation and resentment at being cut off or not being consulted about group decisions. However, Jerry's dominance was never seriously challenged; nor was the lack-of-input issue addressed. There were certainly conflicts over specific issues related to the unit's operation, but the fundamental and threatening issue of Jerry's dominance was not raised. In part, this submergence of the issue was due to members' respect for Jerry: he was quite sure of himself, somewhat combative, and quite competent, so that challenging his control might easily turn into a "bloody" scrap. In part, it was due to Jerry's inability to recognize possible problems with his authority: he couldn't (or didn't want to) see the problem and therefore never brought it out. In part, it was due to an unintended collision between Jerry and the group which kept the issue submerged: "even if things are not perfect now, they are better than if the issue was opened up." Given the group's fragile sense of itself, it probably seemed safer to let sleeping dogs lie. Concerns similar to these exist in almost every group and represent an indirect and hidden use of power to control and channel the emergence of conflicts.

Two types of power resources come into play in issue control. First, *members may make definite moves that direct the group's attention away from an issue.* Control over what information members have access to is the most common means for accomplishing this. In his book *Victims of Groupthink* (1972), Janis notes that certain members of Kennedy's cabinet acted as "mindguards" and prevented the emergence of counterarguments against the CIA's plan for the Bay of Pigs invasion. As a result, the CIA's position was never challenged, and it led to the ill-fated attack. The *forms or types of information* the group works with can also limit the issues it raises.

A study of university departmental budget allocations illustrates this point (Pfeffer, 1978, pp. 78–86). Most people would agree that considerations such as quality of teaching, level of scholarship, and general concern with social values are the criteria that should guide decisions about where a university should spend (or cut back) its money. However, with the advent of computerized information systems that provide "hard" numerical data on enrollment levels, number of articles published (usually without regard for quality), and other performance measures, they have turned away from "soft" criteria judgments of education quality, which cannot be numerically quantified. Although sheer number of students served is not nearly as good a criterion as educational quality, it determines decisions because it can be "objectively" measured; as a result, the hard, soul-searching questions about quality (which can also be threatening to some administrators and departments) are seldom raised and rarely dealt with. The form of information groups utilize has built-in biases that preclude consideration of some issues by omitting them. If the group does not know that problems or alternatives exist, it can't very well raise them or promote open conflict.

The second type of resources involved in issue control function *negatively:* they suppress conflicts by creating fear of raising issues. As in the psychological evaluation unit, one member's power and prominence may keep other members from even broaching a problem. Fear of the unknown—of whether raising an issue will create deep enmities with other members or upset the existing balance of power in the group—can also limit the issues the group raises. Even if there is no single overpowering member, members may fear an unpredictable collective reaction from the group if they transgress a strongly shared norm. Janis's *Victims of Groupthink* reports numerous cases where prestigious Presidential advisors were subjected to ostracism, pressure, and even ridicule for disagreeing with the dominant sentiments of the cabinet.

There is also a *skill factor* in issue control. Because it operates tacitly, skillful issue control requires that the dominant member's power remain hidden. In the Gary pollution control case, U.S. Steel never openly agitated against the ordinance; to have done so would have aroused the community against it. As Pfeffer (1978) notes, this is one reason it is so hard to determine who holds power in organizations: members do not want to divulge their strength because they may become points of opposition for others. Almost as effective, a dominant party may control issues by *manipulating other issues indirectly related to the threatening issue.* Pfeffer (1978) notes that one of the best means of influencing a decision is to control the criteria by which the decision is made. Since this is generally done very early in the decision-making process, its influence on the final outcome is often not apparent. In the psychological evaluation unit Jerry sometimes shaped the unit's decisions in this manner. He would state the issue and talk briefly about what an "effective" decision might look like. Following these comments, he would throw the issue open for discussion. His initial suggestions often had a strong influence on final decisions, despite the low-key manner in which they were delivered.

As with all tactics based on hidden power, *how issue control is managed* can undermine or strengthen the endorsement of the controlling member's power. If control is flaunted openly, other members may band together to counteract that person's dominance. Hence, working quietly and through indirect channels offers the greatest chance to preserve and strengthen endorsement. Issue control tends to perpetuate itself as long as it operates tacitly, because it defines the group's "reality." It restricts members' thought processes and the alternatives people consider and, therefore, rules out challenges to the power base that sustains it.

TACTICS AND THE STRUCTURE OF CONFLICT EPISODES

Tactics do not stand alone. The *pattern of moves and countermoves* and the way in which tactics enter into conflict interaction make a big difference in the effect any given tactic will have. For this reason it is important to consider the *forces* that directly shape conflict episodes and how these influence the development of conflicts.

An episode is "any sequence of happenings in which human beings engage which has some principle of unity" (Harre & Secord, 1973). Episodes are natural units in the stream of behavior. They have a beginning and an end which are set off by symbolic and often physical boundaries. Placing an order in a restaurant is one example of an episode. A conversation between friends is another. Episodes may be extremely short or very long; regardless of length, their common characteristic is that they are meaningful, self-contained units that most people would recognize as such.

Conflicts, like all social events, can be broken into strings of *episodes*. For example, one conflict might consist of the following episodes: (a) a meeting in the hall; (b) a short conversation at which an appointment is made; (c) meeting for the appointment; (d) a discussion in which a difference of opinion emerges; (e) a sharp argument over the difference, terminated by the end of the meeting; (f) another meeting the next day at which apologies are offered; (g) working out a deal. Each episode would have different themes and concerns, a different pattern of development, and different tactical choices by participants. The episodes are the major units of conflict. If a conflict can be likened to a play, episodes would be the scenes and acts of that play. The forces that influence the direction conflicts take do so through their *influence on episodes, by constraining the pattern of moves and countermoves on two levels*.

The first major constraint on conflict moves stems from the *specific content of the episode*. The *context* in which a tactic is used influences how the tactic is interpreted and therefore what force it has. Studies of the sequences of acts in interaction clearly demonstrate the power of context in determining the meaning of actions (Hawes & Foley, 1976; Ellis & Fisher, 1975; Mishler, 1979).

In particular, at least four contextual properties of conflict episodes influence members' interpretations of tactics: (1) *The tactics immediately preceding a tactic* are important, because they set the comparison level by which the meaning of the current move will be assessed. If cooperative tactics have generally been employed, then a direct competitive move will be more noticeable, and will probably seem more hostile, than if competitive tactics preceded it. If members have been escalating a conflict with increasingly serious threats, then a less severe threat may well appear to be a conciliatory move rather than an attempt to force. Similarly, a promise from one who has recently threatened us is likely to seem manipulative, rather than conciliatory.

(2) The *phase* of conflict a tactic occurs in also influences how it is interpreted. As we noted in chapter 1, Ellis and Fisher found that the same acts had very different functions, depending on the point at which they occurred during a conflict. For example, a threat early in the differentiation stage may be a signal for escalation, while a threat during the later part of the integration stage may be interpreted as a bargaining tactic designed to motivate the other to nail down a final agreement.

(3) The *orientation* adopted by a party also influences how the party's tactics are interpreted. If a party has clearly adopted a competitive orientation, even potentially conciliatory tactics may be construed as attempts to manipulate the situation. If a party has clearly adopted an accommodative stance, his or her tactics are likely to be discounted by opponents who assume that the party will eventually give in. Even severe threats or gunnysacking may be interpreted merely as efforts to stave off the inevitable capitulation. In the same vein, other orientations lend a definite flavor to the party's tactics.

(4) Finally, the particular *relationship* between the parties will influence how tactics are interpreted. Between longtime friends, a threat may be taken as a joke and an indirect tactic like labeling may carry far more weight, because the friends have an extensive base of experience that gives the label extra meaning. Between enemies even conciliatory tactics may arouse mistrust or be taken as opportunities for manipulation.

Other contextual factors can be added to these four. However, *preceding moves, phase, orientation,* and *relationship* are the most immediate determinants of the force tactics have in conflict situations.

A second major constraint on tactics comes from *the form episodes take as they develop.* The forces that determine how episodes unfold influence the direction conflicts take by encouraging or discouraging use of certain tactics and types of power. At least eight factors, some of which have already been discussed, influence the development of episodes:

(1) *Climate,* discussed in chapter 3, has profound effects on the evolution of conflict episodes. Since the group's climate sets the general tone for interaction, it facilitates the use of some tactics, while discouraging the use of others. In the psychological evaluation unit discussed in chapter 3 (see Case 3.3), the authoritarian climate discouraged weaker members from using tactics employing direct or direct-and-virtual power, because these tactics would challenge the leader. Moreover, because the leader's control of the group was exercised "under the table," the leader had to employ tactics embodying *hidden power,* such as issue control. The consequences of climate for the development of conflict episodes in the unit are evident in the analysis of chapter 3: open conflict was discouraged and differences were "talked around" or submerged beneath a veneer of consensus.

(2) *Working habits,* discussed in chapter 2, also shape conflict episodes. These habits serve as programs or scripts that move the episode along a definite course. For example, if a group develops the habit of evaluating ideas as soon as they are introduced, evaluation becomes a stage for the conflict. As such it also promotes some tactics over others. Generally evaluation involves indirect use of power, but it may also involve virtual, direct power modes—a negative evaluation can be phrased as a threat, for example. On the other hand, evaluation does not usually involve hidden power, because issues are brought into the open for all to work on.

Like evaluation, the other working habits discussed in chapter 2 limit the types of tactics that can be employed. When this limitation works in destructive directions, working habits become trained incapacities.

(3) The *orientations* or *styles* discussed in chapter 1 are a third important influence on episodes. Depending on how people's orientations mesh, an episode will unfold differently. For example, if both people choose a collaborative style, the episode will develop as a cooperative negotiation through the stages of problem-solving. If one person selects forcing and another accommodation, the episode is likely to develop as a capitulation in which one person is exploited. Obviously, each style and combination of styles encourages the emergence of certain tactics.

(4) A fourth determinant of episodes is the often observed tendency of parties to *match* each other's moves. Leary's (1957) discussion of the "interpersonal reflex" gives a good account of this tendency. According to Leary, people have a subsconscious tendency to respond to others' behavior with behavior similar in level of cooperation or competition. If someone behaves in a cooperative manner toward us, it tends to evoke a cooperative response. The strategies of *reformed sinner* and *tit for tat,* discussed in chapter 1, illustrate matching. In reformed sinner, the person shifts from competition to cooperation and this switch tends to elicit matching cooperation from the other. Tit for tat is a pure matching strategy, and it does tend to lead the other to match in a manner consistent with the demands of climate: in a cooperative situation, people settle into cooperative matching, while in a competitive one they persist in competition. Matching shapes conflict by causing groups to persist along their current courses. It lends momentum to both escalation and de-escalation tendencies, whenever either takes root in the group.

(5) Walton's (1969) discussion of *proliferation tendencies* suggests a fifth determinant of episode structure. In his discussion of third-party interventions in conflicts, Walton notes a tendency of issues to multiply during conflicts. This multiplication makes conflicts more persistent and harder to mediate, because it results in a tangled mass of issues and grievances that reinforce each other. Walton explores two dynamics that underlie proliferation, people's attempts to *legitimate their grievances* and people's attempts to *exaggerate the differences between their positions.* Both lend a definite structure to episodes, and both must be counteracted if the conflict is to be successfully resolved.

Umbrellas are issues one person introduces to legitimate his or her grievances when the original issue is one others would not normally accept as valid. For example, David may be angry at Jim because Jim has gotten a promotion to a position David wanted. For David to express anger toward Jim because of Jim's promotion would seem petty. However, if Jim persistently comes to meetings late, David can legitimately chide him for that. David can then transfer his anger related to the promotion into an attack on Jim for always being late. The lateness issue serves as an umbrella for the anger generated by the real issue. Many of us do this in everyday conflicts: we are angry at someone and use the first legitimate issue that arises as an excuse to vent anger.

Walton calls the second type of tendency *bundling boards,* after a board early American families put up to guarantee the separation of courting couples sleeping in the same bed. Essentially, bundling boards are extra issues used to enhance the apparent distance between people's positions. As more and more issues are added, people see their interests as more and more incompatible. For example, assume

David has lashed out at Jim for Jim's lateness. Jim could respond with a remark such as, "Well, you're not perfect yourself—your reports are always late!" David might then comment on Jim's sloppiness and Jim on David's jealousy, and so on, as the conflict develops into a real "everything but the kitchen sink" fight. Bundling boards are useful in some ways. They allow parties to save face by shifting attention to others' shortcomings. They are one way for members to point out that others share the responsibility for the conflict as well. However, they also contribute to the tangle of issues and can accelerate the conflict.

Proliferation tendencies make it harder to stop destructive spirals, because they mask the issues at the root of the conflict. Since they generally escalate the conflict, they tend to favor tactics which lead toward escalation, such as gunnysacking or threats, and tactics which make direct or direct-and-virtual use of power.

(6) The *phase* the conflict is in also influences how episodes unfold. As we noted in chapter 1, conflicts tend to pass at least four milestones: latency, triggering incidents, differentiation, and integration. Passing through each phase supplies certain requirements for resolving the conflict—the latency phase facilitates recognition of the conflict, the triggering incident brings the conflict out in the open, the differentiation phase enables members to recognize differences, and the integration phase moves the group to a common solution. Depending on how many requirements the group has fulfilled, episodes will develop differently. In the differentiation phase, for example, episodes tend to escalate more than they would in the integration or latency phases. In each phase the group concentrates on different concerns, and this concentration promotes different types of moves and responses.

(7) The last two forces that influence the evolution of conflict episodes will be discussed in the rest of this chapter and the next, so we will simply mention them here. In chapter 5, we will consider the role of *face-saving* in the development of conflicts. Face-saving is a person's attempt to preserve a favorable self-image in response to a perceived challenge. It has a profound effect on conflict interaction. (8) The other force that shapes episodes is power itself. As we will see below, the *balance of power* in a group is of critical importance in understanding how conflict interaction unfolds.

The two sets of forces discussed here can be used to understand and explain how conflict episodes unfold. The four *contextual* features—preceding moves, phase, orientation, and relationship—provide the backdrop against which people formulate their moves and interpret those of others. They influence the meanings moves have for participants and therefore govern which moves people will select. The eight factors that determine the *form* of episodes influence how the actual sequence of moves and countermoves develops. They encourage or discourage the use of certain tactics and therefore govern the direction the conflict can take. Clearly the particular combination of factors involved is of critical importance to understanding the development of conflict episodes. Each combination will result in different pressures on the participants. It is beyond the scope of this book to deal at length with these combinations, but several of the examples discussed earlier, such as the psychological evaluation unit of chapter 3 (Case 3.3) and the creativity committee discussed earlier in this chapter (Case 4.2) illustrate the effects of specific combinations of factors. Being aware of contextual and process forces can help the reader understand and, to some degree, predict the thrust of move and countermove in conflicts.

THE BALANCE OF POWER IN CONFLICT

In discussions of power, group conflict, and third-party interventions, there is widespread agreement that any significant *imbalance of power* poses a serious threat to constructive conflict resolution (Wehr, 1979; Walton, 1969; Rummel, 1976). When one person can exert more influence than others because he or she holds greater power resources, or is more willing to employ their resources, the odds increase against reaching a mutually satisfying solution.

In the creativity development committee for the laboratories described above (Case 4.2) the group initially acted under an assumption of equal power. The project directors believed that the manager was holding his power in abeyance because he had called the group together to read, evaluate, and presumably select a new program for the lab. Interaction in early meetings was premised on the assumption of a balance of power. Members acted and reacted on the basis of their knowledge as researchers. Since every member had experience with research, there was an assumption that all had a say in the outcome. The project directors reported that it never occurred to them to refuse to use the program until after Tom indicated he might make the final choice himself. The shift from a recognized and self-endorsed balance of power to a state of potential imbalance when Tom acted on his managerial rights turned conflict interaction away from a pursuit of a mutually satisfactory outcome. Tom asserted that he could make a choice that others would have very little control over, and the project directors challenged that assertion.

Originally, Tom may have wanted to find a program the whole committee could agree on. It is unlikely that he envisioned a split on the final options. Once the split occurred, however, the decision to act on a basis of power not available to project directors elicited their reciprocal use of power and triggered the beginning of potentially destructive interaction. The relationship between Tom and his subordinates was strained, the quality of research could have been jeopardized, and the project directors' careers could have been threatened if Tom chose to retaliate.

When power imbalances exist in a group, acting on those imbalances can easily escalate conflicts and promote the kind of destructive consequences no one in the research and development committee believed were even remotely possible at first. Stronger and weaker parties in conflict are both in precarious positions as they make moves in the conflict interaction. Although the dangers and problems of being the weaker party may seem more apparent at first glance, stronger parties face as many dilemmas as weaker ones in trying to act in a conflict where a significant power imbalance exists.

THE DILEMMAS OF STRENGTH

Holding more power than others in a conflict is usually seen as a competitive advantage. However, the use of power in conflict interaction is often far more complex and self-threatening than is commonly assumed. To demonstrate this complexity we will consider three dilemmas that the more powerful party in a conflict typically faces.

First, the moves that a more powerful party makes in a conflict are sometimes self-defeating because *any source of power can erode once it is used*. Since power must be endorsed by others in the group to be a basis for successful influence, using the resources one holds can prompt others to begin *withdrawing* their endorsement of those resources. Bachrach and Baratz have suggested two reasons why this erosion tends to take place. First, they note that the use of power can cause "a radical reordering" of the values in the coerced person and undermine the power relationship (Bachrach & Baratz, 1970, p. 29). The person who is the target of a power move may reshuffle his or her values so that the stronger party becomes less consequential. This clearly happened in the creativity development committee case. The project director who decided not to require the program in his unit made a value decision about the relative importance of his role in the lab. He placed a higher value on his right to work as he thought best than on honoring his manager's right to assign the decision-making procedure. The project director had never considered counteracting his superior's orders before the summer committee met. It was Tom's use of power that prompted the project director to question it. Did Tom actually have the power of his position once he used it? In a real sense, he did not. The basis of his power eroded, in his subordinates' eyes, when he *used* the unique source of power he held in this situation. Tom still held the legitimate authority of his position, but that authority was weakened: the endorsement that gave it force over his subordinates was undermined.

Bachrach and Baratz also suggest that power may be exhausted because the constraint or sanction imposed by a powerful party "may prove in retrospect far less severe than it appeared in prospect. . . ." (p. 29). The threat of power may be more effective than its actual use because *the actual constraint may be more tolerable than was ever expected.* Future attempts to influence the "weaker" party or gain compliance may fail because the power has been used once and the weaker party has "lived through" its consequences.

_____ CASE 4.3 _____

This is illustrated by the case of a new copywriter in an advertising department of a large company. A committee of all the copywriters normally approved ads. In this committee one member, Ruth, often dominated discussions. Ruth was extremely forceful and had a habit of making cutting remarks about and shouting down others who disagreed with her. This forcefulness initially cowed Jan and she generally went along with Ruth's positions, however unwillingly. Jan finally decided to defy Ruth when Ruth attempted to revise an ad on which Jan had worked for several months. She attempted to refute Ruth's objections and received what she described as "a torrent of abuse" questioning her qualifications, competence, and loyalty to the department. Jan reported that once Ruth's attack started, she realized it wasn't as bad as she thought it would be. She recognized that Ruth was simply trying to manipulate her. Jan stood firm and, after some discussion, managed to work out a compromise in the committee. After this incident Jan was much less fearful of Ruth and became one of Ruth's leading opponents in the group.

Sometimes members realize that using their power advantage may exhaust it. One tactic in this case is to make *bogus power moves* that only appear to employ power. To protect specific resources, the stronger party follows the "rule of anticipated reactions" (Bachrach & Baratz, 1970): the party anticipates the reactions or preferences of the weaker party and tailors any demands to these anticipated preferences. When this happens, the "weaker" party appears to be influenced by the "stronger," but the stronger party has actually tailored any demands to the behaviors he or she knows the weaker party will accept. When bogus power moves are made, they often reflect the stronger party's fear of exercising power. The use of the power is forestalled but, ironically, the base itself is protected because it has not been put to the test. There is no risk that weaker parties will withdraw their endorsement of the power.

Not only do powerful people face the dilemma of losing power with its use, they also run a second risk, *the risk of making false assumptions about the weaker person's response.* Raven and Kruglanski (1970) suggest, for example, that stronger people often anticipate that those in a less powerful position will resent the power they hold or dislike them personally. This assumption gives rise to an image of the weaker person as unfriendly or hostile. This image, in turn, "convinces" the stronger person that they must take even tougher stands to defend themselves against possible counterattack. The stronger person moves as if the weaker person intends to undermine or challenge their power base, regardless of the weaker person's actual intentions or feelings. In conflict situations, this assumption can quickly promote hostile escalation and can remove the possibility that people will act without using force or threats.

False or untested assumptions about a weaker party are also likely when the more powerful party is *successful.* In research on how people explain their ability to influence successfully, high-status individuals who were able to change others' opinions were likely to believe that the change occurred because of *ingratiation* (Jones, Gergen, & Jones, 1963). Stronger people tend to believe, in other words, that people change their minds because they want to win an influential person's favor. Similarly, Walton (1969) suggests that in unbalanced power situations the stronger person's trust in the weaker is undermined, because the more powerful person may assume others act out of a dutiful sense of *compliance* rather than by their own choice. This belief can encourage a stronger person to mistrust the behaviors of less powerful individuals, and can prevent powerful people from recognizing instances where others act, not out of a sense of duty, but because they see that the more powerful person has expertise.

A third dilemma of strength stems from the stronger person's ability to set the terms for reaching a settlement. In conflicts with significant differences in power, the stronger individual frequently controls how destructive the conflict interaction becomes (Komorita, 1977). This control may stem, not from the stronger person's power moves, but from failure to make de-escalation an attractive alternative to the weaker person. A weaker individual may have little motivation to stop destructive interaction cycles and begin searching for some workable solution to the problem, unless the stronger person demonstrates that this approach may be worthwhile. If the weaker person believes that compromising on an issue will *mean* "total loss" because the more powerful person can *obtain* "total gain" once the weaker person begins making concessions, the weaker person has little incentive to begin negotiating. If the more powerful person demands total capitulation, continued fighting or avoidance of the issue may be more attractive to the weaker person than an attempt to resolve the conflict through negotiation or problem-solving.

In many conflict situations, it is easy for the stronger member to lay an implicit or explicit claim to a desired solution to the conflict and to leave an impression with the weaker member that nothing short of that outcome will be acceptable. This impression can be enough to dissuade a weaker member from pursuing constructive approaches to the problem. The subtle ways in which a more powerful faction in a group can deter a weaker member from working on a conflict is illustrated in the following case of a three-person office group.

_____ CASE 4.4 _____

A small social service agency employed three women to coordinate and plan projects that a large group of volunteers carried out. The agency was a fairly informal, non-hierarchical organization. The women did not have written job descriptions; instead, an informal set of expectations about what the agency's objectives were guided their day-to-day work routines. All these women assumed they had equal say in the projects that were conducted by the office. None of them held the role of director or boss; all three answered to an agency board that was in charge of personnel.

One of the women, Kathy, was a single parent in her mid-forties who had worked at the office for a little over three years. The other two workers (Lois and Janelle) were in their early twenties, had just graduated from college together, were at the office for less than a year, and were good friends when they were hired. The younger women had a great deal of energy to devote to the agency, in part because they had few personal commitments outside of work which would direct their time or attention elsewhere and, in part because they had a well-developed and somewhat idealistic view of the path they wanted the agency to follow. Kathy, on the other hand, found it difficult to support and raise a child while working and, because she had been working at the agency for three years, did not have as much enthusiasm for her work as the other two staff people. The job had become more routine for her and was primarily a way of making ends meet.

Over a period of several months, Lois and Janelle became increasingly dissatisfied with Kathy's work at the agency. They felt she did not complete project reports on time or in sufficient detail and, as a result, they tried to complete or revise a considerable amount of her work. They felt that Kathy had a different perspective on what their jobs entailed and what the goals of the agency should be. They were frustrated by the additional work they were forced to do and by the thought that Kathy was not allowing the agency to change and move in new directions.

In a fairly short time, the two younger women became more vocal about their dissatisfaction with Kathy's work. Although they would occasionally give specific criticism about where they thought her performance was deficient, the larger issue of how much say they would have in moving the agency along faster and in new directions brought them to a quick, defiant stand against Kathy. A position of "Kathy is not doing her work right" quickly became "we want Kathy out." Kathy was aware of her co-workers' feelings and realized that they had different conceptions about the agency and their roles in it. On a day-to-day basis, however, she tended to avoid confronting the issue as much as possible. When questioned about her work, she would typically respond with a question that mirrored Lois and Janelle's resentment and hostility (for example, "How could I do all that when I've been trying to deal with a sick child at home all week?"). Kathy felt that the two women had very little understanding of what her situation was like. She knew that the two younger women saw her as a "bad person" and she felt they did not seek the kind of information that would allow them to see why her view of the job and agency was different than theirs.

Lois and Janelle eventually confronted Kathy with the problem by bringing it up to the agency board. They told the board that in their view, Kathy was not doing what her job required and was resisting the new directions of the agency. When questioned about the situation, Kathy tried to defend herself, but soon became conciliatory. Feeling enormous pressure from the two other women, Kathy resigned from the agency within a few weeks after the board meeting.

Because this office had little organizational structure and few direct lines of authority to evaluate performance formally, the two newer workers at this agency developed a considerable power base. Their friendship and similar views about what the agency should be doing made the pair a strong coalition making Kathy's job at the agency nearly impossible. In taking an early hard-nosed stand and concluding that Kathy had to leave, the women (as the more powerful members in the conflict) provided no incentive for Kathy to work on any behavior that could have made a difference in her performance or could have encouraged possible changes in the program's direction. It is surprising that Kathy did so little to change her behavior in the face of her co-workers' criticism because, as a self-supporting parent, she needed the job badly. Although the two newer employees may have had valid criticism of Kathy's work, their belief that Kathy had to leave the agency was, in effect, a demand for total capitulation. Kathy became convinced that there was little reason to work through the issue. Even if the board had decided she should stay on, it would have been difficult for her to work closely with the other women. The women had the ability to pressure Kathy out of the office and, by leaving the impression that they indeed wanted this outcome, they discouraged any initiatives to work constructively on the conflict.

THE DANGERS OF WEAKNESS

Conflicts are often analyzed by defining the various needs of the participants and noting where these needs seem to be incompatible. In the social service agency described above, for example, the needs of the two newer staff people were basically two-fold: to move the agency in new directions and to have the office run efficiently while maintaining an equal division of labor among the three workers. Kathy's needs centered around the necessity of balancing a difficult home life with a demanding job. This general concern lay behind her need to continue with established programs rather than begin new ones and to work at a slower pace than her co-workers at the office. Although the issue spread fast and became highly personalized, the "problem" underlying this conflict centered around the apparent incompatibility of these two sets of needs. A collaborative or "problem-solving" orientation to this conflict would have led the participants in determined pursuit of a solution that could have met both sets of needs simultaneously. However, problem-solving approaches to conflict are premised on an assumption that participants recognize the legitimacy of each other's needs. When the needs themselves are held in question, there is no reason for the participants to search for some way of satisfying those needs.

In an unbalanced conflict situation, the greatest danger for the weaker member is that *their needs will not be seen as legitimate,* that they will not be taken into account as possible resolutions are sought. When more powerful members discount others' needs, the solutions they seek (for example, firing Kathy) are ones which, by definition, are unacceptable or unsatisfying for other people in the conflict. Indeed, this is more than just a case of the stronger person's needs winning out over those of the weaker. The stronger person can often determine what needs are relevant through his or her ability *to define what the conflict is about,* in other words, to exert *issue control.*

The social service case just mentioned provides an excellent example of the effects of issue control on the weaker party. When the issue was brought before the board it was defined as a conflict over whether Kathy would or could hold up her end of the agency's work and adapt to its new directions. This put Kathy in a defensive position. There were several possible alternative definitions that were not proposed: the conflict could be (1) over whether the agency should expand, or (2) over whether fair and reasonable demands were being made of Kathy, or even (3) over what general life-style the work promotes (Kathy claimed it militated against family time and the two new members wanted the work to play a big role in their lives). Each of these definitions implies a different focus for conflict interaction than the definition presented to the board. Definition 1 defines the conflict as a problem common to all three members concerning the agency's goals, while definition 2 questions the behavior of Lois and Janelle, and definition 3 reorients concerns to "external" issues such as members' overall satisfaction and life plans. Clearly it would be easier for Kathy to respond to any of these issues than to the issue presented before the board, but they were not raised. Lois and Janelle used their power and momentum to press their attack before the board and, by "getting the first word in," set an agenda that Kathy had to reply to. Kathy had little choice but to attempt to defend herself, and this response no doubt made her look bad in the eyes of the board and undermined her own confidence, which was already shaky.

A danger of weakness is that stronger members may be able to *define the terms and grounds of the conflict in their own favor* (Bachrach & Baratz, 1962). This type of definition not only puts the weaker member at a disadvantage, but it may also hurt both people by resulting in an ineffective or harmful solution. The more powerful person often only understands one side of the conflict and his or her grasp of the underlying causes may be imperfect. As a result, the definition of the conflict advanced by the stronger person may not state the problem in terms that would lead to an effective solution. For example, in the social service agency, Lois and Janelle defined the conflict as Kathy's lack of cooperation. This definition pressured Kathy to resign; the social service agency lost Kathy's experience and talent and had to pay for hiring and training a replacement.

The outcome might have been different had the conflict been defined as a conflict over whether the agency should expand. This definition recognizes both sides' concerns by emphasizing the agency, not the members. Although the same issues would probably have come out—Kathy's lack of energy, Lois and Janelle's desire to innovate—they would be discussed in terms of a common issue, and much of the pressure would have been off Kathy. Perhaps, if managed correctly, a problem-solving approach could have generated solutions all could live with, while preserving Kathy's talents for the agency.

A second danger of weakness is its *tendency to become self-perpetuating and self-defeating.* We mentioned above that weak members tend to perceive themselves as powerless. These perceptions can discourage members from attempting to resist or make countermoves to a powerful member's moves. The end result is a reinforcement of the powerful member's control and further proof of the weak member's impotence (Janeway, 1980). This process simply reproduces both members' positions.

When a member becomes convinced that he or she has little influence in the group and is threatened with loss of a particularly valued goal or possession, he or she may feel pressure to commit an "act of desperation" in a last-ditch attempt to avoid the loss. As we noted in the previous section, sometimes the weaker person may be convinced that he or she has little to lose by resisting, and a serious attack —one which threatens the existence of the group—may appear to be the only course for a chance of success. For example, in a charity fund-raising committee, one man with very low power faced the loss of money necessary for the survival of his "pet" project, a community development loan corporation. If the project fell through, the member stood to lose his job as director of the corporation as well as his position on the committee. Believing the committee was about to veto his project, the member threatened to go to the local newspaper and state that the committee gave no support to the local economy. This would arouse a great deal of controversy around the committee and possibly hurt its major fund-raising drive, which was to begin in two months. The committee ultimately worked out a compromise which gave the project partial funding, but considerable anger was caused by the member's move. The committee's cohesion was undermined, and the project was cancelled two years later. The desperation of weakness can motivate "absolute" acts with the potential to destroy a group or lead to worse retributions later on.

BUILDING GROUP-CENTERED POWER BASES

The cases discussed in this chapter suggest that there are two general types of power resources and that they have different consequences for conflict interaction. Members can attempt to influence a conflict by drawing either on the *unique* resources they hold or on sources of power *available to the entire group* and explicitly endorsed by the group as a legitimate basis for influence. When members draw from their unique sources of power, the conflict is likely to turn away from problem-solving interaction and towards heightened escalation. Each move premised on unique sources of power "tells" other group members that an attempt may be made to resolve the issue by means not available to everyone. In effect, use of unique power resources is an attempt to unilaterally control interaction. This message can promote escalation as each member assesses his or her own unique resources and becomes more likely to use them to counter a threat they cannot meet on its own terms.

The creativity development committee case provides an illustration of a group that moved from the use of shared to individual resources. In the early meetings, members' actions were contained by boundaries the group as a whole accepted. The project directors and the manager drew from a set of resources they all shared and saw as a legitimate basis for changing opinions and determining possible outcomes. When the manager indicated that *he* might make the final choice, the moves in the conflict became premised on *unique* sources of power individual group members held (in other words, Tom's power as director; the project directors' power as supervisors of their own units, and so on). Similarly, in the social service agency example, the conflict quickly became premised on unique power bases. The two newer staff people used their friendship and agreement on agency policy to move against Kathy. Kathy drew from her "seniority" and experience as an older worker to justify her positions in response to the challenge she faced. The three women never developed an implicit agreement about what resources could be drawn from to influence each other's behavior legitimately. There was not, in other words, a group-endorsed set of resources that could be drawn upon to try to work through the conflicts over the quality of work in the office and the long-range objectives of the agency. Although differences of opinion on these issues may have been difficult to resolve, the staff's interaction prevented a *group* assault on the problem. In making moves based on their *unique* sources of power, members worked on the problem from their own standpoints and discouraged other forms of conflict interaction from emerging that may have at least allowed for greater clarification of each person's needs or positions.

To safeguard against the dangers that can result from unbalanced power, group members need to forestall making power moves based on unique resources. Individually held resources become less salient and are less likely to be invoked when the group as a whole has established a self-endorsed power base. But what conditions are conducive to the use of group-endorsed power? What keeps members constrained within a set of power moves that the group as a whole sees as *legitimate* attempts at influence? Although there is no cut-and-dry answer to this question, there are several conditions that at least allow for the possibility that a group-centered basis of power will be employed as a means of influence when conflicts arise.

First, *all members must agree on what the primary goals of the group are.* When people share a common conception of what the main purpose of the group is, that shared sense of purpose can be a gauge for judging the appropriateness of any attempt at influence in conflict interaction. Anyone in the group can turn to their understanding of what the group is trying to accomplish to attempt to influence the outcome of the conflict or to assess the legitimacy or possible impact of another's move. Because the group as a whole endorses this aim, the power move, although not always accepted or successful, is at least seen as legitimate, because it draws from a resource base all members share. A common aim or goal gives the group a *center* that can become the driving force behind moves attempted (or challenged) as members try to resolve what appear to be incompatible stands.

The application of group goals to individual issues and decisions is never clearcut; members must be able to articulate what the general goals of the group mean in any given situation. When members look at any given problem and examine alternative (and perhaps incompatible) proposals in light of the group's general purpose, they are engaging in constructive conflict interaction. This process allows the group to check and articulate how it sees its own purpose, to build cohesion around that purpose, and to consistently steer itself, on a decision-by-decision basis, toward the goal it wants to achieve.

Groups that are formed in classes to complete a group project assignment often fail to attain a common goal or purpose. Some students in these groups see the group's major aim as educational; they accept the premise that going through a set of experiences that are directed toward completing a project at the end of the term will be helpful in meeting the instructional objectives of the course. For these students the general purpose of the group is to learn through completing an assigned task as a team. Other students do not "buy into" this educational objective for any number of reasons. Their goal for the group is simply to complete an acceptable assignment that meets the basic requirements for the course and gets a sufficient number of points toward their final grade without spending too much effort.

When these two different goals exist in a project group, differences over how the project should be accomplished, how often the group should meet, or how much time should be spent on each task are ripe for escalation. Without an overarching goal to guide them, members may turn to unique sources of power (for example, noncooperation by less motivated members) to influence the group's choices on these issues. In groups where all members buy into the same goal, there can still be considerable debate over how long meetings should run, and so on, but the group is working toward the same conception of success as it tries to reach agreement on this issue. Members may have to spend considerable time defining what success entails, what the best means for achieving success are, and how much time is needed to reach their goal, but this type of discussion is a constructive form of conflict interaction. It points the group toward a more well-defined conception of itself, and it allows the group to set explicit standards for what behavior is expected from group members.

In the social service agency case described above, the three women never reached an agreement about what the primary goals of the agency should be. There were implicit differences that the two factions never tried to resolve or meld into one shared mission for the office. As a result, differences over an issue like what constitutes "quality work" at the agency were "settled" by members turning to the unique sources of power they held. Sticking to the shared definition of their problem—should the agency expand?—might have helped the three women to identify common goals.

A second condition that is conducive to a group-centered power base is the group's *willingness to make any power resource accessible to all members.* The resource must, in other words, be truly shared by the membership if it is to be an alternative to the use of unique sources. If, for example, knowledge of the past history of the group is endorsed as an important resource for influencing decisions and settling differences about policy matters, and so on, then all members—even new people—must be given access to this knowledge. New members will, of course, be less influential than others at first, because they do not enter the group with a full history in hand. However, there must be an assumption that relevant information will be made available on a decision-by-decision or issue-by-issue basis so that newer members can draw upon the same basis of influence that older members endorse and use. In many groups this is done through formal channels, such as orientation sessions, training in skills valued by the group, and written histories.

Even when all information is available and "access" is given to all members in principle, certain members may consistently be more influential than others because they are more skillful. Some members will be more powerful than others because they may be better able to articulate positions the group recognizes as appropriate or consistent with the direction it wants to take. Insuring access to all does not mean that all members will be *equally able* to use the resource. Some members may be able to apply the resource more quickly or insightfully as new issues arise, and thus their power, their ability to influence the direction of conflicts or determine decisions, will appear to be greater. The difference is, however, that the power these members exercise is seen as legitimate because the group as a whole continues to endorse the resources regardless of who uses them.

The importance of equalizing the power resources available to all members is clear in the social service case. In their coalition, Lois and Janelle had a source of power unavailable to Kathy. If Lois and Janelle had not taken advantage of their alliance and had instead tried to deal with Kathy "one-on-one," they might have been able to work out a more constructive solution. From one-on-one conversation, Lois and Janelle might have been able to understand Kathy's needs and feelings better. They might also have seen her potential and the problems that kept her from contributing. Kathy, on the other hand, would not be intimidated by Lois and Janelle's "united front" and might, herself, see the merits in their case. Once each side understood the other's needs and problems, working out a solution would be easier. Moreover, once Kathy understood that the other two would not use their superior power to force her, she might become less reactive and more willing to work on improving the agency.

A third condition underlies the first two: the group must *recognize that its members are the source of power and that they participate continually in the exercise and renewal of power.* The group must work to see through the myth of power as a possession to the process of *endorsement* that is necessary for any move to be effective. It must acknowledge that this endorsement occurs in members' interaction and that therefore, as Janeway (1980) argues, all power is grounded in "community" among members. This is what democratic nations try to do in their constitutions, and this is what groups must do to build a shared power base. However, just as governments often have trouble remembering their popular roots, so to do group members have trouble remembering the roots of their power. As we noted above, the endorsement process operates to hide the source of power from members. *Long socialization, the mystique of power,* and *subtle interaction processes* veil members' roles in endorsement. To achieve a balance of power in the group, members must adopt structural measures to counteract these forces. Groups have done this in a variety of ways, including rotating leadership regularly, appointing "process watchers" to comment on members' moves and group interaction, setting up retreats and evaluation periods to help members discuss power-related problems, and forcing their leaders to adopt a nondirective style. Whatever the specific steps, they were effective because (a) they made members aware of their community and their responsibilities to the group and to each other, (b) they emphasized admitting all members into discussions on an equal basis, and (c) they de-emphasized the prominence of any particular individual vis-à-vis the group.

A final note: in this section we have emphasized the need to develop shared power bases. We mean this as an ideal or goal to strive for, not as the only effective or justifiable use of power. Some groups have such deep-seated discrepancies that weaker members have no choice but to develop and use unique power bases: the use of force or countervailing resources may be the only way to check or get the attention of the dominant members. The literature on groups and organizations is full of examples of groups with authoritarian leaders who became so oppressively dominant that members saw no choice but to band together and rebel or strike. A forceful countermove was the only way these parties could get a message across to the leader. At the same time we acknowledge cases where unique sources of power may be used beneficially, it is important to remember that they create unstable situations if used over the long run. One side may topple the other, but the other is likely to strike back, no matter how long it takes. Moving to a shared power base greatly enhances the likelihood of a constructive and mutually beneficial solution.

SUMMARY

Power is the architecture of conflict interaction. The moves and countermoves that are made in a conflict are based on people's ability and willingness to use power. Power moves are based on resources members hold that serve as a successful basis of influence in the group. Power must be viewed as a relational concept because in order for resources to be a basis for influence, the resources must carry the endorsement of other members. At first glance, the relational nature of power seems to suggest that weaker members in a conflict always have a way out—they can withdraw their endorsement if more powerful parties apply pressure. There are, however, strong social forces that encourage or sustain the endorsement of various forms of power in groups or organizations. Whatever the distribution of power may be in a group, its balance is critically important in determining the direction of conflict. When power is imbalanced, the stronger and weaker members both face dilemmas as they make moves and step through difficult conflict situations. Stronger members can exhaust their power by its use, they can consciously or inadvertently set terms for a settlement that encourage continued escalation, and they can make faulty assumptions about the likely response of a weaker person. Weaker members may have to live with a definition of the problem that ignores their real needs because they have no hand in determining what issues get addressed. Groups that achieve a successful balance of power develop group-centered power bases: sources of power are employed that are available to the entire group and are explicitly endorsed by the group as a legitimate basis for influence.

REFERENCES

Allison, G. T. Conceptual models and the Cuban Missile Crisis. *American Political Science Review*, 1969, *63*, 689–718.

Apfelbaum, E. Relations of dominance and movements for liberation: An analysis of power between groups. In W. G. Austin & S. Worchel (Eds.), *The social psychology of intergroup relations*. Monterey, Calif.: Brooks-Cole, 1979.

Arendt, H. *On violence*. New York: Harcourt Brace & Jovanovich, 1969.

Bachrach, P., & Baratz, M. S. Two faces of power. *American Political Science Review*, 1962, *56*, 947–952.

Bachrach, P., & Baratz, M. S. *Power and poverty*. New York: Oxford University Press, 1970.

Bowers, J. W. Beyond threats and promises. *Communication Monographs*, 1974, *41*, ix–xi.

Burgess, P. G. Crisis rhetoric: Coercion vs. force. *Quarterly Journal of Speech*, 1973, *59*, 61–73.

Burgoon, J. K., & Saine, T. J. *The unspoken dialogue: An introduction to nonverbal communication*. Boston: Houghton Mifflin, 1978.

Crenson, M. A. *The un-politics of air pollution: A study of nondecision-making in the cities*. Baltimore: Johns Hopkins Press, 1971.

Deutsch, M. *The resolution of conflict.* New Haven: Yale University Press, 1973.

Downs, C. W., Smeyak, G. P., & Martin, E. *Professional interviewing.* New York: Harper and Row, 1980.

Ellis, D., & Fisher, B. A. Phases of conflict in small group development. *Human Communication Research,* 1975, *7,* 195–212.

Emerson, R. M. Power-dependence relations. *American Sociological Review,* 1962, *27,* 31–41.

Evans, G. Effect of unilateral promise and value of rewards upon cooperation and trust. *Journal of Abnormal and Social Psychology,* 1964, *69,* 587–590.

Fisher, R. *International conflict resolution for beginners.* New York: Harper and Row, 1969.

French, R. P., & Raven, B. The bases of social power. In D. Cartwright (Ed.), *Studies in social power.* Ann Arbor: University of Michigan Press, 1959.

Friedland, N. Social influence via threats. *Journal of Social Psychology,* 1976, *88,* 552–563.

Harre, H., & Secord, P. F. *The explanation of social behavior.* Totowa, New Jersey: Littlefield Adams, 1973.

Hawes, L., & Foley, J. M. Group decisioning: Testing a finite stochastic model. In G. R. Miller (Ed.), *Explorations in interpersonal communication.* Beverly Hills, Calif.: Sage, 1976.

Heilman, M. E. Threats and promises: Reputational consequences and the transfer of credibility. *Journal of Experimental Social Psychology,* 1974, *10,* 310–324.

Janeway, E. *Powers of the weak.* New York: Morrow-Quill, 1980.

Janis, I. *Victims of groupthink.* Boston: Houghton Mifflin, 1972.

Jewell, L. N., & Reitz, H. J. *Group effectiveness in organizations.* Glenview, Ill.: Scott, Foresman, 1981.

Jones, E. E., Gergen, K. J., & Jones, R. G. Tactics of ingratiation among leaders and subordinates in a status hierarchy. *Psychological Monographs,* 1963, *77,* 1–20.

Kaplowitz, S. A. An experimental test of a rationalistic theory of deterrence. *Journal of Conflict Resolution,* 1973, *17,* 535–572.

Kelley, H. H. Experimental studies of threats in interpersonal negotiations. *Journal of Conflict Resolution,* 1965, *9,* 79–105.

Kerr, C. A., Schreisheim, C. A., Murphy, C. J., & Stogdill, R. M. Toward a contingency theory of leadership based upon the consideration and initiating structure literature. *Organizational Behavior and Human Performance,* 1974, *12,* 62–82.

Komorita, S. S. Negotiating from strength and the concept of bargaining strength. *Journal of the Theory of Social Behavior,* 1977, *7*(1), 65–79.

Leary, T. *Interpersonal diagnosis of personality.* New York: Ronald, 1957.

Lukes, S. *Power: A radical view.* London: MacMillan, 1974.

Marwell, G., & Schmitt, D. R. Dimensions of compliance-gaining behavior: An empirical analysis. *Sociometry,* 1967, *30,* 350–364.

Meyer, H. H., Kay, E., & French, J. R. P., Jr. Split roles in performance appraisal. *Harvard Business Review,* 1965, 21–29.

Mishler, E. Meaning in context: Is there any other kind? *Harvard Educational Review,* 1979, *19,* 1–19.

Moore, J. C. Status and influence in small group interaction. *Sociometry,* 1968, *31,* 47–63.

Pelz, D. C. Influence: A key to effective leadership in the first-line supervisor. *Personnel,* 1952, *29,* 209–217.

Pfeffer, J. *Organizational design.* Arlington Heights, Ill.: AHM Publishing, 1978.

Raven, B., & Kruglanski, A. Conflict and power. In Paul Swingle (Ed.), *The structure of conflict.* New York: Academic Press, 1970.

Roloff, M. E. Communication strategies, relationships, and relational changes. In G. R. Miller (Ed.), *Explorations in interpersonal communication.* Beverly Hills, Calif.: Sage, 1976.

Rubin, J. Z., & Brown, B. *The social psychology of bargaining and negotiation.* New York: Academic Press, 1975.

Rummel, R. J. *Understanding conflict and war (Vol. 2).* Beverly Hills, Calif.: Sage, 1976.

Sharp, G. *The politics of nonviolent action.* Boston: Porter-Sargent, 1973.

Stogdill, R. *Handbook of leadership.* New York: Free Press, 1974.

Tajfel, H. *Differentiation between social groups: Studies in the social psychology of intergroup relations.* New York: Academic Press, 1981.

Tedeschi, J. T. Threats and promises. In P. Swingle (Ed.), *The structure of conflict.* New York: Academic Press, 1970.

Walster, E., Berscheid, E., & Walster, G. W. New directions in equity research. *Journal of Personality and Social Psychology,* 1973, *25,* 151–176.

Walton, R. *Interpersonal peacemaking: Confrontations and third party consultation.* Reading, Mass.: Addison-Wesley, 1969.

Watzlawick, P., Beavin, J., & Jackson, D. *The pragmatics of human communication.* New York: Norton, 1967.

Wehr, P. *Conflict regulation.* Boulder, Colo.: Westview Press, 1979.

Wilmot, J. H., & Wilmot, W. W. *Interpersonal conflict.* Dubuque, Iowa: Wm. C. Brown, 1978.

Wilson, S. *Informal groups.* Englewood Cliffs, N.J.: Prentice-Hall, 1978.

Face-Saving

FACE-SAVING: A THREAT TO FLEXIBILITY IN CONFLICT INTERACTION

Continued change is often a good sign in conflict. Changes in members' positions and styles, as well as more general shifts in climate and emotional tenor, indicate that the group is successfully resisting tendencies toward rigid perpetuation of conflict interaction patterns. They also decrease the likelihood that the group will lock into the destructive cycles trained incapacities often produce. As uncomfortable as it sometimes is, members should be encouraged by change, because it usually means that the group is still working on the issue and that a breakthrough is possible. Change requires energy; the use of the group's energy to move the conflict interaction in new directions suggests there is still some level of motivation to deal with the unresolved issue. Any signs of stalemate or rigidity can easily paint the first grey shades of discouragement on a colorful, although difficult and emotionally draining, conflict.

The emotional side of conflict is intimately connected with members' flexibility. As we noted in chapter 1, every move in conflict interaction affects relationships among members, their liking (or disliking) for each other, their mutual respect or lack of respect, their beliefs about each other's competence, and a score of other beliefs and feelings. *Face-saving* is members' attempts to protect or repair their relational images, in response to threats real or imagined, potential or actual. It poses a threat to constructive conflict interaction because it halts the group's momentum for change and can limit members' flexibility in taking new approaches to the conflict issue. In addition, because of its relational consequences, face-saving often carries an emotional "charge" which can greatly accelerate destructive escalation or avoidance in conflicts. Like the effects of trained incapacities, face-saving issues often redefine conflicts. Once face-saving becomes a concern, people's perceptions and interaction patterns can lead to a progressive redefinition of the conflict which changes a potentially resolvable difference over some tangible problem into an unmanageable issue centering on the relationships between the members and the images people hold of themselves.

Before exploring face-saving in detail—its causes, and its consequences—it is useful to consider a few illustrations. The following short case examples show three diverse conflict situations where the ability to be flexible and to change approaches, positions, or interaction styles is in jeopardy. At the heart of each case lies a concern with saving face.

In the first case, a university professor becomes increasingly concerned about the way students are likely to see her if she changes her mind about a decision she recently made.

_____ CASE 5.1 _____

An English professor at a Midwestern university was called by the academic appeals referee and told that a student in her introductory writing course filed a grievance about a grade he received last semester. The student was given a "D" in the class because he did not take the final exam in the course. On the day of the exam, the student had left a message with the department secretary saying that he was ill and would not be present for the test. Although the professor received this message, the student did not get back in touch with her until after the grades had to be submitted. When the student did get in touch with the professor, he told her that he had three other final exams scheduled that week and had decided to take those tests to stay on schedule rather than making up the English final immediately. He said he had thought he would be able to contact her again before the grades had to be reported but, as it turned out, he was too slow in doing so. On hearing the student's explanation, the professor decided to stick with her earlier decision to give him the grade he received without any points on the final. The student's grades on the earlier tests and writing assignments were good enough that if he had received a "B" on the final exam, he would have finished with a "B−" in the course.

After receiving the call from the appeals referee, the professor began to question her own decision. Originally she had felt justified in taking the tough stand because she had stated a very clear policy about missing tests and assignments early in the term. She began to believe, however, that she might have been somewhat dogmatic in this case and was leaning towards allowing the man to take a make-up exam and use that score in recomputing his final grade. But as she entered the meeting with the appeals referee and student, she became increasingly concerned about changing her mind. She knew that word travels fast among students, and she was worried that soon she would have a reputation for changing grades or class policy when the right pressure was applied. She was also increasingly bothered by the student's decision to register a formal complaint against her in the college.

In this second example, a group had fears that an outspoken, quick-thinking member would have trouble backing off from a position once she took a stand on an issue. To the group's surprise, she had little concern for face and changed stands once a better argument was made by other members.

_____ CASE 5.2 _____

A group of twelve leaders and activists in the antipollution movement of an eastern city began meeting to discuss strategies for dealing with an attack on water standards that was currently being made in their area. A local business executive was mounting a campaign that could have jeopardized water and waste treatment standards if it gained sufficient support. The group of twelve met to determine what could be done to counteract the business campaign and to coordinate the efforts of environmentalists who wanted to work on the project. They saw their main task as building an effective alliance of people in town who wanted to work for environmental quality at this crucial time.

The people in the group were from a wide variety of backgrounds and professions: some headed smaller civic organizations, some were students, one worked for a local newspaper, one was an elected city official. One member, Ruth, was a woman in her thirties, an attorney, and a longtime activist in local politics. She was an outspoken person who took the floor several times early in the first meeting and spoke in a loud and confident tone of voice. She came to the meeting with well-developed ideas about what the group should do and she was able to argue her position clearly and forcefully, while other members, on the other hand, still seemed to be thinking about what the current situation was like and calculating what should be done as an immediate plan of action.

When Ruth made a strong case for what the group should do in the first part of the initial meeting, the climate in the group grew uneasy and tense. Several people looked at each other uncomfortably and most people seemed hesitant to speak. The group seemed to be "holding its breath" and anticipating that Ruth would be difficult to work with. Although Ruth was obviously bright and had good reasons supporting her suggestions, members feared that she had set ideas and that she would not budge from the proposal she had just articulated so forcefully. The group thought she would feel as if she had lost face if she moved away from her stated position.

After several people made comments that were not related to Ruth's proposal, one man in the group began pointing to possible complications and problems with Ruth's suggestion. Ruth listened intently and when he was finished speaking, she said that she really had not thought of the points he had raised and that she felt they posed a very serious set of problems. She asked the man if he had an alternative suggestion, listened to it, and then shortly began arguing for it. She made stronger and more well-reasoned arguments for the man's proposal than he himself had made, and she was able to clarify questions other people in the group had about the proposed plan without dominating the interaction or intimidating people further.

The group soon saw Ruth as one of its most valuable members. She could carry a line of thought through for the group, lay out a well-reasoned set of arguments for a stand she was taking, but at the same time, was not hesitant to turn 180 degrees on an issue if new information or evidence was presented that she had not previously considered.

In this third example, the group felt its face was threatened by one person who "took charge" without the group's endorsement.

___ CASE 5.3 _____

Four staff members in a personnel office at a large computer corporation were assigned to a rather demanding recruitment project in addition to their regular job of interviewing and placement. They were asked to design and implement an effective program for minority recruitment and placement within the corporation. The project was viewed as one of the top priorities for the department and the workers knew that the success or failure of the project would have a significant impact on their advancement in the organization.

About a month before the project was due, one of the team members asked her immediate supervisor if the group could meet with him. The supervisor agreed, but when the group arrived only three of the four members were present. The group had not asked the fourth member to attend this meeting with the supervisor. The problem the group faced was that the fourth member repeatedly made decisions and completed tasks that the group as a whole had not endorsed. The three staff members felt that these decisions and actions were threatening the quality of the entire project.

The fourth member was a man who had been in the personnel office a year longer than the other three people. He felt he had more knowledge and experience than the other staff, and he made this point to the group on several occasions. He also told the group that he did not want this project to interfere with the time he needed to complete his normal work routine, and so he was willing to make certain decisions about the project on his own to move things along faster. Although the staff felt intimidated by their co-worker's outspoken and evaluative style, they felt that he was bright, hardworking, and that he did have some experience that they lacked. In most cases, however, they felt this additional experience was unrelated to the assignment they were currently given. They saw the man's concern about the project taking time away from his normal work assignment as pure arrogance; they all had the same work schedule to complete each week and needed to find time to work on the recruitment project. The group felt particularly insulted because on several occasions, the man did not show up for meetings that had been scheduled. He did not let the group know that he would not be attending nor did he offer any explanations for his absence afterwards. He made no attempt to get information that he held to these meetings. Thus, the group's work was often delayed. When he was present, meetings were tense and antagonistic and the motivation of the whole group had plummeted because of the problem.

When the supervisor asked the group if they had discussed their reactions openly with the "problem" person, they said they had not. They had wrestled with the idea but decided that the issue may just be too emotional to air openly. They were, however, mad at their co-worker, felt intimidated by him, and wanted management in the department to hear about the problem.

In all three cases, some form of face-saving was a central concern and could have undermined the parties' ability to deal successfully with the conflict. In the grade dispute, the professor had taken a stand on an issue and was reluctant to move from that position, because she might be seen as indecisive or unsure of herself. When she reconsidered her decision, she recognized that the student may have had a good case and that she may have been too harsh in enforcing her no make-up policy. In entering the meeting where the conflict was to be addressed, however, there was a great likelihood that her current beliefs on the problem would not be stated unless something was done to ease her concern about the image she might acquire by following her inclinations. Part of her reluctance to move also stemmed from an already existing threat to face: the image she had of herself as a fair professor had already been called into question publicly by the student's decision to contact the college official.

In the environmental group, the face-saving issue was anticipated by members who heard Ruth make early and forceful arguments. A tense and uneasy climate arose because most members assumed Ruth had made a strong commitment to her position and would be very hard to move. There was a general sense that

Ruth would be a "problem," because others assumed a strong public defense of her position meant Ruth's self-image would be at stake if the group challenged her suggestions. The group was surprised and relieved to find that Ruth's intellectual and verbal abilities could provide information and clear reasoning for the group without being tied to Ruth's self-image. If no one in the group had run the risk of questioning Ruth's initial stand because they feared embarrassing her, the group could easily have become dissatisfied with the decision-making process but remained silent, perhaps eventually splintering into pro- and anti-Ruth factions.

For the staff on the personnel project, face-saving was at least one of their concerns as they entered the supervisor's office. Although the group feared the emotional strain and potential long-range consequences of raising the issue with their co-worker, they felt this person had treated them unfairly. They were made to feel as if their input on the project was unnecessary or even harmful. At least part of their motivation for contacting the supervisor was to restore face: they did not want to think of themselves as incompetent. Nor did they want to see themselves as people who would accept unfair treatment without resistance. If the supervisor agreed with their accusations and assessment of the situation, their face would be restored.

When face-saving becomes an issue, members' ability to remain flexible and shift their modes of conflict interaction is threatened. Face-saving reduces flexibility and the likelihood of change in group conflict situations for two reasons. First, the emergence of a concern with saving face inevitably *adds an issue to the conflict.* The additional problem tends to take precedence because it stands in the way of getting back to the main issue. The group's energy and attention are drawn away from the central issue and are spent on peripheral matters; work may stop on the issues that count most to the members as people deal with a threat to face. In each of the three cases described above, face-saving added issues to the conflict that diverted attention—and interaction—away from the central concern, or exhausted members before an adequate resolution was reached.

In the grade dispute, for example, the main conflict was over the professor's policy on make-up exams and her decision to enforce that policy in the current situation. The professor's reputation as indecisive or soft was really a secondary (although related) issue. In the environmental group, members' attention started to shift from a concern with how the group should go about protecting water standards to how the group was going to deal with a member who appeared to be dogmatic and would likely be threatened by criticism. In the personnel project team, the central conflict was over decision-making rights in the group. In allowing the issue to go unaddressed, the three workers added a face-saving concern: they felt unjustly intimidated by the man and spent considerable time trying to feel better about the situation and attempting to decide whether they had somehow helped elicit the man's arrogant behavior. These additional issues can easily displace the group's focus if they remain salient concerns or if the members fail to address a face-saving issue that is influencing the behaviors in the group.

Besides multiplying issues, face-saving *makes inflexibility likely* because face-saving concerns usually entail the real possibility of a future impasse in the conflict. Motives to save face are difficult to alleviate in conflicts and tend to foster interaction that heads toward stalemates and standoffs. After examining face-saving in a variety of formal bargaining settings, Brown (1977) notes that issues related to the loss of face are "among the most troublesome kinds of problems that arise in negotiation" (p. 275). Several factors contribute to the tendency for face-saving issues to head towards impasse.

Face-saving issues often remain highly *intangible* and *elusive* because people are reluctant to acknowledge that an image they want to preserve or restore has been threatened. The group can sense that something is going wrong, and that positions seem to be tightening, but the face-saving motive may never be explicitly raised. To acknowledge a threat to one's image is, in some ways, to make that threat all the more real. One can maintain a desired self-image despite what others think as long as one can somehow deny what others think. To openly state what the threat may be and risk confirmation of the belief is, in some cases, to remove the possibility of denial. Thus, the threat to one's image may be real and may be influencing the conflict interaction, but it often lies beneath the surface where it will go unrecognized or unaddressed by the group.

The professor in the grade controversy might, for example, go through the entire meeting with the student and appeals referee without raising the issue of her image or without noting that she felt put off by the student's decision to contact the referee about the matter. Although these concerns may never surface, they could prompt her to make strong arguments in favor of her original decision (even though she now doubted its fairness) or make unreasonable demands on the student before moving from her initial stand. An effective third-party appeals referee might anticipate these face-saving concerns and make suggestions which alleviate them, but do not require that the issue be stated explicitly (Shubert & Folger, 1980). Often the mere presence of a third party allows someone to move from a position without losing face because they can attribute any movement they make to the third party: "I never would have settled for that if the appeals referee hadn't pushed for it" (Pruitt & Johnson, 1970; Brown, 1977).

There is another reason why impasses are likely outcomes of conflicts complicated by face-saving issues: conflict interaction becomes highly vulnerable to an "all-or-nothing" approach to resolution when face-saving issues arise. A gambler who loses through an evening at a casino table may feel a need to bet big at the end of the night to restore face with those who have watched him struggle for a missed fortune. When an issue becomes heavily steeped in establishing or protecting face, it is often easier for the participants to "go for broke" or walk away than to remain in a situation that, in an important sense, undermines their self-concept or sense of self-worth. Face, in many instances, is seen as an uncompromisable issue. Personal honor and a commitment to oneself can take precedence over any continued involvement with or commitment to the relationships in the group or the group task.

The staff who worked on the personnel recruitment project were all too willing to let the one man make decisions for them even though they were insulted and upset with his behavior. They expected further embarrassment if they brought the issue to the man's attention; they thought he would defend himself by pointing to his own experience and chide them for ignoring their daily work tasks to work on this project. Rather than risk this confrontation and a further affront to their self-image, members were willing to walk away from the issue even though it meant continued frustration with the project.

CONFLICT INTERACTION AS AN ARENA FOR FACE-SAVING

Face-saving messages are concerned with an image the speaker is trying to establish, maintain, or reestablish in the interaction. Because this image depends on others' reactions, any attempt to save face is an attempt to negotiate the speaker's relationship with other parties in the conflict. Face-saving messages offer information about how the speaker wants and expects to be seen in the exchange. Studies of how communication is used to define interpersonal relationships have noted that this type of "relational comment" (in other words, "This is how I see you seeing me" or "This is how I want you to see me") is carried by any message a speaker sends (Watzlawick, Beavin, & Jackson, 1967). In the case of face-saving messages, however, the relational comment is more salient because it is under dispute; the face-saving message is a defensive response to a perceived threat. The speaker has reason to believe that his or her desired image will not be accepted by other members. As a result, the speaker feels a need for assurance or confirmation and engages in various behaviors, such as those in our examples, to "restore face." Interaction usually cannot proceed without resolution of the "face" problem, and will often be dominated by this problem until the speaker feels satisfied that enough has been done to establish the desired image. It is clearly the speaker's perception of how others are taking him or her that determines when the face-saving issue is lifted from the interaction.

If a member rushes into an important meeting fifteen minutes late and says, "Back-to-back meetings never seem to work out," the comment carries a face-saving message. It asks the group to see the member as someone so busy that he or she may have to over-schedule meetings and end up being late at times. This relational message serves a face-saving function because it surplants a potentially threatening image others could hold; it asks people not to see the speaker as someone who is inconsiderate of others' time or is unconcerned about what may go on at the meeting. Being busy, hardworking, or overtaxed is a positive image; being inconsiderate, slow, or careless about the group is an image the member wants to avoid.

In an insightful analysis of face-saving work in everyday interactions, Goffman (1967) has described how people try to conduct themselves in social encounters to maintain both their own and others' face. Goffman emphasizes that the negotiation and mutual acceptance of face is "a condition of interaction, not its objective" (p. 12). Interaction ordinarily proceeds on the assumption that the faces people want to project are in fact the ones that are accepted as the exchange unfolds. There is a noticeable strain or a recognizable problem when face maintenance becomes the objective rather than a precondition of interaction. Even in nonconflict interaction, then, people feel a need to amend the situation when a face-saving issue arises so that the exchange can unfold without the concern.

In group conflict there is a noticeable difference in interaction when face-saving issues arise and become the objective of the interaction. There is a shift away from group-centered and group-directed interaction and toward interaction focused on the experience of the individual group member and his or her relationship to the group. Conflict interaction is *group*-centered when all parties take into account their membership within the group and continuously recognize that any movement made on an issue must be made *with* other parties in the conflict. Individual positions and stands can be argued (and indeed must be, if adequate differentiation is to occur). However, when the interaction remains group-centered, there is a continual recognition that individual positions are being offered and that all comments are geared toward issues that result from differences in needs or goals of the members. Members never lose their identity and concept of self when interaction is group-focused; the commitment to self and the sense of personal identity becomes secondary to the awareness that the conflict is a shared experience and that change or movement in the direction of the conflict will be *with* other members.

The emergence of face-saving as an issue undercuts this group-centered focus in conflict interaction. By its very nature, face-saving gives prominence to the individual members and their sense of self in the group. Attention is turned toward the experience of the individual in the group because face inevitably raises a question about the way some member is seen by others in the group.

Face-saving issues always cross the line between group- and individual-centered interaction. This crossing reflects an ambivalence about the role of individuals in groups that has been noted repeatedly in analyses of group experience. Several researchers have observed that the

> individual's fundamental attitudes toward group membership are characterized by ambivalence. . . . The basic antagonism is between the individual's commitment to himself—to his own needs, beliefs and ambitions—and his yearning for psychological submersion in a group, for an obliteration of those qualities that make him unique and thus distinct and separate from others. . . . Submersion brings a measure of security and a sense of connectedness and belonging, but it also undermines individual autonomy. . . and may in other respects demand a sacrifice of individual wishes to those of the group. (Gibbard, Hartman, & Mann, 1974, p. 177)

When a face-saving issue arises, an individual's concern is not placed in a secondary role to group issues or disputes. The commitment to self and, in particular, the commitment to establishing a desirable self-image, takes precedence over the sense of belonging and cohesion that exists when members "step into" the group more fully.

What is important about the emergence of face-saving concerns is that they produce a *qualitative change* in the nature of the group's conflict interaction. Group-centered interaction is founded on the assumption or precondition that all are acting and responding primarily as *group members*. In this sense, everyone remains at the same level in the interaction because they all take into account their membership in the group and act on that awareness when they speak and respond to others. When interaction becomes individually focused, one person steps into an "official role" that he or she holds as an individual. Obviously, such a role is always present for each member but it can easily remain dormant while members try to sustain group-centered interaction. The role of the *group member as individual* raises concerns about what the person *looks like* to the group, what *impact* that person, in particular, is having on the outcome of a decision, what *place* he or she holds in the group's power structure, and so on. In a sense, the individual adopts an "authority" position; the individual is, and wants to be seen as, the authoritative representative of an image he or she wants to maintain or a role he or she wants to play in the group's process. There is an awareness of someone carving out an individual figure from the composite interaction that the group has molded. This separation lays the groundwork for the inflexibility discussed above.

The following example, which is an actual transcript of a discussion among four graduate students, illustrates a turn from group- to individual-centered interaction. The students in this discussion were given a topic as part of a class assignment. Believe it or not, their task was to clarify Plato's conception of truth. In the interaction just prior to this segment, the students (who were from the same department and knew each other quite well) joked about the seriousness of the topic and were somewhat eager to go off on a tangent before leaping into the task at hand. As this segment of interaction began, Kathy asks Peggy about her research on sex differences in people's thought patterns. The group recognized that the question is somewhat off the assigned topic, but they were more than willing to pursue it and delay their discussion of truth. The group eventually ties the issue of sex research back to the main topic, but that part of the exchange is not included here. Watch for the turn the interaction takes toward individual-centered interaction.

Kathy: (to Peggy) Are you doing any more work on differences of male-female thinking?
Peggy: (answering Kathy) Uh, hum.
Dave: I have an article.
Peggy: Collecting data as a matter of fact.
Dave: I have an article that is so good. This is off the subject, but let's talk about it for a few minutes.
Peggy: That's right, let's forget truth. I'd rather talk about males and females than truth.
Kathy,
Gary: Mhmmm.
Dave: Candice Pert is into, got into, pharmacology and is now in neuroscience. She is the discoverer of what's called the opiate receptor in the brain. Those are the brain cells which opium have an effect on. The ones they're attracted to.
Peggy: Hmmmm.
Dave: And they've, they've gone from opium receptors to ah valium receptors to any tranquilizer. And she's working now on a marijuana receptor, that the cells hit. And it's so neat . . .
(some laughter while Dave is talking, Gary mimes something and Kathy makes a comment under her breath and laughs)
Dave: (laughing slightly) Now wait a minute, wait a minute. This is fascinating.
(general laughter)
Gary: I've already heard it, so I'm spacing off on my own here.
Dave: She made this discovery when she was a grad student.
Kathy: Then there's hope for me yet.
(general laughter)
Peggy: (pointing to the back of her head) Ah, here are my opiate receptors.
Dave: She's first author, and her male mentor and advisor and teacher is second author.

Peggy: Hmmmmm.

Dave: There was an award given called the . . .

Kathy: (interrupting) And he got it, right?

Dave: (continuing) the Lasky award which is seen as a stepping stone to a, to a Nobel prize, and ah . . .

Kathy: What do opiates have to do with men and women?

Dave: Now wait a minute.

Peggy: (jokingly) Wait, wait have patience, have faith.

Dave: Here's, here's your politics in it to start with.

Kathy: All right.

Dave: She was first author on this paper when this Lasky award was given; it was given to four men.

Kathy: Mhmmm.

Dave: And she was invited to the awards ceremony. That's the extent of it. And she talks about it a little bit.

Peggy: Oh, marvelous.

Dave: But in the interview she talks about the, you know, I can be known as a scorned woman here, but I've done some other things since then that are really important to me. And she, she uses the analogy of the brain as a computer. And although she doesn't talk about what we would commonly call software, that's what you learn, she really, she's looking at what she calls the hardwiring, the circuitry in the brain. And the differences in male/female circuitry.

Peggy: And she's found some?

Dave: She's found some possibilities. Some probable areas. Now there are differences, there are some other differences that are not just male and female. There are differences, say, between what we would consider healthy, normal personalities and say, schizophrenia.

Peggy: Mhmm.

(There's a short three second interruption here as someone enters the room, then Dave continues.)

Dave: Ah, you look at the evolution of language instead of being male-oriented and thinking that men had to learn how to use language so that they could coordinate hunting down a large animal; it was women who were the ones who were staying home.

Kathy: (sarcastically) To get them out of the cave.

(general laughter)

Peggy: To talk to the walls.

Dave: Yeah, you know talk to walls, talk to the kids.

Peggy: Well, that's interesting. I'd like to read that.

Dave: And from the beginning. Yeah, it's really fascinating because there are detectable differences in male and female brains.

Kathy: Hmmm (makes a face)

Peggy: Yeah, I'd like to read that.

Dave: (to Kathy) You act like I'm being chauvinistic.

Peggy: No.

Kathy: No, I'm just, I'm . . .

Dave: (interrupting) Oh boy, this is terrible.

Gary: She'd act a whole lot worse if you were being chauvinistic.

Kathy: Do I act like you're chauvinistic? Yes.

Dave: You made a face.

Kathy: (laughing) I'm trying to see inside my brain to see if there are any differences. That's all.

Dave: Differences. What, from mine?

Kathy: Yes.

Dave: But how can you see mine?

Kathy: Oh, I don't know. I can't see in mine either. Let me be successful here first. No, I was thinking of brains, young Frankenstein you know.

Dave: (laughing) Oh yeah.

Kathy: Twelve years dead, six months dead, freshly dead.

Dave: Yeah, yeah.

Kathy: Sorry, Dave, I'm just not on that level today.

Dave: No, no.

Peggy: Well, I think there are some very definite differences in language use and that would be some clue as to why. I've always talked about it being culture, socialization, and that sort of thing, but, ah . . .

Gary: I wonder if there's a change coming in that with the revolutionary changes in men and women's roles in society—they're now becoming different—and if that will have an effect on this too.

Peggy: Go back far enough and actually you can see that the species will evolve differently . . .

Initially, the group's interaction in this exchange consists primarily of offering and evaluating information about research on sex differences. Although Peggy did not elaborate on her research when Kathy asked her about it, Dave's comments about the brain's sensitivity to drugs held the group's interest and prompted continued interaction on this topic. It became the focus of questions and jokes in the group, and it also raised the issue of how sexual politics becomes involved in research. Dave's summary of the article he had read and his commentary about the possible implications it might have for understanding the evolutionary development of male and female language use set the stage for the turn towards individual-centered interaction that took place in this discussion.

After Dave says "Yeah, it's really fascinating because there are detectable differences in male and female brains," the next twenty speaking turns are focused on Dave's image in the group. These comments deal with Dave's relationship to the group rather than with the topic that had surfaced and engaged the group as a whole. Kathy's facial response to Dave's statement made Dave concerned about whether Kathy or the other group members saw him as a chauvinist. Peggy, Gary, and Kathy all attempt to reassure him (although sometimes lightheartedly and perhaps unconvincingly) that he is not seen as a chauvinist because of the way he summarized the article and reacted to it. In the main, the group handles the face-saving concern by joking about the article, becoming somewhat ludicrous (with the references to young Frankenstein's brain) and finally treating one of Dave's major points (about the possible value of an evolutionary explanation for language differences) seriously. When Peggy and Gary make their comments in the last three speaking turns in this segment, the interaction is turned back to a group focus. The interaction is no longer focused on Dave's experience in the group and the way he is seen by others. Dave lets his concern about his image drop and the group continues with an exploration of the merits and problems with research on sex differences.

Since any group is composed of members with self-concepts and concerns about their roles within the group, group interaction, conflict or otherwise, tends to teeter somewhere between group and individual emphases. It is possible to achieve a healthy balance which eases the "basic antagonism" between individuals' commitments to themselves and the need or desire to move the group along as a group. This balance can allow the group to remain a cohesive unit able to settle disputes, yet at the same time, minimize the threat to individuals and meet individual needs. Needless to say, this balance is difficult to maintain when conflicts occur.

Conflicts provide an arena where the balance of group and individual-centered interaction is easily tipped towards the concerns of individual group members, making face-saving likely to occur. Several factors, in combination, are likely to lead the group away from group-centered interaction once conflict arises. First, the *process of differentiation* is, as we have noted in chapter 2, one that temporarily associates individuals in the conflict with "sides" of an issue and reveals the main differences between members. This differentiation is desirable, because it articulates individual stands and creates an understanding of the differences between members. Clarifying individual positions is, however, a powerful thrust towards individual-centered interaction. People hear themselves argue for a position in front of others and may be hesitant to leave their initial positions once they make a public statement.

Second, there is *a tendency for members to point a finger* at others and assign responsibility for the emergence of the conflict to a single individual or faction in the group. Sometimes this arises from displaced aggression as we discussed in chapter 1. This tactic ignores the fact that conflicts always lie in some incompatibility of goals or needs among all concerned; it also focuses group attention and interaction on the roles or behaviors of individuals in the conflict. The "accused" are put in the paradoxical position of, on the one hand, having to defend themselves against the charges and thus giving continued prominence to their individuality, while, on the other hand, needing to move the interaction towards a group focus if real progress toward reaching a resolution is to be made.

Third, as we observed in chapter 4, parties in conflict often turn to *unique sources of power* during conflict interaction. Any move based on unique power sources gives prominence to the characteristics of individuals in the conflict and promotes countermoves that are also based on unique sources of power. These moves work against members' constructing and using group-endorsed bases of power as a means of influence. When someone uses a unique source of power to try to influence the group, they put an important part of themselves on the line. If the move is not successful, *their* image, not the image of the whole group, is threatened and may need to be redeemed through the use of threats, force or deception.

Besides the effects of differentiation, the tendency to attribute conflict to individuals, and the use of unique sources of power, interaction in groups can also tip toward an individual focus because of *decision-making procedures that groups employ in conflict settings.* If members know that decisions will be made and conflicts settled by, for example, a voting procedure, a group will often "walk" through conflicts with an expectation that the vote will settle things. Voting *labels* people as "winners" and "losers." Each member knows whether they are on a winning or losing side as issues are discussed and solutions chosen by the group. This awareness can heighten members' sense of themselves as allied with, or against, others and promote comments and responses that defend individual positions and self-images. ("I lost out this time, but you can bet it won't happen again soon.")

In sum, conflicts are likely arenas for establishing and defending members' images of themselves. These concerns can easily turn interaction away from constructive work on the conflict issue and toward secondary, but troublesome issues that stem from the individual's relationship to the group. When these concerns arise, they tend to promote *inflexibility* in interaction and prevent the group from approaching the conflict from new directions.

Although these destructive tendencies are likely, it should be noted that there may be times when a turn towards individual-centered interaction is useful or necessary in a group. Some members may need certain images of themselves confirmed, even though the image may not have been questioned by other people in the group. Someone may, for example, have a strong need to know that their contributions are valued by other people in the group. In order to fulfill this need, the group's interaction would have to center on the member's relationship to the group. This turn could serve a useful function, *if* it provides valuable feedback about a member's performance or an incentive for someone to continue with their work and involvement in the group. In most cases, this type of interaction occurs outside of conflict situations, so it rarely becomes problematic for the group.

FORMS OF FACE-SAVING IN CONFLICT INTERACTION

Although there are many ways in which concerns for self-image can surface in interaction, *three general forms of face-saving* tend to emerge repeatedly in conflict settings. Each of these forms reflects a different interpretation the person trying to save face might assign to the situation. These interpretations act as "mind-sets" to promote defensive, face-saving behavior. Each type of face-saving has recognizable symptoms that distinguish it from the others and each requires different corrective measures. Two of these forms have been studied by researchers who focused on competitive contexts such as negotiation and bargaining settings. We have alluded to them in the earlier cases, but they deserve more explicit attention because they pose a serious threat to constructive conflict interaction. We will also discuss a third form of face-saving that has not been studied by previous researchers; this form is unique to more informal conflict settings (like most work or group decision-making contexts) where the interaction is premised, at least initially, on the assumption that people will act cooperatively to make decisions and settle differences. Few researchers have studied these noncompetitive contexts.

Resisting unjust intimidation.   Brown (1977) and others (Deutsch & Krauss, 1962) have suggested that face-saving often results from a need to "resist undeserved intimidation in order to guard against the loss of self-esteem and of social approval that ordinarily results from uncontested acquiescence to such treatment" (Brown, 1977, p. 278). When people feel they are being treated unfairly or pushed in a way that is unjustified, they are likely to make some attempt to resist this treatment. Interaction can turn towards a defense of the individual's self-image as the individual tries to establish that he or she will not accept intimidation without resistance. There is an "I don't have to take this" or "Any fair-minded person wouldn't stand for this" message to the other group members.

When this form of face-saving message is sent, it always carries two components. First, there is an *accusation* that others are in fact treating the person in an unfair or intimidating manner. In some cases the other group members will recognize (although perhaps not admit) that there may be some grounds for the accusation. The response in this case is likely to be a defense of the behaviors or charges made against the person who is trying to save face. For example, in a local health department, an assistant administrator conducted several surprise inspections that made employees very nervous and defensive and came near to causing a labor dispute. When the supervisor of one unit that had been inspected by the assistant administrator confronted her with this problem and challenged her fairness, she refused to discuss the issue. Her responsibilities, she argued, forced her to "tighten up the ship" and increase work quality by whatever methods she had available.

In other instances, the accusatory face-saving message may take the group by surprise and may elicit either an initial defensive response ("We never did that to you") or total avoidance because the group is unaware or doesn't believe that some person or faction in the group has grounds for feeling unjustly intimidated. Regardless of the response it receives, this type of face-saving message necessitates a reaction because it carries an accusation. It is the accusatory nature of the message that prevents it from remaining an isolated event in the stream of interaction; rather, it becomes a force which redirects interaction because it necessitates a response from other group members. Even active avoidance means that the group has decided to allow future interaction to be influenced by the unacknowledged, but real effects of an issue that the group has decided to ignore.

The second important component of this type of face-saving message is the sense of *adamant resistance* it conveys. The speaker suggests, in effect, that "business as usual" cannot continue until the concern has been addressed. This sense of resistance often accompanies messages that are sparked by perceived threat (Gibb, 1961). The major impact this component of the message has on interaction is its potential for *altering the climate* in the group. Once this type of face-saving message is sent, other members may feel that it is no longer safe to allow the interaction to continue in the present direction or to suggest new questions or issues for discussion. The defensive member has claimed the right to define the immediate topic of conversation and to insist that it remain until he or she is satisfied with the outcome of the exchange. Other members can challenge this claim, but the move would be immediately recognized as a challenge and thus contribute to an air of threat; it would increase the chance that the group may splinter. Messages which suggest someone has not been treated fairly (like those sent by the workers in the personnel department who felt unjustly treated by their co-worker) may also imply that members are not committed to one another. It hoists a warning flag signalling problems with trust and responsibility in the group. If this issue is not met head on, the group may have difficulty sustaining an image of itself as a united and functioning unit committed to making members feel good about their participation.

Regardless of whether the claim is justified or not, when one or more members feel a need to resist what they see as undeserved intimidation there are usually *important consequences* for the group. Whether these consequences are ultimately destructive depends on how the group deals with the issue. *When the issue is ignored, destructive consequences often threaten the group:* a woman who had planned on leaving a job in a food distribution company for unrelated personal reasons, decided to stay on six months longer to "fight it out." She did not want to leave feeling like she was the cause of some problem that led to her departure. In the personnel staff project discussed above, the three intimidated workers spent considerable time and effort trying to feel better about themselves. This time could have been spent on the project if the issue had been addressed at an earlier point.

When this type of face-saving issue goes unaddressed it is also common for the threatened person to contact an *outside party* for help, hoping that a neutral outsider might understand and perhaps exonerate them. Although a third party can help in many instances, when the person who is trying to save face contacts the outsider it may subvert any legitimate effort to mediate the problem. The group as a whole has to recognize the problem and agree on a need for outside help before any intervention is likely to be successful. Finally, if this type of face-saving issue is left unaddressed, people who are trying to save face are left with a need to explain the *causes* behind the unjust or intimidating treatment. Since the group has not supplied any reasons or denied that the threat exists, the party may begin attributing the intimidation to some set of causes that may or may not be true. These unchecked attributions can shape the comments the member makes from that point on and lead to a more serious set of problems that are impenetrable. For example, in the food distribution company mentioned above, three people were involved in the conflict (including the woman who stayed six months extra); all three incorrectly assumed the others hated them and were attacking them for reasons of personal incompatibility. Actually, all three were merely responding to each other's aggressive behavior, and their responses fed on each other, thereby escalating the conflict.

The key to alleviating face-saving concerns that emerge from feelings of unjust intimidation lies in members' ability to give feedback without eliciting further animosity. Members who feel they are being unjustly treated or intimidated must be able to state the basis for their feelings in a way which does not prejudge other members or discourage them from explaining their behavior. Escalation and stand-offs are likely when criticism is handled poorly as a face-saving issue is addressed. Although many prescriptions have been given for constructing feedback, most discussions of constructive criticism stress that feedback must be *timely* (in other words, offered at a point that is both relevant and least disruptive to the group's progress) and centered on *descriptions of group members' own feelings* rather than assumptions about what the other intends (for example, "When you didn't show up for the scheduled meeting the group felt put down" rather than "You wanted to teach the group a lesson by not showing up for the scheduled meeting").

Face-saving concerns that stem from feelings of unjust intimidation can best be managed if the group has set aside time for *regular evaluations* of its own process. Setting aside five or ten minutes at the end of each meeting for an evaluation session can allow group members to raise issues early before they become impasses and give positive or negative feedback to each other without interfering with the group's work during a meeting. Resentment and hostility is less likely to build and affect other issues if the group as a whole knows it has set time aside to address relational issues or concerns about interaction during the meeting.

Stepping back from a position. A second form of face-saving is based on members' fears that they will *compromise* a position or stand they have taken on some issue (Pruitt, 1971; Brown, 1977). Members often remain committed to a stand or solution even in light of convincing refutations, not because they still believe it is the best option, but because they believe moving away from that position will harm their image. When this form of face-saving emerges, a member believes that conditions in the group are such that reversing one's stand or stepping back from a position is unsafe.

There are many reasons why this fear may become real for group members who are involved in a conflict. In their analysis of the forces governing commitment to decisions, Janis and Mann (1977) have suggested that people may remain committed to an undesirable decision because they believe that they will look indecisive, erratic, or unstable if they retract or reverse their choice: "To avoid perceiving himself as weakminded, vacillating, ineffectual and undependable, the person turns his back on pressures to reconsider his decision and sticks firmly with his chosen alternative, even after he has started to suspect that it is a defective choice" (p. 283). For example, Epstein (1962) reports that novice parachutists, fearing loss of face, often go through with their decision to jump, even though as the time draws near, their desire to skip what many see as a dangerous and senseless endeavor increases. Fear of losing face is a stronger motive in this case than their own judgment at the moment. If a group places a higher value on *consistency* than accuracy, this fear may prevent people from changing their minds or remaining flexible as new information is given and new proposals are considered during conflict interaction.

Janis and Mann also suggest that there is a certain *momentum* behind reaching a decision or articulating a position in public. This momentum stems from the difficulty of reversing a decision once it is made or retracting a position once it is stated. It simply takes more work and effort to explain why one has changed one's mind than it does to leave a previously stated position on the table. If the member is at all uncertain about the reversal, he or she may not make the effort necessary to feel comfortable reversing a stand.

Goffman (1967) discusses a similar motive for this form of face-saving. He indicates that people's fears of moving from a position can rest on a belief that they will not be taken seriously in the *future* if they step away from a position they have taken on a current issue. In this case the member believes that *his or her credibility in the group will suffer* if he or she moves on an important issue or decision. The group has established a climate—or at least the member believes that a climate exists—where reversal will be costly in future situations. Ideas or suggestions the person makes will be overlooked or considered less seriously, if the group believes that ideas are not developed fully enough to warrant continued commitment. There is a fear that future suggestions will be seen, in all cases, as potentially problematic so they will be given less weight in the discussion when they are offered.

Finally, Brown (1977) and other researchers (Tjosvold & Huston, 1978) point to a somewhat different motive for this type of face-saving in adversarial contexts, such as bargaining and negotiation sessions. Whenever people make initial settlement offers and then try to negotiate an agreement without losing much ground, they are often reluctant to move from their initial position because they may be seen as weak bargainers. In a negotiation context, people often want to appear tough as long as it is to their advantage. If the opposing side believes they will give in easily, the opposition may hold their ground because they believe they can obtain concessions (Stevens, 1963). When group conflict interaction becomes competitive, and members believe that the outcome will produce *winners and losers,* this belief becomes a possible source of face-saving concerns. If members believe that their goals are inherently incompatible and that they cannot find a solution that meets everyone's needs, then the *appearance of strength or weakness* influences the moves people make in the conflict.

Whatever the motivation, whether people feel comfortable in changing a stated position is ultimately tied to *expectations* members have about how ideas (in other words, suggestions, information, proposals) are treated in the group. As we noted in chapter 3, the group's climate tells members how ideas should be proposed to the group and, perhaps more importantly, how they will be taken once they are offered. Members have a sense, for example, of whether exploratory questions will be valued or discouraged. In the same vein, the group may welcome or discount suggestions that are not fully developed. Ideas that are offered tentatively can be seen either as a waste of the group's time or as a sign that members feel comfortable making comments that may not be complete but could spark ideas in other members. Some groups seek or value "authoritative" statements—statements well-supported by reliable evidence or proposals that have known consequences. If the group expects authoritative statements, the members may feel more closely bound to any position they take or idea they offer. Since the group works under this shared expectation, once an idea is offered it is easy for members to convince themselves that they would not have offered it unless the idea was worth continued support.

Statements like "I really haven't thought this through but I'd like to suggest . . ." or "I don't know exactly how I feel about this but we could try . . ." may be an indication that members feel they have to apologize for "half-baked" ideas. They may indicate that the group does not encourage or accept tentative suggestions. At the same time however, these type of phrases may *promote* a more exploratory climate in the group. In effect, speakers who use these phrases are attempting to establish that it is all right to offer tentative ideas. The statements can provide a frame or context for the interaction which says, in effect, that the group is in an exploratory frame of mind. Ideas can be offered and evaluations can be made without committing an individual (or the group) to any suggestions. A tone can be set that helps preserve flexibility and the possibility of continued change when conflicts arise.

Suppressing conflict issues. In groups that assume they should be able to reach agreement without conflict or that they can handle any conflict without seeking outside help, members may strongly discourage each other from admitting that a conflict exists or is beyond the group's control. If a member attempts to acknowledge the existence of a conflict or raise the possibility that the group seek third party assistance, he or she may lose face in the eyes of the group. The member may be seen as someone who causes problems for the group or is eager to find fault with the way the group operates. This threat may deter members from engaging in adequate differentiation, and it may promote prolonged and destructive avoidance of an issue.

If someone decides to raise an issue in such a group, conflict interaction may unfold on more complicated grounds than necessary. An issue will have been added to the conflict—the person's threatened relationship to the group; a turn toward inflexibility and stalemate may be imminent if the person feels his or her image must be defended at all costs ("I don't care what you think of me for raising this issue, I think we need to address it."). These complications may mean that the group cannot differentiate successfully or that integration is unattainable.

Academic appeal referees at colleges and universities are assigned the task of mediating disputes that arise between students and faculty about grades, financial aid, discrimination, enactment of departmental or university policies, and so on. One referee at a large university reports that students there are often reluctant to raise conflict issues and, as a result, conflicts are not addressed until the issues have gotten out of hand. Students are often hesitant to raise their concerns with a third-party because they fear loss of face in the eyes of their mentors. In university settings student-faculty relationships are premised on a cooperative assumption: students (especially graduate students) and faculty are expected to work and learn together to advance knowledge in their academic fields. When a conflict arises over such issues as grading, or interpretation of departmental policy, students feel that if they take the issue to a third party (even one that the university endorses), they may threaten or destroy their relationship. The student fears that the faculty will see him or her as someone who is unwilling to work through difficulties cooperatively and who may be trying to make the professor look bad in the eyes of a representative of the institution. Third parties who work in this context need to address this threat to face and help restore an atmosphere of cooperation so that the relationship can continue after the specific issue has been resolved.

In these types of conflicts, the threat to face stems from a fear of being seeing as someone who is willing to jeopardize a "good" relationship by bringing a conflict out in the open. This fear is almost inevitably founded on a belief that the very emergence of conflict is always harmful or destructive.

SUMMARY

Face-saving concerns are, at base, concerns about the relationship of individual members to the group as a whole. When interaction becomes centered on these concerns during a conflict, members are negotiating how they will see each other; each message and response establishes whether a desired image will be allowed to stand in the eyes of other group members. Since these images are closely tied to people's self-concepts, face-saving interaction has a strong influence on how comfortable people feel in the group and how successful the group will be at resolving conflicts constructively.

Groups often benefit when the role of individual members and their sense of self becomes the focus of interaction. Relationships can be improved and people can feel better about themselves because others have confirmed a self-image they value. When the need to *save* face emerges, however, interaction in the group can head towards destructive escalation because a member's self-image is under dispute. Uncertain that a desired self-image is accepted by the group (or certain that an undesirable image has been established), a member seeks confirmation of a new relational image. If the acceptance of this bid is problematic for the group, moving on from this issue may be difficult. Attempts to redirect the topic or shift back to group-centered interaction may be thwarted by feelings of resentment or a preoccupation with the group's resistance to changing its view. When face-saving issues go unresolved, making any decision or addressing any issue can be a highly volatile task for the group. Unsettled issues about members' images of themselves can be played out in other more substantive contexts with potentially disastrous effects for the group.

____ REFERENCES _____

Brown, B. R. Face-saving and face-restoration in negotiation. In D. Druckman (Ed.), *Negotiations.* Beverly Hills: Sage, 1977.

Deutsch, M., & Krauss, R. M. Studies of interpersonal bargaining. *Journal of Conflict Resolution,* 1962, *6,* 52–76.

Epstein, S. The measurement of drive and conflict in humans: Theory and experiment. In M. R. Jones (Ed.), *Nebraska Symposium on Motivation.* Lincoln: University of Nebraska Press, 1962.

Gibb, J. Defensive communication. *Journal of Communication,* 1961, *2,* 141–148.

Gibbard, G., Hartman, J., & Mann, R. *Analysis of groups.* San Francisco: Jossey Bass, 1974.

Goffman, E. On face-work. In E. Goffman (Ed.), *Interaction ritual.* New York: Anchor Books, 1967.

Janis, I., & Mann, L. *Decision making.* New York: Free Press, 1977.

Pruitt, D. Indirect communication and the search for agreement in negotiation. *Journal of Applied Social Psychology,* 1971, *1,* 205–239.

Pruitt, D., & Johnson, D. Mediation as an aid to face saving in negotiation. *Journal of Personality and Social Psychology,* 1970, *14,* 239–246.

Shubert, J., & Folger, J. *The role of face saving in non-adversarial disputes: Legal communication in an alternative setting.* Paper presented to the annual convention of the Speech Communication Association, New York, November 1980.

Stevens, C. M. *Strategy and collective bargaining negotiation.* New York: McGraw Hill, 1963.

Tjosvold, D., & Huston, T. Social face and resistance to compromise in bargaining. *The Journal of Social Psychology,* 1978, *104,* 57–68.

Watzlawick, P., Beavin, J., & Jackson, D. *The pragmatics of human communication.* New York: Norton, 1967.

_____CHAPTER 6_____

Action and Intervention

Until now we have been concerned primarily with understanding the forces behind conflicts. Understanding, however, is of little value unless it can be put into *practice*. This chapter suggests measures members can take to improve their group's chances of dealing with conflict productively. We will consider two types of activities, involving two distinct types of participants. First, *group members may regulate their own conflicts as they work*. This self-regulation is the optimal method of managing conflict: because it is motivated from within the group, members are more likely to accept necessary measures and the measures are often more appropriate and effective than those suggested by outsiders. Alternatively, a formal third party—most often brought in from the outside, but sometimes a member specially-appointed for the task—may facilitate or mediate the group's attempts to deal with conflict. Third parties may do many of the same things members would, but because of their special role, their actions often have a significantly different impact. Third parties have a different viewpoint on the group and can be the source of many novel and innovative suggestions.

This chapter attempts in two sections—one concerned with *self-regulation* and the other with *third-party interventions*—to go beyond the principles and explanations presented in previous chapters to develop *guidelines for working through conflict*. These guidelines will not be pat answers, because there are simply too many variables in conflicts. To present formulas would be both wrong and misleading. In each case we will explore the rationale behind the principle in question and consider problems and needs governing its use in groups and organizations.

SELF-REGULATION OF GROUP CONFLICTS

Self-regulation refers to group behavior which checks destructive conflict interaction and turns it in a constructive direction. The previous discussions of the forces shaping conflict—trained incapacities, climate, power, and face-saving—suggest action principles to counteract whatever negative influence these forces

168

may exert and to turn them into positive influences. In order to work with the four forces members must be able to (a) diagnose emerging problems, and (b) act on their diagnoses to successfully alter group interaction patterns. Accordingly, this section will present suggestions for both diagnosis and action for each force. Before proceeding, however, here are two reminders:

First, it is often difficult to determine when group interaction has made a turn in a destructive direction. As we have seen, conflict interaction can develop by gradual and often subtle steps. A group can suddenly find itself caught in an escalating spiral without suspecting it. The cues for recognizing destructive conflict which were outlined at the end of chapter 2 can help members avoid such situations. *Members must be constantly on the alert for signs of destructive patterns and act quickly to alter them.*

Second, changing conflict interaction patterns require *structural* change in the group. Often, discussing a problem in the group will prompt members to apologize and promise to change their attitudes and feelings about others: "Really, it's just a matter of taking a different perspective and respecting each other's opinions." This change in attitude is admirable and represents an important first step, but more often than not it is ineffective. In order to alter a group's methods of dealing with conflict, *it is necessary to structurally change the group's interaction patterns by altering its working habits, its climate, its power relations, or its members' need to save face.* Changes in attitude are important, but they are usually insufficient to sustain more productive patterns of conflict interaction. Too easily, existing structures re-exert their influence on member interaction and undermine resolutions made in more reflective moments. This occurred in the Riverdale Halfway House conflict discussed in chapter 3. After talking with the consultant, both George and Carole attempted to put a new face on things and take more constructive attitudes toward each other. Over the long run, however, their attempts proved fruitless, because the suspicious climate at Riverdale prevented serious work on their problems. After a while both George and Carole fell back into their old patterns of sniping and misunderstanding, which persisted until George left. Only when the *forces* moving group interaction in destructive directions are eliminated or neutralized is lasting change possible. For this reason, the principles we discuss are oriented toward *unfreezing and changing* the structures which shape group interaction.

WORKING WITH TRAINED INCAPACITIES

Trained incapacities are work habits inflexibly applied in response to conflict. The key to diagnosing the effect of trained incapacities is therefore to examine the group's "standard operating procedures"—its habitual methods of conducting its affairs—for traps. The discussion in chapter 2 of task requirements, the five incapacities, and the problems they imply supplies a systematic set of starting points for this search: groups can monitor discussions for problems due to goal-centeredness (such as insufficient analysis of problems underlying the conflict), evaluative tendencies, dependence on objective standards, destructive redefinition, or reliance on procedural rules. This monitoring process must go on continually, because groups can slip into harmful patterns without recognizing it. Because trained incapacities are "second nature," they are subtle and hard to detect: members know something is wrong, but they cannot put their finger on the source.

The chair of an administrative committee in one midwestern social service agency keeps a checklist of possible problems to help her overcome this difficulty. It includes questions such as the following: "Is there too little dissent to have a balanced discussion?" "Are votes being used to suppress minority views?" and "Are differences discussed in win-lose terms?" The chair goes over this list (or parts of it) during and after every meeting, carefully monitoring the group's process. Although her answers are negative for most meetings, the list has turned up several unexpected problems that could have been damaging if unchecked.

One dangerous symptom of trained incapacities is a high level of tension in the group. Recall from chapter 2 that differentiation of positions in the early stages of a conflict creates tension which can lead to inflexible behavior and reinforce trained incapacities. Although there is not a perfect cause-effect relationship between tension-level and the problems of trained incapacities, tension increases their likelihood immensely. Situations which create tension—a serious threat from outside the group, a rapidly-approaching time limit, or a severe and important disagreement—are ripe for the dangers discussed in chapter 2.

The most straightforward method of counteracting trained incapacities is for the group to adopt *procedures that correct* for the biases they introduce. The widely-used *Reflective Thinking Process* for group decision-making is one such procedure (Scheidel & Crowell, 1979, pp. 25–51; Gouran, 1982, pp. 29–30). Basically, the Reflective Thinking Process is designed to avoid three errors that may be produced by trained incapacities: (1) over-focusing on solutions before the problem is thoroughly understood (which stems from goal-centeredness), (2) premature evaluation of ideas (which stems from the tendency to evaluate), and (3) destructive redefinition of disagreements. The process avoids these problems by positing a five-step problem-solving procedure and requiring the group to go through the steps in order, keeping deliberations on each step separate:

1. Definition of the Problem or Task—the group assesses the nature of the problem before it and determines if the problem is significant enough to act on.
2. Analysis of the Problem—once the problem is defined, the group analyzes its causes. Only after these are understood, does the group move on to step C.
3. Suggestion of Possible Solutions—the group researches and develops a wide array of possible solutions. No serious evaluation or elimination of solutions occurs at this stage.
4. Solution Selection—the group evaluates and selects the best solution.
5. Implementation—the group plans how to put the solution into effect.

This procedure closely parallels logical thought processes and is the basis for most group decision-making methods (see also, Etzioni, 1968) and conflict management sequences (see also, Filley, 1975). By requiring the group to analyze the problem prior to developing solutions and to develop a long list of solutions prior to evaluating them, it counteracts over-focusing on solutions and premature evaluation. By focusing the group's attention on a well-defined pattern of thought about a common problem, it also helps avoid destructive redefinition.

Hall and Watson (1970) present another procedural format that works against the ill effects of trained incapacities. Rather than focusing on *what* the group talks about at particular stages of decision-making, they attempt to develop a set of ground rules for *how* members should work on a problem. Their *consensus-seeking rules* (p. 304) are designed to help groups work through differences and disagreements in a constructive fashion:

1. Avoid *arguing* for your own position. Present your position as clearly and logically as possible, but consider seriously the reactions of the group in any subsequent presentations of the same point.
2. Avoid *"win-lose"* stalemates in the discussion of positions. Discard the notion that someone must win and someone must lose in the discussion; when impasses occur, look for the next most acceptable alternative for both parties.
3. Avoid changing your mind *only* to avoid the conflict and to reach agreement. Withstand pressures to yield which have no objective or logically sound foundation. Strive for enlightened flexibility; avoid outright capitulation.
4. Avoid suppressing conflicts by resorting to voting, averaging, coin-flipping, and the like. Treat differences of opinion as indicative of an incomplete sharing of information and viewpoints and press for additional exploration and investigation.
5. View differences of opinion as both natural and helpful rather than as a hindrance in decision-making. Generally, the more ideas expressed the greater the likelihood of conflict will be, but the richer the array of resources will be as well.
6. View initial agreement as suspect. Explore the reasons underlying apparent agreements; make sure that people have arrived at similar solutions for either the same basic reaons or for complementary reasons before incorporating such solutions in the group decision.

These rules encourage members to air and work out differences rather than to come to agreement quickly. They counteract several problems of trained incapacities, including over-evaluation, premature convergence on a single solution (from goal-centeredness), and reliance on objective standards where none exist. Hall and Watson tested these procedures and found that groups trained in the rules produced better answers on a problem-solving task than did untrained groups. They attributed this to a "synergy bonus" from the procedure which allowed trained groups to make use of all their members' skills and knowledge. Untrained groups fell prey to difficulties which precluded effective involvement of all members.

Although these and other formats are invaluable in helping groups to avoid trained incapacities, it is important to remember that they can themselves become procedural incapacities. Neither format is appropriate under all conditions. For example, Reflective Thinking does not work well when members have fundamental disagreements over values, because it presumes agreement on criteria used to evaluate solutions. The consensus-seeking rules would not be appropriate for members with long-standing dislike of each other. In such cases sticking to either procedure would only compound the conflict; although protecting against some possible problems, they can unintentionally introduce others.

The effectiveness of procedural formulas is limited by the fact that they can only counteract those trained incapacities which are *explicitly* permitted in their rules.

Reflective Thinking, for example, does nothing to control overemphasis on objective criteria because its rules do not take this incapacity into account. A much more effective method is to give the group *critical tools for recognizing and surmounting trained incapacities, whatever their particular form might be.* Trained incapacities feed on the group's lack of self-awareness; critical methods that make members *conscious* of their own possibly narrow thinking offer a powerful means of controlling destructive habits.

In response to this need Volkema (1981; 1983) developed the *Problem-Purpose Expansion Technique,* a critical method to help members recognize and transcend their own narrow thinking. Volkema argues that the effectiveness of any conflict management strategy depends on how people *formulate* the problems they face. Problem formulation has at least two effects on conflicts. First, it channels members' thinking and can severely limit the range of solutions considered by the group. In the research and development case discussed in chapter 4 (Case 4.2) the problem was expressed as "selection of the best possible procedure for making decisions in the research meetings." This problem formulation constrained members to search for a *single* procedure to be used by *all* project teams, a problem that provoked the conflict. The formulation implicitly ruled out several solutions that would have allowed members to work on common grounds, such as adopting two procedures and testing each in half of the project teams or adopting several procedures and allowing the project directors to choose whichever they liked best. As we have seen, groups tend to converge on solutions prematurely, and an overly-narrow problem formulation encourages this. Second, problem formulations also influence conflicts by setting up the relationship between people when a conflict emerges. The research committee's problem formulation set up a win-lose situation once members became divided over the two candidate programs. Since only one program could be adopted given this approach, a win-lose fight became inevitable with the manager forcing an end to the conflict.

Volkema shows that problem formulations vary along a continuum from a very narrow scope to a very broad scope. For the research and development committee, the formulation "Selection of Tom's procedure for the project teams" would be the narrowest scope possible, because it focuses on a *single* solution and specifies *what* must be done in that solution, that is—selection. Problem formulations of a broader scope ask the question "What are we trying to accomplish by the narrower formulation?" So the formulation given in the previous paragraph "Selection of the best possible procedure for making decisions in the research meetings" is a bit broader than the first, because it encompasses what selection of Tom's procedure would accomplish. Notice also that the second formulation admits a greater number of possible solutions than the first, because it does not specify *which* procedure should be chosen and opens up a range of possibilities. The second formulation also focuses the group's attention on a different set of actions than does the first. If we take the first formulation, the group is likely to focus on how it can get project teams to like Tom's procedure; if we take the second, the group concentrates on searching for alternative procedures and choosing one. A still broader problem formulation than the second would be "selection of the best possible procedures which can be used by the teams." Broader still is "To make the best possible decisions in the project teams." Both of these formulations open up a wider range of possibilities and imply different actions than do the first two (indeed, the fourth opens up the possibility of chucking the procedures altogether).

Volkema argues that in every conflict some levels of formulation promote better and more acceptable solutions than others. Exactly which formulations are best varies depending on the group, the nature of the conflict, the group's environment, and other factors; at present we do not know enough to identify the best formulations. However, our discussion of trained incapacities suggests a way to identify which formulations are *not desirable,* namely, those that promote trained incapacities.

The trained incapacities at work in a group are usually evident in its problem formulations. When groups are goal-centered, they begin discussions of the problem by suggesting specific solutions. Goal-centeredness could lead a discussion of problems with an office record-keeping system to an early consideration of specific changes before all of the real difficulties with the system are identified. If discussion begins with the suggestion of specific solutions, problem formulation is likely to be excessively narrow and focused on only one aspect of the problem. If group members fall prey to the objectivity incapacity, they assume that there are objective or "correct" standards that the solution must meet, when, in fact, the problem requires a judgment call based on the values or preferences of the group. If the group operates under this misconception, the formulation of a problem can easily reflect the objective standards the group hopes will resolve the problem. For example, a group in conflict over whether to hire a male or a female for a position might phrase its problem as "to hire a person who can raise productivity by 10 percent in three years," in an attempt to get around the issue. When destructive redefinition is likely, the formulation will often be so narrow as to preclude a cooperative solution (as in the research and development committee) or phrased in either-or terms (such as "To decide whether a man or woman can best fill our needs"). Such formulations can undermine even the best procedures, because they can easily slip in undetected during a problem definition step.

Identification of problem formulations is a complex process. For one thing, problems are not always explicitly stated by a group. Sometimes, in fact, groups consciously *avoid* clear problem statements in an attempt to avoid bringing the conflict out. In these cases members must try to infer the group's definition of the problem from its discussions. Figuring out the definition is fairly easy once one is familiar with some examples of problem formulations: hypothetical examples can be compared to the group. An additional complication is introduced by the fact that problem formulations may change as the group works on an issue. In the research and development committee the problem was initially "selection of the best possible decision-making procedure for the project teams" but over time shifted to "should we adopt the manager's preference?" which implied confrontation. Clearly these shifts reflect significant occurrences in the conflict and changes in the relationship of members to one another. Indeed, several researchers have proposed that group work is nothing more than a series of redefinitions and reconceptualizations of problems leading gradually toward a narrow solution statement (Lyles & Mitroff, 1980; Poole, 1982). Members must be sensitive to these shifts and their implications for the direction the conflict takes.

Volkema has developed a method called *Problem-Purpose Expansion* to help groups generate a range of formulations. The method makes members aware of their assumptions and makes it possible to recognize trained incapacities by comparing different levels of problem formulations. The *Problem-Purpose Expansion Method* (PPE) has two basic parts. The first is a format for stating the problem.

The format is as follows: an infinitive + an object + a qualifier. For example, if the problem is presently thought to be how to convince the residents of a neighborhood that a sidewalk should be installed along their block, the problem might be stated as:

to convince	neighbors	that a sidewalk is needed
Infinitive	Object	Qualifier

This statement then becomes the focus of an initial brainstorm of solutions (see Figure 8).

The second part of PPE expands this problem by reformulating it so that a brainstorming of solutions can be repeated at another level. This is done by asking the following:

What are we trying to accomplish by this?
We want (Most recent formulation)
In order to (Reformulation)

The group might decide it wants to *convince neighbors that a sidewalk is needed* in order *to get neighbors to pay for sidewalk installation*. This reformulation becomes a second level and can be brainstormed. This process is then repeated to generate a whole set of formulations and solutions (see Figure 8). Comparison of the levels can enable the group to recognize where its thinking was narrow and what incapacities may be operating. By making the group aware of different formulations, PPE can disclose the values and assumptions hidden in the group's

---

Figure 8

A hierarchy of expanded problem statements

	Problem Statements	Possible Solutions
Increasing Problem Scope →	TO CONVINCE NEIGHBORS THAT A SIDEWALK IS NEEDED	Gather data; hold public hearings; go door-to-door
	TO GET NEIGHBORS TO PAY FOR SIDEWALK INSTALLATION	Go to the Transportation Department; sue neighbors; introduce a resolution at City Hall
	TO GET A SIDEWALK INSTALLED	Pay for sidewalk yourself; install sidewalk yourself
	TO MAKE THE AREA WHERE A SIDEWALK WOULD GO PASSABLE	Level off area; build boardwalk
	TO MAKE PEDESTRIAN TRAFFIC SAFE	Reroute auto traffic; partition off part of street; stop auto traffic for pedestrians; put up caution signs for autos

From Volkema (1982)

current way of looking at its problem and suggest innovative viewpoints that cut through existing tangles.

PPE can also be used when the problem in question is "about" the group itself rather than about something the group might do. For example, in the Riverdale Halfway House case (chapter 2) the problem was formulated as how "to resolve the animosities between George and Carole." PPE might lead to other formulations more conducive to constructive dialogue, such as how "to clarify lines of authority at Riverdale" or how "to create a more supportive climate at Riverdale." In both cases the broader reformulations change the focus of the problem from Carole and George to the group as a whole and provide a common problem the entire group can work on.

PPE moves the group out of its well-worn, unreflective channels and encourages it to consider new ideas. As we noted in chapter 2, a surprising or startling move can also do this. A former chair of the board of General Motors is reputed to have said during a particularly docile meeting, "Well, it appears as if we're all in agreement. Why don't we all try to work up some conflicts over the weekend so when we come back on Monday we'll be able to think this proposal through thoroughly?" The chair's statement was designed to surprise the other members and jolt them out of their premature convergence. Because it is surprising it is also likely to arouse members to shock, laughter, or incredulity; as a result of this increased energy, when members return to their task they most likely will do so with greater concentration and renewed vigor.

Finally, trained incapacities may be neutralized by reducing the tensions which sustain them. There are, in principle, three ways to reduce tension in conflicts. One method involves *removing the parties from the conflict situation,* in the hope that distance from the conflict will allow them to calm down and recompose themselves. The well-known tactics of a "cooling off period" and of "taking time out" are designed to facilitate this process. The second tack is the opposite of the first: *members are encouraged to vent their tensions* as a means of working through them. This approach is used in some training groups employed by consultants to build cohesive management teams. Obviously, it can easily run out of control, and must be handled very skillfully. The third approach involves reducing tension by *reassuring members that their tension is natural* and does not represent permanent problems or rifts in the group. In one group engaged in planning an educational conference, numerous conflicts arose over the format and scheduling of events. One member was instrumental in enabling the group to confront and work out its differences. She played a "parental" role, reminding other members that each was valuable in his or her own right and that she cared about everyone. This reassurance noticeably reduced tensions and enabled the group to confront and resolve issues it was reluctant to deal with.

WORKING WITH CLIMATE

Diagnosis of climates was considered at great length in chapter 3 (p. 101), so this section will advance three measures for *changing* climate to influence conflict interaction. Our earlier analysis of climate clearly implies the first principle: *small, cumulative changes in interaction can eventually result in major changes in climate.* For example, many members report that their first feeling of belonging to their group occurred when members began using "we" when talking about group activities. This subtle difference signals a change in identification from "individual" to "member"; it promotes a more relaxed climate in the group by indicating to members that others are well-disposed toward them and that there is a common ground for working together. In the psychological evaluation unit analyzed in chapter 3, Jerry maintained his dominant position and the group's authoritarian climate through a series of moves which enabled him to control the issues the group worked on. In the same way members could have changed the group's climate by being more assertive and making "bids" to have a say in controlling the group. Jerry might not have noticed these changes, but they will gradually alter the group's climate to encourage more equal participation by members.

A second tactic for working on climates is *to discuss openly themes which trouble members.* Much of the climate's influence on group interaction depends on members' inability to recognize it. If they can bring its effects out in the open and consciously move to counteract them, climate can be used to channel conflict interaction in constructive directions. Often this "consciousness raising" is done by one insightful member.

––––– **CASE 6.1** –––

In a small, twelve-person consulting agency, two important members, the program coordinator (Joe) and the publications manager (Jim) were having serious problems getting along together because an outside business they had been running for three years was failing. Joe and Jim decided not to bring up their problems in front of the group, because they believed it could only disrupt the operations of the ordinarily harmonious group. Their suppression of the problems certainly kept their antagonism from becoming an open issue in the group, but it did not prevent their tensions from influencing the group's climate. The agency's weekly meetings were marked by uncomfortable pauses and evasions of pressing issues. Relationships in the group became cautious and artificial; authority relations were also ambiguous because two central members, Joe and Jim, were reluctant to talk to each other and fought over small issues. Finally, at one tension-filled meeting another member, Karen, openly stated that she felt uncomfortable and that she wanted to talk about Joe and Jim's problems and its effect on the group. In the ensuing discussion many issues and feelings emerged. Members were relieved to talk openly, and both Jim and Joe were able to unburden themselves and get support from the group. The tension between Joe and Jim did not subside as a result of Karen's intervention (in fact, it continued until Joe left the agency), but the group's climate improved markedly and members were better able to cope with their co-workers' relationship problems.

There are also formal procedures for member evaluation of the group's climate and functioning (Auvine, Densmore, Extrom, Poole, & Shanklin, 1979). Self-evaluation questionnaires on which members rate their own and others' performance and weaknesses are often used (see Johnson & Johnson, 1975, for several good forms). The questionnaire provides a structured and legitimate way to raise criticisms of the group and open them up for discussion. This "survey-feedback" process can be used to set goals for changing the group's interaction and, ultimately, its climate.

A third tactic for altering a group's climate was mentioned in chapter 3—a member can create a *critical incident* that shifts the entire direction of the group's climate. Recall the example in chapter 1 of the faculty brown bag discussion where the student suddenly challenged the speaker: the climate shifted from congenial to tense. In the same vein, members can attempt to create critical incidents to alter unfavorable climates. Several considerations must be taken into account in order to do this effectively. For one thing, *timing* is critical. Members must be able to recognize propitious moments for acting on the group's climate. Bormann (1972) gives a good example of the importance of timing. In the groups he studied he found a certain point in discussion at which one member would venture a favorable comment or joke about the group. In cases where the other members responded with other favorable comments or followed up on the joke, the group generally developed an open, inclusive climate. When members let the favorable comment drop, the group usually took a much *longer* time to develop cohesion, if it did so at all. Timing is vital in these cases; if the critical moment passes it is gone and members may not get another chance.

Along with timing, *salience* is also important. The move must hold the group's attention if it is to be a watershed. The student's attack on the brown-bag lunch speaker captured the attention of other members; thereafter, they were reacting to the student's move, and their reactions reinforced the tension his statement originally interjected. There are many ways of enhancing the salience of a move—including raising the volume of one's voice, using colorful or symbolic language, being dramatic, or saying something surprising. Used properly, these tactics increase the probability that the move will prove effective. Finally, a member who aspires to create a critical incident should have *credibility and respect* in the eyes of other group members. The actions of a respected member are likely to receive attention from other members and therefore have a good chance to influence the group's interaction. In addition, making an effort to change the group's climate can be interpreted as manipulation; moves of a respected and trusted member are unlikely to be rejected as self-serving.

Of the three approaches, creating a critical incident is the most *uncertain.* It is hard to do, and it has the potential to backfire: other members may reject the person who attempts to maneuver the group. When effective, however, it brings results quickly and it can be initiated by a single member without having to rely on others. Small, cumulative changes and open discussion are more certain, but also have problems. Small changes operate piecemeal through day-to-day group interaction; therefore, it is easy to lapse back into old patterns. To use this technique successfully requires a clear sense of purpose and patience. It does not work quickly and is of limited utility in situations where climate is causing an immediate crisis in a group. Open discussion works much more quickly than cumulative change, but it may add fuel to a conflict by introducing a new issue: members satisfied with the present climate may side against those who are dissatisfied. The emotions associated with discussions of power relations or the group's supportiveness may generalize to the conflict and intensify disagreements on other issues. In using any of the approaches it is important to be aware of possible problems and take measures to circumvent them.

WORKING WITH POWER

There are a number of barriers to accurate diagnosis of the role of power in conflicts. For one thing, members are often unwilling to talk about power or to provide honest and accurate assessments of their own or others' power, for several reasons. Given our culture's emphasis on democracy and equality, the open use of power is not socially sanctioned. Members may be unwilling to admit that they use "force" or that their group is controlled by only a few members because they believe it makes them look bad. Further, since power depends on endorsement, powerful members often try to keep their power unobtrusive, in order not to alienate those they influence. If weaker members cannot see the member's power, or if they do not understand how it "works," they can do nothing to upset the present balance. In addition, as we noted in chapter 4, many moves (such as issue control) use power indirectly and it is hard to determine how power figures in or who is influencing the situation. Finally, power and endorsement processes depend on relationships *between* members rather than being properties of individuals, so it is often hard to grasp where the source of power is. If power stems from relationships it is often misleading to try to identify a particular person who holds power. The more important question may be who assents to the use of power or who withholds endorsement.

These barriers make the assessment of power a complex process for which there can be no set formula. It is best to look for several different types of indicators to determine which one works best in a given situation. One approach for assessing power is to *determine the possible power resources in the situation and identify who holds them*. This involves identifying both obvious resources like status, knowledge, personal attractiveness, or formal authority *and* more subtle sources of power, such as confidence or ability to predict the other's behavior (Frost & Wilmot, 1978). A second, complementary approach is to *identify power through its effects*. Those members whose *preferences consistently win out* and who are accommodated by other members are generally those who control influential resources and use them effectively. As Frost and Wilmot (p. 60) note, the *ability to label the conflict* is also a sign of power. If a conflict could be interpreted either as a minor difference of opinion or as a major matter of principle, and it ends up being interpreted as a minor difference, the members who favored this view are likely to hold the high ground. A third indicator of power is *conservatism*. If power is relational, then changes in existing relationships generally alter the balance of power, while stability preserves it. Members who are against change are likely to believe they will lose by it, and these are generally the members with power under the status quo.

None of these three indicators is foolproof and each can support mistaken assessments. However, as a set they provide a good starting point for thinking about power. Judgments about power ultimately rest on knowledge of the group or organization, its particular history, and the nuances that signal dominance and subordination. Diagnoses cannot be programmed and must be continually revised in light of ever changing relationships in the group.

In chapter 4 we illustrated how conflict interaction can head toward destructive escalation when members draw upon *unique* resources as a basis for influence. We also discussed several ways that a group can encourage its members to use resources that the group as a whole *shares* when any attempt at influence is made.

More specifically, we suggested that the group can try to develop consensus on what the major goals or objectives of the group are, work toward making power resources accessible to all members, and increase awareness that the members, as a community, are the source of power in the group. In one sense, these suggestions are preconditions; they are what must be in place in a group if the members can hope to develop shared power resources and use them as a basis for moves in any conflict interaction. In another sense, these suggestions offer long-term intervention strategies; they are areas that the group can work on in the long run and can establish as part of the general expectations for how the group operates. They can govern what members consider doing when they try to sway each other's thinking about any issue that is in front of the group.

What happens, however, when these preconditions have not been established in a group or they fall through when some particular conflict issue arises that is so important to some member that he or she draws upon resources as a basis for influence that the group as a whole does not share? Although no intervention is guaranteed of success in this situation, there are several approaches members can take to help prevent the possible escalation that can result from this type of move.

Members of the group may need to *anticipate and state* what the group's likely reaction to the member's use of unique resources may be. It may be wise for members to acknowledge explicitly, for example, that they are likely to have trouble seeing the member as someone who has the best interest of the group in mind if such an attempt is made. Or they can warn of possible escalation because they feel that the power move may lead other members to believe that they have no alternative but to use their own unique power resources to regain control. Although this approach is an attempt to encourage members to reflect on how moves are being made in the conflict rather than introducing structural changes in the way people are actually behaving, it can at least force the group to recognize that its interaction may be about to shift dramatically. It also points to the possible dangers or pitfalls that might result when the shift occurs.

A second approach is aimed at developing structural changes in interaction when power moves are based on uniquely held resources. Chapter 4 shows that one of the most effective tools for changing the influence of power in conflicts is to increase members' *awareness* of their own role in creating and sustaining power relations. If members become aware of how their endorsement is shaped by social categorization, the mystique of power, and their own interaction, they are well on their way to "seeing through" the existing power structure. Their understanding enables them to withdraw their support from unwarranted power and work to change the group's power structure. The value of "consciousness-raising" is illustrated by the support groups that spring up in professions which are undergoing rapid change and its accompanying struggles. These groups, which range from groups of female executives in male-dominated corporations to groups of nurses and medical orderlies attempting to gain more input into hospital decisions, give their members a chance to share problems and fears and give each other advice. Members help each other understand how the dominant groups maintain their positions, work out ways of being more effective, and build resolve and courage to face difficult situations. They encourage members to question what was previously unquestionable, the taken-for-granted relations of authority and obedience, strength and weakness in the group. Nor are formal support groups the only thing that can serve this function: a conversation over drinks after work can have the same effect and lead to important insights.

Just realizing they are not alone and comparing experiences is an important step for members who wish to change their group.

As Janeway (1980) observes, in addition to awareness, mutual support is another way for weaker members to counterbalance stronger ones. People generally associate coalitions with open shows of strength and solidarity against others, as in a union vote, but open shows may be ineffective in group and organizational contexts. By raising a flag of defiance, members may threaten the stronger members and cause them to overreact, sending the conflict into an escalating spiral. Those who have greater resources stand to lose if the current balance tips in a new direction, and they will fight against moves they perceive as harmful. A coalition is more likely to be successful in moving a conflict in a productive direction if it is unobtrusive. The pact between members should not be openly displayed, and, if possible, any coordination or support should not be obvious. In addition, a coalition is more likely to turn conflict in a productive direction if it aims for a balance of power with shared endorsement, than if it tries to win. If the powerful members' interests are not threatened, and if they do not face serious losses, they are more likely to cooperate with efforts to achieve a balance of power.

WORKING WITH FACE-SAVING ISSUES

The key to diagnosing face-saving issues successfully lies in members' ability to recognize two major symptoms in group interaction. First, when face-saving is a concern, *the interaction in the group becomes centered on a secondary issue, and this issue prevents members from addressing substantive decisions and agenda items.* The substantive problems the group must resolve are buried by statements and reactions that indicate members are resentful of each other, or are clouded by arguments that defend individuals' positions but do little to advance the group's understanding of the problem or decision it faces. Since the secondary, face-saving issues are related to the more substantive problems the group is addressing, they can consume a group's energy and predominate the interaction before the group realizes that a face-saving issue has diverted its attention. For example, members can defend alternative solutions to a problem in what appears to be a heated debate. But the members may do so only because they feel that if they back away from their positions, they will carry less weight in future discussions or decisions. In this case, the most pressing issue, the one that has greatest influence over the interaction is, "how will the group treat members who change their minds?" However, the content of the discussion remains focused on an agenda item in front of the group. If members fail to see that a secondary issue is driving the interaction, the face-saving concern can produce destructive escalation and threaten the working relationships in the group.

Second, as we noted in chapter 5, *face-saving issues turn members away from group-centered interaction and toward individually centered interaction.* This is an important symptom in diagnosing face-saving issues. When face-saving is an issue, the relationship between an individual member (or several members) to the group as a whole becomes salient and the interaction becomes focused on this relationship. The relationship issue (that is, how the group will view the member) is being raised even though the group may not make any explicit comments about the fact that it is being raised or about how it should be resolved. There may be, in other words, no explicit attempt to talk about what the relationship of the individual member to the group is or why it is in dispute even though the members are negotiating how someone will be seen.

A concern for the image of an individual in the group is not always problematic; it becomes problematic when it prevents members from pursuing a discussion of more critical issues or ignites those discussions into heated but pointless arguments. If there is a prolonged focus on the relationship of the individual to the group, issues can become easily personalized, members can become overly cautious about making any comments, or the group may make little progress on important issues despite heated discussion. Any of these symptoms suggest that some action must be taken to redirect interaction that has been triggered by face-saving concerns.

Establishing *climates that prevent face-saving concerns from emerging* is, perhaps, the most effective means for eliminating the potentially destructive influence of these issues. The climate established in the group plays a critical role in determining whether face-saving concerns will emerge and become problematic for the group. Members have shared expectations about whether it is safe to move away from a stated position, whether conflict issues can be raised without threatening the group, and whether a member's feelings of unjust treatment can be discussed openly. These expectations arise from events that have occurred in the group— from previous reactions that the group has had to members' comments and concerns, or assumptions people make about how the group would react, to concern about a member's image in the group. While establishing a "healthy" climate is something the group can work towards on an act-by-act basis, the difficult interventions are those that are needed when *a preventative climate has not been established or when some event in the group calls the climate into question* (when, for example, a member is unsure about whether he or she can step back from a position and still be seen as an important, contributing member).

Interventions that attempt to stop the destructive effects of face-saving issues must be built on a recognition that face-saving centers around the *negotiation* of a member's image in the eyes of the group. All three forms of face-saving we have discussed carry a "statement" about an image that the speaker does not want to have the group assign to him or her. Consider the following characterizations of these statements:

Resisting Unjust Intimidation: "Don't see me as someone who accepts unfair treatment or intimidation."

Stepping Back from a Position: "Don't see me as someone who is indecisive" (easily beat, weak, and so on).

Raising Unacknowledged Conflict Issues: "Don't see me as someone who is willing to *cause* problems by raising conflict issues."

Each of these statements makes an assumption or guess about the likely reactions of the group and each indicates that the member feels threatened by the image he or she assumes will be assigned by other group members. However, because each of these statements is founded on an assumption about how the group will react, these assumptions can either be confirmed or rejected by other group members. The interaction that occurs when face-saving is an issue is always a negotiation; it is an attempt to settle what image the speaker can assume the group will hold of him or her.

Interventions that treat *the face-saving issue as a negotiation process* may have the greatest chance for success. We see three steps that can be taken to help facilitate this process. First, the negotiations can occur with less chance of continued escalation *if defensiveness is reduced.* A person who is trying to save face is always under some perceived threat—the threat of having an undesirable image assigned to him or her by the group. Defensiveness is a likely reaction to perceived threat (Gibb, 1961). People feel they must be on guard because a mistaken move on their part can bring about some undesirable consequence. Research by Rapoport (1960) suggests that defensiveness can be reduced by having an opponent indicate an understanding of another's stand on an issue and recognizing some area of validity in the other's position. In the face-saving context, group members can show that they understand why someone feels unfairly treated or worried about appearing weak or indecisive. They can also recognize ways in which the belief may actually be legitimate. If the group has handled similar incidents poorly in the past, acknowledging that these incidents occurred can show a sympathetic understanding for the members' concern. Acknowledging another's position as legitimate and indicating an understanding of it does not ensure that the issue can be settled easily, but it does allow for the possibility of an open discussion as the negotiation unfolds.

Second, the negotiation of a face-saving concern can be facilitated *if the group opens the door for an exchange of concessions on the issue.* Pruitt (1971) has demonstrated the importance of letting both parties in a negotiation tell each other (either implicitly or explicitly) that an exchange of concessions is possible and safe. The parties need to know that there will be some reciprocity of moves if both sides begin making offers toward a settlement. Although face-saving issues are not the same as formal bargaining situations where offers can be made in increments, it is useful to think of the negotiation of a face-saving issue in the same general terms. Take as an example, the face-saving situation where someone is hesitant to step back from a position. The person who is concerned about losing face needs some assurance that moving away from a position is a safe move. A member who is afraid of losing face in the eyes of the group if they back away from a stand needs some assurance that shifting positions will not reduce their role or importance in the group. Comments or reactions that give a member a "way out" of these fears are likely to reduce the concern for face that may be keeping someone from moving from a position they, themselves, no longer want to defend. To encourage an exchange of concessions, there are several tacks members in the group can take: they can acknowledge the importance of the concerned member by requesting information from him or her about important issues that the group is addressing, they can stress the importance of the member in the group's current or future work, or they can actually increase the member's role in future projects. A supervisor in a large record-keeping office at a corporation recently dealt with a difficult face-saving issue by trying to reassure a concerned employee that it was safe to back away from a position.

_____ CASE 6.2 _____

An office worker was assigned the task of putting together an extensive report that described the productivity and performance of people in various divisions of a corporation. When the report was printed, a copy was sent to each division head for their inspection before the book was distributed generally in the corporation. One division head called the research office after reading the report and was irate about an error that he found in the description of his department. He saw the mistake as a significant problem that could cause considerable damage to his division's reputation and future development.

The complaint was discussed by several supervisors in the research office before it reached the person who had actually compiled the book. When this person was told about the error, she became very defensive and argued that the information that appeared in the book was accurate. It was clear to her supervisors that the information was in error and that the employee was trying to save face. The worker was defending her position, not because she firmly believed that it was correct, but because acknowledging that she had made a mistake could mean that she would be seen as incompetent.

The approach her immediate supervisor took in handling this situation was to point out to the employee that compiling the report was an immense and difficult task because the information had to be drawn from so many different sources and often had to be inferred from sketchy notes or letters that various people in the departments submitted to the records office. She congratulated the employee for putting together a catalogue that had ten thousand pieces of *correct* information. These comments allowed the woman to admit the error because it reduced the threat of being seen as incompetent and, more importantly, it allowed the two of them to begin discussing possible ways that the error could be handled so that the irate division head would be satisfied and accurate information would be disseminated about the unit.

Signalling that an exchange of "concessions" is possible is important in the other two face-saving situations we have discussed, although the way this signalling occurs would, of course, be different. The person who is trying to save face because he or she feels that they have been treated unfairly by the group is often preoccupied with making this point known. Letting others know that they feel they have been mistreated can take precedence over any desire to discuss whether or how the treatment occurred. As a result, other members in the group must provide some assurance that if the concerned person stops "saying" that he or she has been treated unfairly, the issue will not be lost or forgotten. There has to be assurance that the group is willing to discuss the matter in order for the person to concede that they have made their point known. This is often more difficult than it may appear at first glance. If a member feels they have been treated unfairly in the past, it may be difficult for that member to believe that the group actually wants to address the issue. But until this assurance is given, the face-saving issue may continue to escalate as the member criticizes the group without allowing for a productive discussion of the issue.

When someone raises a conflict issue in a group that typically avoids potentially devisive issues or believes that none occur, a concern for face can continue as the conflict is being addressed. The member can believe that they are being seen as someone who is the cause of the group's problems rather than someone who raises an issue that was already present and affecting the group's interaction. If this concern for face is not alleviated, the member who raises the issue may feel less a part of the group or could be hesitant to address the conflict openly during differentiation. At least *one* other member in the group must step forward and say that they believe it is important that the issue be addressed. If such a signal is not sent, the person who is concerned about his or her image in the group has no assurance that the group does not still hold him or her responsible for the conflict. The group has to offer some signal that it is beginning to *own* the conflict.

If defensiveness cannot be reduced, or if the group cannot facilitate negotiation through an exchange of concessions, there is a third step that can be taken to help stop the possible destructive effects of face-saving interaction. One or more members can *stress the consequences of not settling the issue that is in front of the group.* This strategy is frequently offered as a way to increase tension or sharpen a conflict so that members will become more motivated to deal with the issue (Walton, 1969). When face-saving is an issue, increasing tension by pointing to the consequences of an unresolved conflict can encourage the member who is concerned about face to care more about the substantive issue that is in front of the group than the potential threat to his or her image. It can, in other words, help direct the interaction away from an individual focus and toward a group focus.

RELATIONS AMONG THE FORCES

It should be clear that the forces are often interrelated and that work on one can be counteracted by the effect of others. Climate pervades everything that happens in the group, so an unfavorable climate can undermine work in other forces. A competitive group with great differences in members' influence and little supportiveness will have great difficulty avoiding destructive redefinition and problems related to face-saving. At the same time, forces that shape immediate interaction can prohibit changes in climate, because climates depend on interaction. The use of unique sources of power may reinforce an authoritarian and suspicious climate, despite the best efforts of members to relax the climate. Premature evaluation may anger members and introduce a competitive atmosphere as well as face-saving concerns. In the same way all four forces may intersect and reinforce one another under certain circumstances. It is important to take this possibility into account when attempting to turn conflict in productive directions.

THIRD PARTY INTERVENTIONS

Third party interventions have a very different quality from members' own attempts to work with conflicts. Even when a third party takes exactly the same measures members could take for themselves, the third party's actions are often much more effective by virtue of his or her special position. Third parties can have special legitimacy and credibility in the eyes of the group, because the group has requested that they come in. In addition, third parties often have special knowledge or skills—for example, training in conflict management techniques, managerial experience, or a background in mediation—which further enhances the group's respect for them. As an outside observer the third party is free from the problems and traditions group members are steeped in; therefore the third party often has a clearer view and can bring fresh ideas. The third party is also (at least initially) in a position of neutrality. He or she is outside the group and, hence, in an excellent position to maintain an even hand with all parties to the conflict. If the third party can maintain neutrality, his or her actions and recommendations are much more likely to be adopted by the group: they will not be seen as self-serving or manipulative, or as favoring any side unjustly. That the group calls in an outside party at all is a sign of its recognition of a need for change, and this may be the third party's greatest asset. If he or she can capitalize on this tension for change, the group can often be mobilized to reorganize itself and take a wholly new approach to dealing with conflict.

This description of the third party is obviously the ideal case, "the best of all possible worlds." In practice, third parties are not always invited by the entire group, and some members may actively resent the intrusion of outsiders, however knowledgeable. These members would not recognize the legitimacy, neutrality, or insightfulness of the third party; at best they might see the third party as a meddler who can only confuse things, and at worst as an ally brought in to help the member who introduced them. Sometimes, too, it happens that a third party makes a move that undermines the group's belief in his or her legitimacy, expertise, and neutrality. What started as a hopeful intervention can very easily turn into a nightmare of recrimination and distrust. Both cases illustrate the work that a third party must do to maintain a viable role in the group. Although third parties can capitalize on the reputation implied by the ideal third party, they must make this ideal happen in their own particular situation. Most third parties devote at least as much effort to maintaining their credibility, legitimacy, neutrality, and expertise in the eyes of the group as they do to actually working with the group's problems. Success in establishing a relationship with the group is inextricably bound up with success in helping the group work through problems. For this reason we will concentrate on establishing the third party role as well as on what third parties actually do to help a group.

GENERAL APPROACH

When planning and carrying out an intervention, effective third parties usually have in mind a definite ideal for how the group should work through its conflicts and what the third party's role in this process should be. This ideal is a working "theory" of how conflict should be managed and of what role a third party should adopt to best facilitate conflict management. The latter part of this theory, the third party's preferred role, is of particular importance, because it dictates certain basic choices that shape the intervention as a whole.

Roles. The first choice pertains to the third party's authority, that is, the amount of control the third party has over how the conflict is resolved (Fisher, 1972). At one end of the spectrum lies the *arbitrator* role, in which the third party is given authority to hear both sides of the case, discuss it with each, and then make a final, binding decision on how the dispute will be settled, much like the judge in a legal case. An arbitrator often has special background knowledge which enables him or her to grapple with the specific issues underlying the conflict. For example, arbitrators are often used for highly technical disputes such as labor contracts, which require knowledge of both economics and labor law. Arbitrators can also be used for "hopeless" cases, where a decision must be made, but agreement is impossible. Arbitrators have been employed to decide grievances over job assignments in school systems where teachers and administrators disagree over fairness.

Less authoritative than the arbitrator is the *mediator* role, where the third party is still assumed to have special knowledge about the issue at hand, but the final decision as to how the conflict is to be resolved still rests with the parties themselves. Mediators have been used extensively to attempt to resolve environmental disputes (Wehr, 1979; Goldmann, 1980). In such disputes there are a number of parties involved—the government, citizens, industry—and the object is to help them negotiate an acceptable resolution; the *process* of reaching a settlement is essential to winning the parties' commitment for the solution. In this case, having a third party empowered to actually make decisions would be positively harmful, because it would encourage the parties to avoid responsibility for a solution and hand it to the third party. A mediator, who is accorded respect by virtue of his or her knowledge and formal position, helps and encourages the parties to negotiate, yet does not give them the out of resorting to an outsider.

The least authoritative role is that of *facilitator,* who is a "process" expert, but has neither extensive expertise related to the issues under discussion nor the power to make a final decision (Auvine et al., 1977). A facilitator is brought in when the group believes it can reach a resolution of the conflict through direct negotiations, but needs help managing the negotiation process. The facilitator is a resource person, but does not act as the "center" of group interaction. Instead, the facilitator helps the group members work more effectively with each other. The impetus for proposals and compromise arises from the members themselves, and the facilitator merely guides it. The third party called into the Riverdale Halfway House (see chapter 3) was a facilitator. He chaired several meetings at which members tried to talk out their problems and offered assistance in clarifying needs and proposals, but did not try to direct the discussion in any forceful or intrusive way.

Which of the three modes of intervention is chosen depends on negotiations between the third party and group members. Each method can be effective, if used in the right situation, and the group's attitude and expectations are important in determining third party effectiveness. For this reason it is important that group members and the third party explicitly negotiate a *mandate* for the intervention. A mandate sets out what the third party's role and powers are to be; it sets a limit on what the third party can do (Delbecq Van de Ven, & Gustafsen, 1975; Auvine et al., 1977). Perhaps most important, it clarifies the group's expectations about the third party. A clear mandate enhances the group's understanding of the invention and legitimates third party moves by giving them the stamp of group approval. With a mandate members are less likely to expect miracles from the third party and more likely to explicitly express their desires.

There is a second basic choice, in addition to determining the third party's formal role. Third parties must also decide on their level of emotional involvement with the group. Some intervenors prefer to keep their distance on the assumption that they can retain some degree of insight and insure their own neutrality if they do so. Becoming emotionally involved with the group may cloud the third party's judgment and introduce biases, because it is very difficult to be equally close to all members. Other third parties attempt to forge a close relationship with the group. They reason that an emotional bond enhances the group's trust in them and encourages members to confide problems they might hide from a more formal outsider. They doubt whether a third party can really understand a group's problems unless he or she can identify with the group. There are clear advantages to both views; the choice is a matter of what style the third party is most comfortable with. However, although emotional involvement is primarily decided by the third party, the group can play a role, as well: members may prefer one style over another. We have seen several interventions fail due to rejection of third parties by members dissatisfied with their "coldness" *or* their over-involvement.

Process.   As we noted at the beginning of this section, the third party's "ideal" refers not only to his or her role in the group, but also to how the group should manage its conflict. Third-party views on this issue are quite diverse, but the points raised by this book suggest some criteria for effective conflict management processes. Regardless of its particular details, an "ideal" conflict management process would do the following:

1. Facilitate the differentiation of positions in the conflict and establish the legitimacy of these positions and the needs they represent for all members.
2. Provide a structure for moving from differentiation to integration that promotes creative generation of solutions and acceptance of these solutions by the members.
3. Neutralize or eliminate climatic elements which are worsening the conflict.
4. Move the group toward a shared power base (or, at least, balance power among members).
5. Prevent face-saving issues from producing inflexibility and adding secondary issues to the conflict.
6. Promote an attitude of self-reflection among group members so that they can recognize their own contribution to the conflict cycle and curtail counterproductive behavior.

The principles of self-regulation discussed in the previous section are designed to promote these criteria and can, of course, be implemented by a third party as well as by members themselves. In a later section we will consider a number of additional measures that third parties can take to facilitate conflict management.

It should be evident that a wide range of interventions could produce the conditions just outlined. There is no magic formula for conflict management. All that is necessary is that the third party mold or adapt his or her theory of intervention to the needs and expectations of the group. This adaptation is harder than it sounds, however, because any theory is also a potential trained incapacity; it may keep third parties from recognizing important problems and lead them to believe certain measures are appropriate for the group when, in fact, they are not. In order to adapt effectively third parties must do two things: they must gain an understanding of the group's problems and needs and their own reactions to the group without being blinded by their ideals; and they must draw from the repertoire of third party moves those necessary to move the conflict in a productive direction. If the third parties can accomplish this in a way that maintains their legitimacy, credibility, and neutrality, the intervention is likely to be effective.

DIAGNOSIS

How can third parties construct an understanding of what is happening in a conflict? What methods can they use to find out about the nature of the conflict, and what are the relative advantages and shortcomings of these methods?

At the most basic level, third parties use their background knowledge about how groups in general, and this group in particular, usually operate to figure out what might be wrong. The third party relies on his or her intuition, or at least the ability to empathize with the group. The danger here, of course, is that the third party may be mistaken in his or her analysis of the group. Observers often presume they have an omniscient view of things. They assume they can objectively identify the meanings of interaction and the problems the group faces. However, this assumption is not always true; observers are quite often mistaken in their diagnoses and, if they press their case too strongly, can anger and alienate those they are attempting to help. In one day-care center with a serious internal conflict, members rejected a third party who misdiagnosed the situation. The third party observed two staff meetings and decided that the center's manager was too authoritarian (the third party was very committed to worker participation and therefore may have been predisposed to fasten on to this particular diagnosis). Having confided this observation to several group members, the third party suggested participative leadership training for the manager. Members believed this measure might be helpful, but also felt it did not strike at the heart of the problem, which they saw as the high stress from responsibility over so many young children. Notwithstanding members' objections, the third party continued to put pressure on the manager to change her style. After one lengthy discussion several members came to the manager's defense; the third party was eventually attacked by several members for "browbeating" the manager. Soon after, the group terminated its contract with the third party. Third parties must be careful not to let a pet theory distort their view of the conflict. Every conflict is distinctive, and understanding it requires continual investigation and questioning of one's conclusions and theories. It is dangerous for a third party to *assume* he or she automatically understands.

Accurate observational techniques can eliminate many problems of understanding. Observers who take notes and attempt to reconstruct the meeting in as much detail as possible immediately after it is over often have a better grasp of the conflict than those who simply "wing it" and assume they can assimilate what is happening intuitively. Often a second observer can be brought in to cross-check accounts and diagnoses. Particularly helpful are informational interviews, in which the third party asks members for their interpretations of the meeting and compares perceptions, checking for member reactions to his or her observations. Any source of information for verifying the third party's interpretations can be an invaluable aid to understanding.

Third parties can also try small "experiments" to ascertain the group's feelings and positions. In the midst of a particularly sharp argument, one third party asked the two sides to stop and state how they were feeling. To their surprise, both said they were unhappy about fighting, but believed the other was attacking them. This "experiment" showed the third party that much of the conflict was based in defensiveness and that members could be encouraged to talk about it; it also gave the members important insights into their own relationship. The advantage of this method—in which the intervenor asks "What would happen if I . . .?"—lies in its bringing out overt responses from members. It may give the third party information that the members themselves would not readily give if simply asked. The disadvantages lie in the potential for abuse and manipulation this technique offers.

It is quite easy for third parties to place too much confidence in their own insight and presume they can try experiments without hurting members, when in fact they may be seriously injuring the group's trust and respect for them.

EXAMPLES OF THIRD PARTY ADAPTATION

To illustrate these points we will consider several cases where third parties selected strategies for intervention.

_____ **CASE 6.3** _____

The first concerns a third party called in to mediate a conflict between two managers of a food distribution company. The conflict began as a quarrel over book-keeping procedures and soon developed into a fight over lines of authority. In the midst of a stalemate where neither manager would talk to the other, the other managers decided to call in a third party. The third party, Richard, was a distinguished-looking man in his late forties. He held a Ph.D. in economics, had written several books, and had a local reputation as a knowledgeable and impartial mediator. Richard first interviewed each party separately; in these interviews he discovered that the roots of the conflict lay in one manager's emotional needs. The more blustery combatant, Thad, had a great need for warmth and support from his coworkers, a need he traced all the way back to bad experiences with his family and his first wife. Thad was not getting the support he needed and believed the others were purposely freezing him out (although Richard found no evidence that this was being done). Thad's anger was channeled toward Marlena, the second party. The jurisdictional dispute had rapidly escalated into a bitter, brutal fight which fed on itself. Thad and Marlena could not even work in the same room without harassing each other.

In determining his strategy, Richard took the following facts into account: (1) A serious emotional problem, which might take years to untangle, underlay the conflict. Other members probably were not aware of this problem, and it was uncertain whether they would be sympathetic or not. (2) The conflict was long-standing and sides were very clearly drawn. Parties were going to have a difficult time moving from their entrenched positions. (3) The conflict was very damaging for the company. It had been going on for four months and was beginning to hurt the business financially. Something definite had to be done. (4) The managers of the company were all young; they tended to look to Richard for help and accorded him considerable respect.

These considerations led Richard to adopt what he termed a "paternalistic style." He took on a role very close to that of arbiter and in a caring, yet somewhat domineering way, told the managers what they should do. He took the other managers aside and told them, "Thad is in pain; he needs support." They tended to scoff at this initially, but Richard did notice that they were more supportive in later meetings. Richard also wrote a formal report with definite recommendations and urged the company to adopt the recommendations and enforce them "from the top down." By taking this tack, Richard hoped to break the conflict by catching the participants "off balance" and push them to change before they could draw back into their well-worn positions. Quick action would mean a quick remedy for the company's problems. The paternalistic approach also protected Richard's position as a third party. This conflict was highly charged, and anger or frustration could easily be turned on the third party; the paternal role is characteristically slightly distant and kept Richard one step removed from the "action" of the conflict.

_____ CASE 6.4 _____

In another intervention, two private consultants, Louis and Sue, were called in by a radio station with administrative problems. Lines of authority among the programming, advertising, and engineering departments were not clear. As a result, conflicts often arose over the scheduling of radio programs, the development of new programming, the scheduling of commercials, and the purchase of air time. Workers at the station concluded that a reorganization was needed to clarify what departments were responsible for decisions and to establish procedures for making decisions in an orderly fashion. One of the managers in the advertising department knew Louis and Sue and obtained permission to invite them to a meeting.

Through observation of the meeting and interviews with several members, Louis and Sue discovered that the station was operating effectively and was in no immediate financial trouble. Workers felt a strong need to do something about their problems, because the constant friction over decisions was beginning to create more personal animosities among members. Their decision to act had been crystallized by a shouting match between the director of advertising and two disc jockeys. This incident had disturbed several workers, and they brought the problem out during a station-wide staff meeting; after kicking it around for a while, the staff had then decided to try a reorganization. The staff held a goal-setting meeting in which workers raised problems and then drew up a list of possible changes. Because the changes were rather complex and members were not sure they could manage the change process themselves, they called in the third parties.

Faced with this situation, Louis and Sue decided to adopt a facilitative style. The group obviously recognized a need for change and had a sense of direction. Members were able to talk out their differences and saw the importance of good relationships for effective work. Even during tense discussions workers attempted to offer emotional support to each other. It was clear that the staff had the skills and sensitivity needed for constructive work and that the third party's role was to help the staff channel its own efforts and initiatives. Moreover, there was ample time for the staff to work through the conflict at its own pace. The station was in no immediate danger; a relatively slow, measured process of discussion and consensus-building was feasible. The third parties recognized the value of facilitating the group's efforts to develop its own unique solution "from the inside" because it would greatly increase members' commitment to the reorganization plan.

The facilitative style also carried three additional advantages. As facilitators, Louis and Sue took a neutral stand toward any particular proposal for restructuring; they managed the negotiations and let the members work out proposals on their own. This enabled them to avoid being perceived as favoring the member who invited them in; as "process managers" they were able to distance themselves from partisan proposals and help the workers come to mutually acceptable conclusions. Louis and Sue also found facilitation a more comfortable style than those requiring a higher degree of control, such as arbitration. Both Sue and Louis believed strongly in participatory management. As facilitators, they were in a position to maximize member participation. Because the facilitative style was consistent with their values, Sue and Louis were able to fit into the restructuring process in a way that felt natural and appropriate to them. This allowed them to relax, and they believe it contributed greatly to the ultimate effectiveness of the intervention.

Finally, the facilitative role was more in line with the staff's expectations than a more authoritative style would have been. The staff had actively worked with its problems and had considerable knowledge about communication and group process. Members had a definite idea of the part they wanted the third party to play: they wanted someone to guide their decision-making processes, but they wanted control over the form and content of the solutions. An outsider—even an expert—who tried to take over the restructuring process would likely have been perceived as overly controlling and condescending and would have been set up for rejection. By adopting a facilitative style, Louis and Sue achieved legitimacy almost immediately, because they filled the staff's needs. Moreover, having demonstrated they were in tune with the staff, the third parties were later able to criticize the group's ideas without creating resentment. They took advantage of what Hollander and Julian (1969) have termed the "idiosyncrasy credit," where by conforming in their early relations with the group, members establish "credits" that excuse later disagreements of deviations from group norms.

These cases illustrate several factors that determine the style a third party should adopt during an intervention. Research on third party interventions and leadership (Tannenbaum & Schmidt, 1973; Walton, 1969; Pruitt & Johnson, 1970; Kerr, Schriesheim, Murphy, & Stogdill, 1974; Stogdill, 1974; Bartunek, Benton, & Keys, 1975; Morley & Stephenson, 1977; Frost & Wilmot, 1978), as well as our own research, suggests the following guidelines:

1. If there is little time to resolve the conflict and if a quick solution is required for survival of the group or organization, a highly authoritative style will be more effective than a less authoritative style.
2. If there is a long-standing conflict in which opposing positions have been clearly and definitely drawn, and the two sides express little hope in their ability to work out a solution, a highly authoritative style is more likely to be effective than a less authoritative one.
3. If the conflict is sharp and bitter, with highly charged emotions, a highly authoritative style will be more effective in getting parties to cease hostilities than will a less authoritative style (Walton, 1969). (Once parties have "cooled down," less authoritative styles may be effective.)
4. The greater the third party's credibility, legitimacy, and respect in the eyes of members, the more successful the third party will be in his or her attempts to adopt a highly authoritative style.
5. If the group members have the bargaining and communication skills necessary to work out a solution, a less authoritative style will be more effective than a more authoritative style.
6. The group's expectations are the most important determinant of the appropriate style. A style that matches the group's expectations of how a third party should act is most likely to be effective, at least in the early stages of the third party intervention (Stogdill, 1974). Once the third party has shown the group he or she can meet its expectations, deviations from these expectations are more likely to be effective (Hollander & Julian, 1969).

A longer list would be helpful, but these propositions are the only ones we can be confident of, given the existing research base. Despite its critical importance, the third party role has received very little attention from social scientists.

SHARPENING CONFLICTS

Regardless of the role and style that a third party adopts, an intervenor's most important and difficult task is to "sharpen" the conflict for the group. A sharpened conflict is one that results from a successful differentiation phase; when a conflict is sharpened, members have an accurate (an often painful) understanding of the issues, they see the consequences of not resolving the problem, and they have some understanding of what a solution must do in order to reach the needs of all involved. The success or failure of an intervention ultimately rests on whether the third party can guide the members through a differentiation phase without letting previous interaction patterns move them toward stalemates or escalation that prevents the group from successfully dealing with the issue on its own.

A third party can control how the group interacts as it makes an attempt to resolve a troublesome issue. In effect, the intervenor has been given the right to say to the group "Let's go through it again, this way . . ." The third party attempts to structure interaction in differentiation so that a clear definition of the problem can emerge without locking parties into solutions that have stifled creative thinking, produced inflexibility, or promoted escalation. Although the specific techniques that a third party employs to achieve this general goal must be guided by the specific conflict and group he or she is working with, we see four intervention objectives that underlie a third party's ability to successfully sharpen a conflict:

Unearthing the historical roots of the problem. By the time a third party is called in to help members work through a conflict, the parties may easily have lost sight of important facts or events that played a significant role in shaping the problem. As the parties argue for solutions that they want adopted and "fight things out" at this level, some of the dimensions of the problem itself can be lost. Having the group walk through the conflict again chronologically may seem pointless to the members at first but often provides important breakthroughs; it encourages the group to write a more careful definition of its own problem.

Providing a safe climate. As we have seen in chapter 3, conflicts may not be well defined because members feel it is not safe to state their positions or express their emotions. The belief may be that if honest statements are made, "things will get out of hand" or personal animosities will develop that may be irreconcilable. How can a third party provide a safe climate so that conflicts can be sharpened? In part, the mere presence of a third party can change conditions considerably in the group. When a third party arrives, there is a sense that the group needs to "perform well" for the intervenor, to look good or earnest in his or her eyes. Although this performance may seem inauthentic at first glance (and can fade fast once the group starts interacting), it often encourages people to be more careful about their word choice and style of presentation. People may be more descriptive than evaluative and less likely to blame others as they define the issue. The group begins to recognize that more care is being taken in how people are stating their positions and making evaluations to each other. This becomes a sign that people are trying to work on the problem without escalating the interaction. Even though people may suspect that this care is being taken because the third party is present, it can still allow for a greater clarification of issues than has ever been achieved previously.

A third party can also intervene to help ensure that interaction proceeds in a safe climate. The third party can set time limits on how long people can talk, arrange agendas so that more explosive issues are surrounded by innocuous or mundane topics, choose a place for a meeting where threatening behavior is less likely because it seems inappropriate (such as a church or library) or talk to members individually beforehand so that people who need to release potentially destructive emotions or save face can do so before work on the problem begins in the group.

Encouraging a statement of needs rather than a fight over solutions. Successful differentiation depends on a clarification of members' needs. Any solution that a member advocates is seen by that person as a solution because it meets some set of *needs* they have. A problem exists in a group not because people are pressing for different solutions but because none of the solutions that are being considered or advocated meet all people's needs. Conflicts, in other words, lie in the apparent inability of the group to meet diverse needs of its members on some issue. The continual fight over solutions is a symptom that all members' needs will not be met if any of the solutions being considered is adopted.

Third parties can take an active role in having members confront the incompatibility of needs that defines the problem they face. This often requires that the intervenor a) force members to clarify what their needs are, b) discourage individuals from seeing each other as the cause of the problem, and c) prevent people from suggesting solutions before all members' needs are clarified. The process of clarifying needs in a conflict can be straightforward and explicit. The third party can turn to each member and ask "What needs of yours must any solution fulfill?" or "You have suggested that the group do X. Why do you want to see this solution adopted? What needs of yours would it meet?" It is often beneficial to put people's "need" statements on paper or a blackboard in front of the whole group. This method can allow for greater depersonalization of the conflict because specific needs become less associated with the members who stated them. People can begin to "see," almost in a literal sense, that the problem they need to address lies above the needs of any one individual and rests in the incompatibility of positions across the group. There is a problem "out there" that the group as a whole can attack.

Cutting through multiple issues. For the differentiation phase of conflict to be successful, issues must be clarified. Often parties are unable to work through their own conflicts because the issues seem overwhelmingly complex. There may be multiple layers of problems that never get discussed separately or issues may appear confused or ambiguous because people's aggression is displaced: frustrations and anxiety from other unaddressed problems drive the interaction. A third party is sometimes in a better position to see the multiple layers of problems than the parties themselves. An outsider can break the problem down into smaller, more manageable parts and separate areas that the group already agrees on from areas that still remain unsettled (Guetzkow & Gyr, 1954; Avery et al., 1981). To cut through multiple issues, the third party must watch for cues indicating that aggression or frustration is displaced. Heated discussions that seem to get nowhere or comments that imply a relational or face-saving problem (such as, "I'm sorry I can't answer that question because I feel like you're talking to me like a three-year-old") are cues that aggression is displaced. The third party can talk to people individually to see if there are problems that have not been raised but are influencing the interaction. If these problems are critical to a successful resolution of the conflict, the third party can raise these issues and explain why the members themselves were hesitant to address them. Through a careful introduction of the problem, the discussions can start under a more cautious light. The third party can place constraints on the interaction to help control issues that may be extremely volatile or allow people to vent frustrations and emotions before the group as a whole addresses the issue.

INDUCING INTEGRATION

When a conflict is sharpened successfully, the group has moved through a productive differentiation phase. The members have a clear understanding of the differences among them, the needs of each member, and the likely consequences of not finding a solution. Moving the group from this phase to integration and the acceptance of a solution that meets all members' needs is often a difficult task for a third party. We will consider three methods third parties can employ to induce integration: suggesting common goals, defining the integration process, and inducing cooperation.

Suggesting common goals. In many conflict situations, there is often more agreement than members realize. People become heavily focused on points of disagreement and lose sight of the commonality that exists among them. A third party can stay attuned to the points of agreement that have been reached and remind members of these points at crucial times during the interaction (Avery et al., 1981). Groups often share a common goal but differ over the means to achieve this goal. If the third party focuses attention and discussion on the shared goals when conflicts become escalated, the tension of the moment can be relieved and members may reexamine their commitments to specific solutions. Comments that point to shared goals allow the group to see its own strength and can offer significant encouragement to members who may feel discouraged, exhausted, or frustrated.

Defining the integrative process. In suggesting common goals the third party attempts to integrate the two sides around a shared issue. The second approach assumes that the parties must define issues and move toward integrative solutions themselves, but attempts to control the *process* by which they do so. In essence the third party sets up an agenda for the areas the two parties will discuss and ground rules for how they will discuss each area. By controlling the process, the third party tries to get the two sides to talk without letting the conflict escalate or de-escalate.

There are a number of procedures for integrative conflict management. Probably the best known is Filley's (1975) Integrative Decision Making (IDM) technique. This technique is premised on several assumptions. First, it assumes people must untangle the substantive and emotional issues surrounding the conflict before they can develop a solution. Second, it assumes that people must have certain attitudes in order to successfully manage conflicts—including a belief in the possibility of a mutually acceptable solution, a belief that the other's position is legitimate (if not acceptable), trust of the other, and a commitment to work for an integrative outcome. Finally, in line with our earlier discussions, the IDM model assumes that problem definition should be separated from solution generation. Based on these assumptions Filley (1975, pp. 92–106) outlines a six-step technique for finding integrative solutions:

1. *Review and adjustment of relational conditions.* In this step conditions conducive to a cooperative climate are set up. These conditions are discussed in chapters 1 and 2 and in the section on climate earlier in this chapter.
2. *Review and adjustment of perceptions.* Here the members use procedures outlined by Filley to clarify the factual basis of the conflict to establish the beliefs held by each member.
3. *Review and adjustment of attitudes.* Members clarify their feelings and attitudes. Here parties state and clarify emotional issues in the conflict and how they feel about each other.
4. *Problem definition.* The mutual determination of the depersonalized problem. Techniques discussed earlier in this chapter, such as Volkema's Problem Purpose Expansion, could be employed at this point.
5. *Search for solution.* The nonjudgmental generation of possible solutions to the problem.
6. *Consensus decision.* The evaluation of alternative solutions and the agreement on a single solution.

The first four steps of IDM are designed to untangle conflict issues. Attitudes consistent with IDM are fostered throughout, but especially by steps 1–3. Finally, problem definition is separated from solution generation in steps 4–6, which are modelled on the Reflective Thinking Process discussed earlier in this chapter (indeed, Reflective Thinking may be substituted for steps 4–6 to give more thorough coverage). Specific recommendations for carrying out the six steps are discussed at length by Filley. We refer the reader to his excellent account for more details.

Third parties impose ground rules like the IDM method in order to regulate interaction between the parties. Such regulation is useful for several reasons. First, it makes them discuss areas that must be clarified to attain an integrative solution. Often parties are simply unaware of what things have to be worked out to resolve a conflict; this agenda lets them know what they have to cover. Second, it constrains them to limited areas of discussion at any one time. This eliminates chaotic, "kitchen-sink" fights where both sides toss in any comments or issues they think are to their advantage. Finally, ground rules offer tangible evidence of the third party's activity and willingness to intervene in the conflict. This can reassure the parties that they are not at each others' mercy and that there is an impartial mediator to regulate the interaction.

Inducing cooperation.   In the third approach the third party enlists one side as an ally in moves designed to get both sides to cooperate. A lack of trust and willingness to cooperate often prevents people from endorsing some solution that "on paper" seems to meet everyone's needs. Solutions may not be endorsed because they do not trust that everyone will carry through on the commitments the solution requires. There is no assurance, in other words, that people are willing to cooperate even if they give their assent to some proposed solution or agreement. This lack of trust can easily prevent groups from moving past differentiation and towards integration; moreover, it often is a catalyst for competitive escalation.

Osgood (1959, 1962, 1966) studied the problem of continued escalation in conflicts and developed a plan (the *GRIT* proposal—graduated and reciprocated initiatives in tension reduction) that is intended to induce mutual cooperation and establish trust. Although the plan was written as a proposal for de-escalating the international arms race, the procedure has been applied in less global conflicts and Lindskold (1978) has recently summarized the game theory research that supports the effectiveness of the main suggestions in the GRIT proposal.

GRIT is a series of steps that one member can take when the group in conflict is "locked in a bond of mutual distrust" and "any innocent-seeming action is perceived as manipulative and threatening" (Lindskold, 1978, p. 777). In this type of climate, the GRIT proposal asks that one participant begin making concessions without demanding any reciprocal moves from others. The theory behind GRIT is that once a member makes a concession and demands no immediate reciprocal response, trust can begin to develop. When one carries through on a promised concession, the sincerity of the offer has been demonstrated and a climate has been established for reciprocal moves. If it is in the best interest of the opposing member to de-escalate as well, the door is open for a conciliatory response and the reversal of a threatening cycle of mistrust and competition.

The person who wants to initiate a cycle of de-escalation follows these beginning steps in the GRIT proposal:

1. Make a sincere, public statement that he or she wants to reduce tension and turn the conflict around.
2. Clarify what conciliatory gesture they will make. Specifics must be given about what, when, and how the action will be taken.
3. Carry out the concession as stated.
4. Invite others to reciprocate but do not demand that such a response is necessary for the promised concession to be carried out.
5. Concessions must be made over a period of time, even though there is no reciprocation. The GRIT proposal notes that the concessions made should not put the person in an extremely vulnerable or indefensible position.

In the case of a clearly competitive standoff, a third party could talk to the individuals independently and suggest that they try to follow such steps in an effort to reestablish trust. Knowledge of the beginning steps in the GRIT proposal may be most useful to a third party, however, in cases where one of the conflicting members wants to initiate concessions, but is afraid to do so or is not being clear about their willingness to make concessions without a promise of reciprocity. In this instance, the third party can make sure that others recognize that a promise of concessions is being made, and that the concession is not linked to a demand for similar moves by others. The third party can also remind others when the promised concessions have been carried out and thereby point to the willingness of some to make a sincere effort to settle the issues. The third party's active involvement in clarifying the implicit steps in a GRIT-like offer can help establish a climate of mutual trust. The third party is a witness to the group's willingness to respond appropriately once a sincere conciliatory move has been made. If others fail to respond with reciprocal concessions or moves, it can be read by the third party as a sign of poor faith. There is some pressure on the responding members to make reciprocal concessions or risk losing the third party's involvement in the process.

SUMMARY

Any intervention in conflict interaction is difficult and risky. In this chapter we have viewed interventions from the point of view of the participants themselves and from the standpoint of third parties who try to settle others' conflicts. Our aim has been to summarize general principles and specific techniques of self-regulation and third party interventions that emerge from our previous discussions of the forces influencing conflict interaction.

There are a number of ways that group members can diagnose their own conflicts and act to redirect them. Members can expand the definition of a problem so that a broader array of alternative solutions can be considered. They can change a group's climate by a series of small changes in interaction, a discussion of climate themes, or the use of some critical incident. They can assess power differentials in the group and develop ways to deal with power imbalances. They can view face-saving interaction as a negotiation process and then facilitate this negotiation by reducing defensiveness, allowing for an exchange of concessions, or stressing the consequences of not reaching a resolution of the face-saving problem.

Third party intervenors must decide what their role in the conflict will be. They must determine how much control they seek from the group over the ultimate resolution of the conflict, and how active they will be in shaping the interaction of the parties. These decisions require careful diagnosis of the conflict the group faces and a strategy for adapting to the specific characteristics of the group the third party is assisting. Regardless of the style of intervention, third parties often try to achieve two main intervention objectives. First, they try to sharpen conflicts by having the group trace the historical roots of the problem, by providing a safe climate for discussions of difficult issues, by encouraging the members to define the problem in terms of their needs, and by cutting through multiple issues that the parties cannot untangle. Second, third parties try to move the group from differentiation to integration—from a common understanding of the problem to a solution that all can accept. This step often means building mutual trust and inducing cooperation so that parties will make concessions and endorse solutions that come closest to meeting all members' needs.

REFERENCES

Auvine, B., Densmore, B., Extrom, M., Poole, S., & Shanklin, M. *A manual for group facilitators*. Madison, Wis.: The Center for Conflict Resolution, 1977.

Avery, M., Auvine, B., Streidel, B., & Weiss, L. *Building united judgment*. Madison, Wis: The Center for Conflict Resolution, 1981.

Bartunek, J., Benton, A., & Keys, C. B. Third party intervention and the bargaining behavior of group representatives. *Journal of Conflict Resolution,* 1975, *19,* 532–557.

Bormann, E. G. Fantasy and rhetorical vision: The rhetorical criticism of social reality. *Quarterly Journal of Speech,* 1972, *58,* 396–407.

Delbecq, A., Van de Ven, A., & Gustafsen, D. *Group techniques for program planning.* Glenview, Ill.: Scott, Foresman, 1975.

Etzioni, A. *The active society.* New York: Macmillan, 1968.

Filley, A. *Interpersonal conflict resolution.* Glenview, Ill.: Scott, Foresman, 1975.

Fisher, R. J. Third party consultation: A method for the study and resolution of conflict. *Journal of Conflict Resolution,* 1972, *16,* 67–94.

Frost, J. H., & Wilmot, W. W. *Interpersonal conflict.* Dubuque, Iowa: William C. Brown, 1978.

Gibb, J. Defensive communication. *Journal of Communication,* 1961, *2,* 141–148.

Goldmann, R. B. *Round table justice: Case studies in conflict resolution.* Boulder, Colo.: Westview Press, 1980.

Gouran, D. S. *Making decisions in groups.* Glenview, Ill.: Scott, Foresman, 1982.

Guetzkow, H., & Gyr, J. An analysis of conflict in decision-making groups. *Human Relations,* 1954, *7,* 367–381.

Hall, J., & Watson, W. H. The effects of a normative intervention on group decision-making performance. *Human Relations,* 1970, *23,* 299–317.

Hollander, E. P., & Julian, J. W. Contemporary trends in the analysis of leadership processes, *Psychological Bulletin,* 1969, *71,* 387–397.

Janeway, E. *Powers of the weak.* New York: Morrow-Quill, 1980.

Johnson, D. W. & Johnson, F. P. *Joining together.* Englewood Cliffs, New Jersey: Prentice-Hall, 1975.

Kerr, S., Schriesheim, C. A., Murphy, C. J., & Stogdill, R. M. Toward a contingency theory of leadership based upon the consideration and initiating structure literature. *Organizational Behavior and Human Performance,* 1974, *12,* 62–82.

Lindskold, S. Trust development, the GRIT proposal, and the effects of conciliatory acts on conflict and cooperation. *Psychological Bulletin,* 1978, *85,* 772–793.

Lyles, M. A., & Mitroff, I. I. Organizational problem formulation: An empirical study. *Administrative Science Quarterly, 25,* 1980, 102–119.

Morley, I. E., & Stephenson, G. M. *The social psychology of bargaining.* London: George Allen and Unwin, 1977.

Osgood, C. E. Suggestions for winning the real war with communism. *Journal of Conflict Resolution,* 1959, *3,* 295–325.

Osgood, C. E. *An alternative to war or surrender.* Urbana: University of Illinois Press, 1962.

Osgood, C. E. *Perspective in foreign policy.* Palo Alto, California: Pacific Books, 1966.

Poole, M. S. *A multiple sequence theory of decision development.* Paper presented at Conference on Small Group Communication Research, Pennsylvania State University, April 1982.

Pruitt, D. Indirect communication and the search for agreement in negotiation. *Journal of Applied Social Psychology,* 1971, *1,* 205–239.

Pruitt, D., & Johnson, D. F. Mediation as an aid to face saving in negotiation. *Journal of Personality and Social Psychology,* 1970, *14,* 239–246.

Rapoport, A. *Fights, games and debates.* Ann Arbor: University of Michigan Press, 1960.

Scheidel, T., and Crowell, L. *Discussing and deciding.* New York: Macmillan, 1979.

Stogdill, R. *Handbook of leadership.* New York: Free Press, 1974.

Tannenbaum, R., & Schmidt, W. H. How to choose a leadership pattern. *Harvard Business Review,* 1958, *36,* 95–101.

Volkema, R. J. *An empirical investigation of problem formulation and problem-purpose expansion.* Unpublished Ph.D. Thesis, University of Wisconsin, Madison, 1981.

Volkema, R. J. *Problem-purpose expansion: A technique for reformulating problems.* Unpublished manuscript, University of Wisconsin, Eau Claire, 1983.

Walton, R. *Interpersonal peacemaking: Confrontations and third party consultation.* Reading, Mass.: Addison-Wesley, 1969.

Wehr, P. *Conflict regulation.* Boulder, Colo.: Westview Press, 1979.

Index

Acknowledgments

CHAPTER 1

Morton Deutsch, *The Resolution of Conflict.* New Haven, Connecticut: Yale University Press, 1973.

Calvin S. Hall, *A Primer of Freudian Psychology.* New York: World Publishing Company, 1954.

Kurt Lewin, *Field Theory in Social Science: Selected Theoretical Papers.* New York: Harper & Brothers, 1951, p. 241.

"Sixteen Compliance-Gaining Techniques with Examples from Family Situations" from "Dimensions of Compliance-Gaining Behavior: An Empirical Analysis" by Gerald Marwell and David R. Schmitt in *Sociometry*, December 1967. Reprinted by permission of the American Sociological Association and Gerald Marwell.

William Skidmore, *Theoretical Thinking in Sociology,* 2nd ed. New York: Cambridge University Press, 1979, pp. 105–106.

"Five Conflict-Management Styles and Their Relationships" from "Developing a Forced-Choice Measure of Conflict-Handling Behavior: The "MODE" Instrument" by R.H. Kilmann and K. W. Thomas in *Educational and Psychological Measurement*, Vol. 37, 1977. Reprinted by permission of Educational and Psychological Measurement and Ralph H. Kilmann.

CHAPTER 2

Richard E. Walton, *Interpersonal Peacemaking: Confrontations and Third-Party Consultation.* Reading, Massachusetts: Addison-Wesley Publishing Company, 1969, p. 105.

Abraham S. Luchins and Edith H. Luchins, *Rigidity of Behavior.* Eugene, Oregon: University of Oregon Press, 1959, p. 19.

From *My Dinner with André* by Wallace Shawn and André Gregory. Copyright © 1981 by Wallace Shawn and André Gregory. Reprinted by permission of Grove Press, Inc.

Hannah Arendt, *On Violence.* New York: Harcourt, Brace & World, 1969, p. 44.

CHAPTER 4

Elizabeth Janeway, *Powers of the Weak.* New York: Alfred A. Knopf, 1980, pp. 77, 126.

Matthew A. Crenson, *The Un-Politics of Air Pollution: A Study of Non-Decisionmaking in the Cities.* Baltimore, Maryland: The Johns Hopkins Press, 1971, pp. 76–77.

Peter Bachrach and Morton S. Baratz, *Power and Poverty: Theory and Practice.* New York: Oxford University Press, 1970, pp. 29, 39.

CHAPTER 5

Analysis of Groups, **Graham S. Gibbard, John J. Hartman, and Richard D. Mann,** eds. San Francisco, California: Jossey-Bass, Inc., Publishers, 1974, p. 177.

Irving L. Janis and Leon Mann, *Decision Making: A Psychological Analysis of Conflict, Choice, and Commitment.* New York: The Free Press, 1977, p. 283.

From "Face-Saving and Face-Restoration in Negotiation" by **B. R. Brown** in D. Druckman (Ed.), *Negotiations.* Beverly Hills, California: Sage Publications, 1977.

CHAPTER 6

From "The Effects of a Normative Intervention on Group Decision-making Performance" by **J. Hall and W. H. Watson** in *Human Relations*, Vol. 23, No. 4, 1970. Copyright © 1970 by Tavistock Institute of Human Relations. Reprinted by permission of Plenum Publishing Corporation.

From *Interpersonal Conflict Resolution* by **Alan C. Filley.** Copyright © 1975 by Scott, Foresman and Company.

Material from "An Empirical Investigation of Problem Formulation and Problem Purpose Expansion," unpublished Ph.D. thesis by **Roger J. Volkema** at University of Wisconsin, Madison, 1981 and "Problem Purpose Expansion: A Technique for Reformulating Problems" by Roger J. Volkema. Reprinted by permission of the author.

DATE DUE

MAY 1 8 2006			
MAY 1 4 2007			
JUL 0 3 REC'D			
GAYLORD			PRINTED IN U.S.A.